The Decade of the Multilatinas

Latin American multinationals (multilatinas) have been central in the rise of emerging markets in the last few decades. Their development comprises part of the global shift of wealth and power between nations. The rise of firms in a broad range of sectors – including construction, oil, telecommunications and the aeronautical industry – as important regional and global players is spreading: companies in Brazil, Mexico, Colombia, Chile and many others are part of this increasing phenomenon. This book analyses the trends, the countries and the firms involved, and explores the implications for the USA, China, Spain and the rest of Europe. In particular, Javier Santiso examines how Spain might profit from positioning itself as a unique hub between Europe and Latin America. *The Decade of the Multilatinas* includes a wide range of statistical data which will be useful to scholars, policymakers and commentators on Latin America in particular, and international business and emerging markets more generally.

JAVIER SANTISO is Professor of Economics at ESADE Business School and Vice President of the ESADEgeo think tank. He is also a managing director in a major global telecom multinational and the founder of Amerigo, a VC network fund in Colombia, Chile, Brazil and Spain with $300 million of capital mobilised. Previously he has held the position of Chief Economist and Director General of the OECD Development Centre, responsible for emerging markets. He has also been Chief Economist for Emerging Markets of BBVA and advisor on emerging markets for Pfizer in New York and Lazard in Paris.

The Decade of the Multilatinas

JAVIER SANTISO
ESADE Business School

CAMBRIDGE UNIVERSITY PRESS
Cambridge, New York, Melbourne, Madrid, Cape Town,
Singapore, São Paulo, Delhi, Mexico City

Cambridge University Press
The Edinburgh Building, Cambridge CB2 8RU, UK

Published in the United States of America by Cambridge University Press, New York

www.cambridge.org
Information on this title: www.cambridge.org/9781107034433

First published 2013

Printed and bound in the United Kingdom by the MPG Printgroup

A catalogue record for this publication is available from the British Library

Library of Congress Cataloguing in Publication data
Santiso, Javier.
[Década de las multilatinas. English]
The decade of the multilatinas / Javier Santiso.
    pages cm
Translation of the author's Década de las multilatinas published in Madrid by
Fundación Carolina in 2012.
Includes bibliographical references and index.
ISBN 978-1-107-03443-3 (hardback)
1. International business enterprises – Latin America.   2. Latin America – Commerce.
3. Investments, Spanish – Latin America.   I. Title.
HD2810.5.S2513   2013
338.8′898 – dc23   2013001831

ISBN 978-1-107-03443-3 Hardback

For Susana and Eliana, with infinite love

Contents

Figures

Tables

Foreword

MAURO F. GUILLÉN
Director, Lauder Institute
and Dr Felix Zandman Professor of International Management,
The Wharton School

Latin America has come of age. After decades of ups and downs, the region seems to have abandoned the ghosts of the recent past and embraced globalisation. Although not every country is equally on board, the most important economies, from Mexico to Chile and from Colombia to Brazil, are riding the wave of economic growth and transformation that is sweeping the emerging world.

This renewed economic bonanza is not just due to the commodities boom. It has to do, most fundamentally, with the rise of a middle class of consumers and with the strong showing of a large number of companies, both large and small, known as the *multilatinas*. In this book, Javier Santiso takes the reader on an exhilarating journey across the Americas and around the world, tracing the origins of these companies to the peculiar historical and institutional trajectories of the various Latin American republics, and following them to the foreign locations in which they have established operations in search of inputs and markets.

Javier Santiso is no neophyte to the topic. Over the course of two decades, he has observed and researched the economic and business evolution of Latin America at close range, first as a chief economist for a major international bank, then as the chief economist for the Organization for Economic Cooperation and Development's Development Centre, and presently as a scholar at ESADE Business School and a managing director in a major telecom multinational. His unique experiences in the worlds of business, multilateral organisations and academia place him in an excellent position to analyse the phenomenon of the new global competitors from Latin America.

Santiso offers a wide-ranging analysis rooted in an extensive use of the available statistics on trade, foreign direct investment and firm-level operations. One of the main strengths of the book is that he makes a connection between the rise of the multilatinas and the recent influence of Spain and China throughout the region. Spanish companies have invested heavily in infrastructure and services since the 1990s, while Chinese firms have become major trading partners, especially in commodities. The arrival of these new investors and traders has transformed the region, laying the foundations for a new breed of Latin American firms to emerge.

Santiso offers a view into the future for Latin America. The region has changed rapidly, and become much more differentiated than in the past. Mexico, Central America and the Caribbean have become much more integrated with the United States, while South America has developed strong ties to China and the rest of Asia. After nearly two decades of macroeconomic stability, Brazil has emerged as the giant of the region. Brazilian firms are now in a position to expand around the world on the basis of proprietary technology and know-how and brands, in sectors as diverse as foodstuffs, cosmetics, aircraft, mining, oil and biofuels.

The rise of the multilatinas is just one more indication of Latin America's enhanced stature in the world, and yet another signal that the global economy has changed dramatically since the turn of the twenty-first century. Because of its population size, expanding middle class, vibrant consumer markets, natural riches and formidable companies, the region is poised to become a major player in global economic and financial affairs. This book offers the best analysis to date of this new phenomenon.

Introduction

The wealth of nations is experiencing an unprecedented transformation. With the new millennium, emerging markets have gained economic prominence and become motors for growth. In contrast, the OECD countries plummeted with the crisis that broke out in 2008. Since then, we continue to witness the progress of the emerging countries with awe; meanwhile the European economies remain immersed in a deep crisis.

In 2013, the bulk of global growth will no longer come from the OECD countries, but from the emerging markets. And this will not change radically throughout the present decade. The Banco Bilbao Vizcaya Argentaria (BBVA) anticipates that the EAGLEs, the 'emerging and growth-leading economies' – that is, the emerging economies that lead global growth – will be responsible for half of the global growth over the next ten years, whereas the G7 will only contribute 30% of the growth.[1] Standard Chartered, however, predicts that by 2030 more than two-thirds of global growth will come from emerging markets and these will continue to benefit from the super cycle of raw materials. China will contribute to most of this growth (22%), followed by the European Union (15%) and the United States (14%). All of Latin America will make a contribution to global growth comparable to India (9%), followed by Central Asia (4%), the Middle East (5%) and Africa (5%).[2]

---

[1] See www.bbvaresearch.com/KETD/ketd/esp/nav/eagles.jsp; and in particular, the presentation made by Alicia García Herrero at ESADE Business School, in Madrid, in 2011: www.bbvaresearch.com/KETD/fbin/mult/110214_BBVA_EAGLES-ESADE_tcm346-246602.pdf; and BBVA, *Who Are the Eagles? Driving Global Growth for the Next Ten Years*, Madrid and Hong Kong, BBVA Research, February 2011.

[2] See Standard Chartered, *The Super Cycle Report*, London, Standard Chartered Global Research, 2010. Available at www.standardchartered.com/media-centre/press-releases/2010/documents/20101115/The_Super-cycle_Report.pdf.

The new economic and financial balance does not always lead to an identical transformation in terms of prosperity. The Legatum Institute reminds us of this in an index that measures not just wealth but also development and prosperity. Although China and Brazil are already economic superpowers, they only hold positions 58 and 45 respectively in this ranking, behind Singapore (17) and Chile (32). In Latin America, Uruguay stands out at 28.[3] Although China caught up with Japan in 2010 as the second largest economy in the world, this emerging market is lagging far behind Japan in terms of development, and is forty positions behind Japan in the Legatum Institute ranking. Moreover, although Brazil exceeded Spain in economic terms in the year 2010, it is twenty-two positions behind in the Legatum ranking.

This new balance is incomplete and it will take years to close some of the gaps. However, in many areas, changes are taking place at a rapid rate. This is especially true in the area of business and two symmetrical movements can be observed.

Firstly, multinationals in the OECD countries started making investments and aggressive bets on emerging markets. This was the case, for instance, of the Spanish companies that went international – many of them through Latin America – and in the process became multinationals. This phenomenon was not isolated: the 600 main OECD companies listed in the Dow Jones increased their exposure to emerging markets on average from 9% to 20% of their total revenue between 1990 and 2010.[4] Companies such as Unilever or Telefónica generated in 2012 half of their income in emerging countries; others already have a totally 'emerging' DNA, such as the 'British' bank Standard Chartered or Vedanta (obtaining 71% and 85%, respectively, of their income from emerging countries). Goldman Sachs analysed this phenomenon in detail by examining the fifty largest companies with activity in emerging countries and found that an average of 30% of

---

[3] See www.prosperity.com/rankings.aspx/. This institute forms part of the initiatives promoted by Legatum, an investment fund based in Dubai which also donated $50 million to establish an innovation and development centre at MIT. See www.legatum.mit.edu/. It also developed a venture capital fund for developing countries, called Legatum Ventures. See www.legatumventures.com/.

[4] See Schroders, *Emerging Markets Investments: Exploding the Myths*, London, Schroders, 2011. Available at www.schroderstalkingpoint.com/?id= a0j50000000u972AAA; and Schroders, *What is the Best Method of Gaining Exposure to Emerging Markets? Exploding the Myths*, London, Schroders, June 2011. Available at www.schroderstalkingpoint.com/files/Exploding% 20the%20myths%20Jun%202011.pdf.

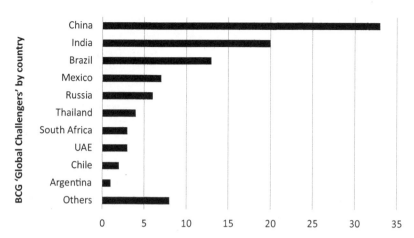

Figure 0.1 The most important emerging multinational companies (by country).
Source: BCG, 2011. *Note:* 'Others' includes Egypt (1), Hungary (1), Malaysia (1), Saudi Arabia (1), Indonesia (2) and Turkey (2).

their sales or income already come from these economies.[5] All of these companies significantly increased their international exposure: today the top 100 companies in the FTSE obtain 70% of their income from outside the nation where their headquarters is located. At the same time, these firms have also globalised their production and supplier centres, particularly in the emerging countries: 94% of the components and labour costs involved in creating the Apple iPhone come from outside the United States.[6]

Secondly, the multinationals from emerging markets began an accelerated course towards other markets, many of them also emerging, and also moved towards the OECD markets (Figure 0.1). As the emerging economies, headed by China, India and Brazil, began to make their way onto the world stage, their companies started globalising and making an increasingly large place for themselves on the international business stage. These companies have tended to perform better than their OECD counterparts who invested in emerging

[5] See Goldman Sachs, *Revisiting our BRIC Nifty 50 Baskets*, New York and London, Goldman Sachs, May 2010.
[6] See Schroders, *Fragmentation in the Global Village: The Paradoxes of our Increasingly Connected World*, London, Schroders, 2011. Available at www.schroderstalkingpoint.com/files/VMaisonneuve%20Fragmentation%20in%20the%20Global%20Village.pdf.

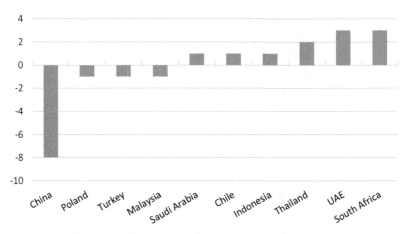

Figure 0.2 Change in the number of companies in the BCG index, 2011–2008.
Source: BCG, 2008 and 2011.

markets and boast share returns of nearly 470% between 2001 and 2011, compared to 130% for their counterparts in the OECD.[7] The story of the emerging multinationals is just starting. It is very likely that by the end of the present decade many of these multinationals will have strengthened their positions as leaders in each of their sectors, including technology – as we will see.

The rise of the multilatinas that we will be analysing in detail is, therefore, part of a wider phenomenon that includes the emerging multinationals in their search for expansion. The Boston Consulting Group (BCG), in its most recent report on the top 100 emerging multinationals, entitled 'Global Challengers', points out that this phenomenon is massive. Today, a total of sixteen countries have multinationals among the 100 main multinationals identified by BCG.[8] Asia dominates, with China and India accounting for a total of fifty-five companies. To these, we must add another seven companies from Indonesia, Thailand and Malaysia. Emerging Asia represents nearly two-thirds of these multinationals (Figure 0.2).

---

[7] See www.schroderstalkingpoint.com/?id=a0j50000000u972AAA.
[8] See BCG, *BCG Global Challengers. Companies on the Move: Rising Stars from Rapidly Developing Economies Are Reshaping Global Industries,* Boston, BCG, 2011. Available at www.bcg.com/documents/file70055.pdf.

However, the phenomenon is not only Asian. Multinationals have also emerged in Africa, Turkey and the Middle East (eleven). Latin America accounts for a formidable twenty-three multinationals, mostly from Brazil and Mexico, but also from Chile and Argentina. In addition, BCG created a separate category for *emeriti* – that is, companies that already resemble their OECD counterparts – which are five in total, including two from Latin America: Vale and Cemex. Latin America now accounts for one in every four emerging multinationals.

The BCG list is questionable, like all exercises of this type. For instance, no multinational companies from Singapore, Korea or Taiwan are included – and all of these countries have world champion firms. In addition, the ranking by country can vary. For example, in the case of Chile, there is no mention of Cencosud, which should be alongside Falabella. Also not included in the ranking is Colombia, which may have multinationals on this scale. In any case, these details have no bearing on the core message: we are witnessing an unstoppable and unprecedented progress of these multinationals. In the first edition of this report in 2006, there were only fourteen countries with ranked multinationals. In addition, China and India dominated even more so, accounting for sixty-three multinational companies in the ranking. Since then, this number has fallen, particularly for China. Meanwhile, Latin America has progressed: in 2008, there were only twenty-one Latin multinationals; yet by 2011, there were already twenty-five (if we add the conglomerates Vale and Cemex). Argentina continues to have just one company in the ranking (Tenaris); however, Chile has doubled its number of companies in the ranking (in 2011, there were two: Falabella and LAN; in 2008, there was only one: CSV). As for Brazil and Mexico, they continue to boast fourteen and seven, respectively. Some have changed: in 2011, Mabe and Mexichem made their way into the ranking for Mexico, and Magnesita and Brasil Foods for Brazil (the latter company results from a merger of two companies that were in the ranking in 2008: Sadia and Perdigão).[9]

BCG estimates that in 2020 these *global challengers* will generate $8 trillion, that is, the equivalent to what is generated today by the

---

[9] See BCG, *The 2008 BCG 100: New Global Challengers. How Top Companies from Rapidly Growing Economies Are Changing the World*, Boston, BCG, 2008. Available at www.bcg.com.cn/export/sites/default/en/files/publications/reports_pdf/New_Global_Challengers_Feb_2008.pdf.

500 main OECD multinational companies represented in the S&P 500 index. In the Fortune 500, the number of emerging multinational companies has skyrocketed, multiplying by nearly five over the past decade (up from twenty-one to ninety-two). In the Forbes 2000, the number has also tripled; there were nearly 400 emerging multinational companies in this ranking in 2010. The United States has lost the most relative weight, and emerging countries have gained a larger presence. Throughout the decade 2000–10, income from these companies has grown an average of 18%, or three times more than their OECD counterparts in the S&P 500, while still maintaining margins (Figure 0.3).

This progress has meant an unprecedented process of business consolidation and internationalisation. These companies no longer aim just to take control of competitors in domestic markets or neighbouring markets. Over the decade 2000–10, emerging multinational companies carried out 60% of takeovers in developed countries. Takeovers in OECD countries were on average valued at more than $550 million, more than the average of the acquisitions carried out in emerging markets ($340 million). The appetite and investing capacity of these multinational companies, including the multilatinas, have spilled over from their immediate regions and become a more global process. It was shown in 2000 by the mega operations of Cemex (when taking over an Australian company), of Mittal (taking over a French company) or of Lenovo (buying an American company), that no OECD market can resist their appetite.

The focus on OECD countries has intensified with the crisis of 2008–12. The emerging multinational companies have taken advantage of the weakness of their OECD rivals to carry out mergers and acquisitions (Figure 0.4). More than 70% of operations since 2010 have been concentrated on acquiring rival companies in OECD countries (compared to 60% during the previous two years). Although this activity was reduced in 2009 owing to the effect of the crisis, in 2010 the emerging multinational companies started taking over firms at a rate similar to the pre-crisis year (2008 was a record year with 135 transactions). Brazil and Mexico provide excellent examples of this phenomenon and we will later examine these in depth. Everything pointed to 2010–12 being another year of strong investment by these multinationals, as indicated by the data we analysed for Latin America, and which we will also delve into in the following chapters.

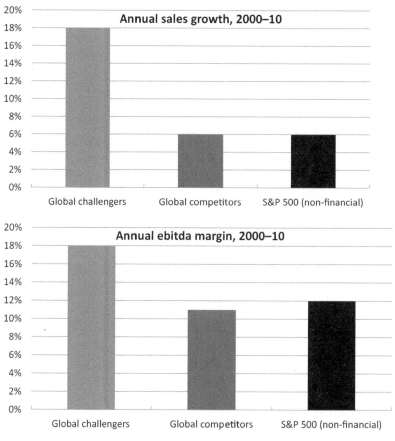

Figure 0.3 The emerging multinational companies: world champions, by sales and margins.
Source: BCG, 2011. *Note:* 'Global competitors' refers to multinational companies based in advanced economies that operate in the same industries as the 'global challengers'.

Therefore, the history of the multilatinas is not an isolated adventure. In the first chapter, we will see how it is framed within a broader phenomenon linked to the progress of the emerging economies, and in particular those of Latin America.

This growth is not limited to Brazil, the Latin variable of the BRICs (a term used to describe Brazil, Russia, India and China) that has gone from being a promise for the future to becoming a present power.

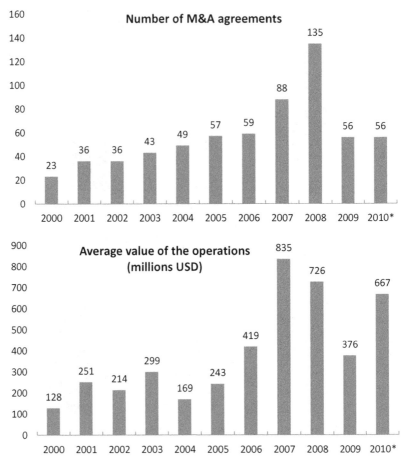

Figure 0.4 Cross-border mergers and acquisitions (M&A) by global challengers, 2011.
Source: BCG, 2011. Note: Data referring to operations with public information. *Until August.

Growth is now extending to other economies on the continent, which are 'graduating' one after the other, and becoming members of the OECD club of countries (such as the case of Mexico in 1995 and Chile in 2010); or are obtaining investment grade rating (more than 80% of the Latin American GDP in 2012), the most recent nations to obtain this rating being Peru and Colombia.

This economic progress has led to business development, as we will see in Chapters 2, 3 and 4. Although the decade 2000–10 witnessed the emergence of several multilatinas that tended to invest mostly in the Americas, in the decade 2010–20 these firms are already exploring new European, Asian, African and Arab markets. Growth in the Americas in the previous decade is now being followed by globalisation. As a result, the decade 2010–20 is that of the multilatinas, with a large role for Brazilian companies (Chapter 3), as well as for the Mexican, Andean and Argentinean firms (Chapter 4). It is also important to stress that the pioneers, the very first multilatinas, were from the Spanish-speaking countries (Argentina in particular), which went abroad much earlier than their Brazilian counterparts. Nevertheless, Brazilian firms are the ones now making the greatest inroads.

We will see in Chapter 5 that this progress is not solely restricted to the sectors of raw materials or the agricultural-industrial sectors. Some multilatinas are already making waves in the field of technology. The major rebalancing of the world towards emerging countries is not only economic and financial, but will also be technological. In this sense, the great business challenge of the continent will be to retain a hold on the technology launched at great speed by the Indian and Chinese growth drivers. The development of venture capital and Latin American startups is encouraging and could lead to a future with more 'Multilatinas 2.0' (IT, software, telcos, startups from Latin America), or who knows, with the emergence of a Latin Facebook in the future.

In this journey towards more value added industries, the path of Latin America will be bumpy: the rules of the game are not (yet) written, but the challenges abound, one of them being precisely also the major event that has boosted Latin American economic development since 2010: the rise of China. As we will stress in Chapter 6, this is a major event for the region. It is both a blessing and a challenge. The rise of Latin American exports is linked to the rise of China, and of Asia more widely. The increasing ties between both regions are good news, but they are also challenging. Multilatinas find new markets for their products in China and Asia, but these markets are commodity related. At the same time multinationals from China are becoming stronger competitors for manufacturers of the region. In this context, for Brazil and other Latin countries, climbing the value chain and also being a technological and innovative powerhouse will require an industrial rebalancing of relations with China. The rise of China now goes well beyond trade; it also involves investments. China has become one of the largest foreign direct investors in the region since 2010. This new entrant now competes with US and Spanish traditional heavyweight investors in the region. More than ever the landscape is changing for traditional Western investors.

At the same time, multilatinas are on the rise, creating new challengers. The progress of the multilatinas invites us to rethink relations with Europe, and particularly with Spain, which is an aspect that we will touch on in the final chapters (7 and 8). Given this dynamic, we can soon expect to see some of these multilatinas emerge with a strong presence in Europe. This could represent an opportunity which could become the platform for entrance into Europe for the multilatinas (and Latin American startups). Petrobras is looking for partners in Europe; the Brazilian banks are eager to open beyond Brazil's borders; and in Chile and Mexico, many companies need or aspire to diversify their markets. For now, these firms are exploring opportunities in Lisbon, London or Paris. Why not imagine, however, that, just like the Mexican Cemex or the Brazilian Gerda in their day, these companies locate themselves in Madrid, Barcelona or Bilbao?

The progress of the emerging countries, and the multilatinas in particular, represents a challenge and an opportunity. Without a doubt, the privileged business relations that Spain has managed to weave in the past with Latin America are a solid foundation. It will be necessary to rethink relations with the continent and open its investment opportunities, as Latin America did with Spain in the past. In the end, the world that is emerging is a more balanced world. The unilateral relations of the past (Spain investing in Latin America) have ended, giving way to bi-directional relations (Spain continues to invest in Latin America, but the multilatinas also invest in Europe). Indeed, this new world is an opportunity, a bias for hope.

1 | *A Novus Mundus*

The phenomenon of the multilatinas that are emerging in Latin America cannot be understood unless it is placed in the context of the overall boom of emerging markets.

This is framed within a three-way trend: firstly, the phenomenal growth of the emerging markets in general; secondly, the economic consolidation of Latin America; and thirdly, the prosperity of the multilatinas.

In this chapter, we will take a look at how this growth is framed within a broader phenomenon, the boom of the emerging markets and Latin American economies. The internationalisation of the multilatinas, which began decades ago, has occurred at great speed, propelled both by the economic booms of the emerging markets, and by that of Latin America in particular.

The world in which these multilatinas are doing business is a very different economic space from that of previous decades – more multipolar, without a centre or a periphery – as we shall see. This represents a *Novus Mundus*, a New World, like the one that Amerigo Vespucci[1] discovered and named in the year 1500, a global world 3.0.[2] Emerging markets now account for the majority of the world's growth and foreign direct investments (FDI). It is above all a world where South–South relations are gaining a new prominence and relevance, a world in which multinationals and emerging investors increasingly invest

---

[1] The continent discovered by Columbus was given its name by another Italian, Amerigo Vespucci, who would be the first to insist that what was discovered was not a new route to the Indies but a new continent, a new world. See the letter of the founding of America dated from 1500, a translation of which can be found at http://memoriapoliticademexico.org/Textos/1Independencia/1500ENM.html.

[2] See Pankaj Ghemawat, *World 3.0: Global Prosperity and How to Achieve It*, Boston, Harvard Business Review Press, 2011.

in other emerging regions – while also doing business in the OECD countries.

In this new business world, a multinational such as the Spanish giant Telefónica already generates the bulk of its income from emerging markets, and Latin America in particular, where it has more customers and employees than in all of Europe. In this new world, a German multinational such as Daimler Benz already has 20% of its capital in the hands of emerging investors and obtains 40% of its income in these same regions.[3] Emerging multinationals are taking over leading positions in many sectors, including technology sectors. The Chinese company Huawei overcame its European and North American rivals to become the world's top telecommunications industry supplier in 2012, while its compatriot Tencent is already positioned as one of the largest Internet companies in terms of market capitalisation, just behind Google and Amazon. In 2012, Chinese PC maker Lenovo took the world leader position ahead of the US tech firm HP.

In the case of Latin America, the region has become more interconnected, and above all with Asia, Africa and the Middle East. At the commercial level, the OECD countries that used to be Latin America's main partners have now given way to new powers, Asian in particular. Meanwhile, the multilatinas are investing strongly in other countries in the region. Some multilatinas, such as the Mexican companies Cemex and América Móvil or the Brazilian companies Embraer, Petrobras and Vale, have become world leaders in their sectors, and respected peers of their OECD competitors.

Nevertheless, Europe and the United States have not disappeared from the investment map of these multilatinas – quite the contrary. However, a great deal of confidence has been placed in emerging regions, whether in Latin America or, in a more incipient way, in Asia, Africa or the Middle East. Throughout the decade of the 2000s, the multilatinas embarked on an accelerated process of internationalisation that was largely a process of focusing on the American continent (North and South). In the decade of the 2010s, we are seeing a new trend emerge, a process that is no longer just internationalisation, but a globalisation that extends across the American continent, Europe, and beyond.

---

[3] See http://maps.ghemawat.com/.

An Olympic effect

One of the most important economic phenomena of the last quarter of a century has been the emergence of new powers that have arisen from the so-called 'developing economies', now reclassified as 'emerging economies'.[4]

The multinationals that established themselves in the developing markets imported everything except cheap labour and raw materials. However, this has changed radically. During most of the last century, investing in the Third World was a risky venture; at the end of the twentieth century it became a wager on the future; and at the beginning of the twenty-first century, it has become an imperative. At the same time, the emerging multinationals have begun to globalise; and in addition to cheap labour and raw materials, they offer the same technical know-how as Western multinationals.

The global crisis of 2008–12 has become a catalyst for the transition that began at the end of the last decade towards a world where emerging markets play a greater role. As a symbol of this progress, in 2010 the World Cup was held in an emerging country, South Africa, two years after the Olympic Games were held in China. In 2014, Brazil, another of the major emerging economies, will host the World Cup, and in 2016, for the first time in its history, it will host the Olympic Games. Meanwhile, Qatar will host its first World Cup before the end of this decade.

These events symbolise a massive overturning of the world economic order. At the end of 2009, the investment bank Goldman Sachs, which coined the term BRIC to describe the main emerging markets (Brazil, Russia, India and China) at the beginning of 2000, recalculated its projections of the world GDPs because of the financial crisis that has overtaken the developed countries. The result points towards an acceleration of the trends predicted by economists in 2003 – it is now anticipated that China will catch the United States in 2027, that is, fourteen years earlier than the initial forecast. As early as 2012,

---

[4] The term was coined by Antoine van Agtmael in 1981. See his essay on the rise of multinationals and emerging economies, *The Emerging Markets Century: How a New Breed of World-Class Companies Is Overtaking the World*, New York, Free Press, 2007.

China would exceed Japan as the world's second economy according to Goldman Sachs (something that in reality had already happened in 2011).[5]

The main surprise, however, came from a Latin American country, Brazil, whose GDP (in dollar terms) exceeded Italy by the end of 2010, that is, fifteen years before initially projected in the exercises carried out by Goldman Sachs in 2003. In 2029, Brazil could be on par with Germany (seven years earlier than initially anticipated) and on par with Japan in 2034, something that was not even considered previously. These projections involve many questionable assumptions and methodological obstacles. However, they point towards an acceleration of a global shift in favour of emerging markets, and in particular of the BRICs. Brazil is now an emerging power rather than an eternal promise.

With the progress of the emerging markets, we are also witnessing an unprecedented increase in the South–South relations. For instance, since 2009, Brazil's main trading partner is no longer an OECD country, but an emerging economy (China). The same is also happening in India, South Africa, South Korea and Indonesia. In other words, Europe and the United States have ceased to be the *centre*, while the rest of the world is the *periphery*. The world is becoming multipolar, with more trade and investment flows between the emerging countries. Since 2009, trade between emerging countries exceeds their trade with OECD countries – proof of a major revolution in the world economy.

A recent HSBC report points out that, for Brazil, South–South trade already represented approximately 60% of total trade in 2010, and that in 2050, it will represent approximately 83%.[6] The United Nations Conference on Trade and Development (UNCTAD) highlights that 70% of direct investments made in 2010 by emerging countries took place in other emerging regions. In addition, there is a

[5] See Goldman Sachs, *The Long Term Outlook for the BRIC and N-11 post Crisis*, London and New York, Goldman Sachs Global Economics Papers 192, 2009. Available at www2.goldmansachs.com/ideas/BRIC/long-term-outlook-doc.pdf.
[6] See HSBC, *The Southern Silk Road: Turbocharging South South Economic Growth*, London and New York, HSBC Global Research, 2011. Available at www.research.hsbc.com/midas/Res/RDV?p=pdf&key=WZnyWSIf38&n=299714.PDF.

Table 1.1 *Projections in 2050: change the centre towards the South.*

Origin	Destination	2010 total exports (%)	2010–50 growth (%)	2050 total exports (%)
China	Total	100	361	100
	South–South	47	621	73
	Ex-continent/region	16	759	20
	Others	53	132	27
India	Total	100	504	100
	South–South	58	761	83
	Ex-continent/region	29	823	45
	Others	42	147	17
Brazil	Total	100	431	100
	South–South	58	651	83
	Ex-continent/region	36	901	68
	Others	42	121	17
Russia	Total	100	343	100
	South–South	19	1066	50
	Ex-continent/region	19	1066	50
	Others	81	174	50

Source: ESADEgeo, 2012; based on HSBC, 2011.

growing attraction towards these countries: 50% of the foreign direct investment (FDI) of OECD multinationals is aimed at emerging markets (Figure 1.1, Table 1.1).

The effects of the Olympic Games or the World Cup will undoubtedly reinforce these trends, helping fuel the economies of the host countries. In a recent analysis of 196 countries between 1950 and 2006, two economists, Rose and Spiegel, from the University of Berkeley and the Federal Reserve of San Francisco respectively, found that the Olympic Games tend to have a positive effect on the exports of the host country, increasing them by 30% on average. Imports also register similar effects.[7] In the more specific case of Latin America, this means that the role of Brazil will continue to develop as the Olympics and the World Cup unfold.

[7] See Andrew Rose and Mark Spiegel, 'The Olympic Effect', National Bureau of Economic Research Working Paper, Boston, 2009.

Multinationals in developing economies

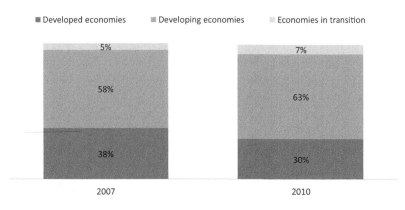

Multinationals in developed economies

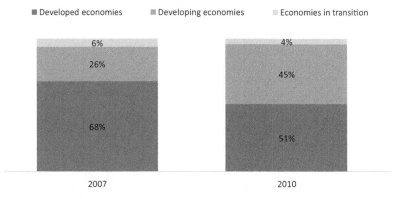

Figure 1.1 Distribution of projects by FDI, by country of origin, 2007–10. *Source:* ESADEgeo, 2012, based on OECD data.

As a result of this new balance, commercial relations between emerging countries are noticeably intensifying. Proof can be found in export dynamics, over which attention is (almost always) divided, as well as import dynamics. Since 2000, imports from emerging countries have increased an average of 17%, exceeding the worldwide increase in imports (13%) and, above all, the increase in imports in developed countries (10%). The weight of imports in emerging economies in the world total increased significantly, jumping from less than 30% at the beginning of 1990 to 45% in 2012. In other words, internal demand in emerging countries is accelerating global demand, and trade between emerging countries is intensifying.

The choice of Río for the Olympics is certainly a milestone for Brazil, and another victory for its president, Lula, who in 2010 was elected by *Time Magazine* as the world's most influential head of state and leader – ahead of Obama or any other leader. This choice marks the first time that Brazil has been designated as the host of the Olympic Games. The Games will be celebrated just eight years after those organised by China in Beijing. Costs are estimated to be $11 billion and it is anticipated that the positive impact on the Brazilian economy will be more than $50 billion (3.5% of the current GDP) between 2012 and 2025, according to a study by the Foundation Institute of Administration at the University of São Paulo (FIA) that was commissioned by the Brazilian Ministry of Sports.

True or not – we will only find out once the Olympics have been held – these numbers show that the BRIC nations are on a roll that will continue through the next decade. The announcement of Brazil as Olympic host represented a celebration for the emerging countries, and the good news for Latin America is that the entire region will also be affected, with Brazil dancing centre stage.

Farewell to the old world

The economies of Europe and the United States are losing importance. This does not mean that they are going to disappear from the map – on the contrary, they will continue to be top economic powers. However, and this is important, they will have to share the limelight and make room for the emerging countries. As a consequence, this will lead to a rethinking of relations between North and South, or in other words between 'developed' and 'developing' economies. Unilateral relations will be substituted by more bilateral and balanced relations, where countries nourish each other in terms of commercial flows, investments and good practices.

The traditional categories of 'OECD countries' and 'emerging countries' have to be reset. Within the OECD, there are already various emerging countries (Mexico, Turkey, Poland, Israel, Chile, to mention a few). The organisation itself, reportedly called the 'Rich Country Club', has members that are poorer and less developed than the

United Arab Emirates or Singapore. What is more, its top director, Ángel Gurría, comes from an emerging country (Mexico). With the crisis of 2008–12, we are also seeing how the OECD countries, previously seen as exponents of 'best practices', can also reveal the worst practices, and are currently suffering economic and financial crises that were only thought to occur in emerging markets (such as those plagued in the 1990s by sudden crisis or financial meltdowns).

The years 2008–12 have seen an increasingly quick change in the wealth of nations as the European dominoes fall, one after the other. The financial crisis of 2008–12 continues to multiply the paradoxes. The OECD countries saw their debts skyrocket, opening the door to comparisons with the emerging markets of the 1980s and 1990s. Meanwhile, the emerging markets tempered their enthusiasm for international investments. Latin American nations are achieving investment grade ratings: first Brazil, then Peru, and more recently, in June 2011, Colombia. During the same period, the OECD countries suffered as their debts and sovereign risks were reclassified by the rating agencies.

In 2011, yet another domino and taboo fell. For the first time, the rating agencies, Standard & Poor's and Moody's, insinuated that the United States could lose its triple AAA rating, meaning that it might lose its status as the world reference for international bonds (a threat executed in August of 2011, when S&P lowered the rating of the United States). The news is significant and the crisis of the summer of 2011, when the budget debate in the US Congress almost led to a suspension of payments, has magnified the news value. US Treasury bonds were previously considered the most secure in the world, even risk-free, according to the markets. These bonds play crucial roles in the international financial system, being the most liquid, a safe haven for assets in times of stress, and an absolute reference for putting a price on the rest of the world's bonds. When Brazil and Russia issue debt, the reference price is established according to US bonds. The whole financial industry is based on the premise (the fiction?) that US Treasury bonds are the bonds of reference and the most secure.

After 2008, the risk premiums of many OECD countries began to converge with those of the emerging markets. Whereas the former saw their premiums increase, and therefore their ratings decline, the latter saw their premiums fall and their ratings rise. In 2011, Greece was on par with Argentina, considered by the markets as one of the countries with the greatest probability of default or sovereign debt restructuring. Brazil boasted a risk premium far lower than its former coloniser Portugal. In April 2011, the former president Lula went so far as to imply that Brazil could rescue Portugal by buying Portuguese bonds; while the *Financial Times* proposed, with a certain irony, that Portugal agree to be annexed by Brazil to resolve the crisis and reduce its risk premium. This shift in international financial risks is leading companies and investors to redefine risks and opportunities.

One of the largest asset managers and investors in the world, Blackrock, introduced a new sovereign risk rating in 2011 that showed China as safer than the United States for investing, Chile safer than Germany, and Brazil safer than Spain.[8] In another previously unimaginable event, markets and investors began to speculate in 2010, 2011 and 2012 on the risk of sovereign default by OECD countries, including the United States.[9] Such an event used to be a risk that only emerging markets faced. Meanwhile, levels of debt in emerging countries ranged between 49% and 55%, while figures for the OECD countries were much higher at between 65% and 90% (or more). The result was a reassignment of financial investment portfolios.[10]

The emerging markets have become the main players in global finance and the international economy. In 2012, the largest holders of US bonds were no longer other OECD countries; half of the ten largest holders were emerging countries. China is in the lead now, followed by Japan and Great Britain, with more than $1.15 trillion in US Treasury bonds held. Therefore, having just learned the news from S&P, Beijing quickly called on Washington to be careful and ensure that Treasury bonds were not reclassified – that is, China gave Washington advice about how to handle the crisis. However, China is not the only emerging country with large US Treasury bond holdings: just behind Britain is Brazil, with nearly $200 billion invested

---

[8] See Blackrock, *Introducing the Blackrock Sovereign Risk Index: A More Comprehensive View of Credit Quality*, New York and London, Blackrock, June 2011. The report by the consultancy firm is available at www2.blackrock.com/webcore/litService/search/getDocument.seam?venue=PUB_IND&source=GLOBAL&contentId=1111142235.

[9] See JP Morgan, *The Domino Effect of a US Treasury Technical Default*, New York, JP Morgan Research, April 2011. Available at www.jpmorgan.com/pages/jpmorgan/investbk/solutions/research.

[10] See Pierre Yves Bareau, *Emerging Markets Debt Coming of Age*, London, JP Morgan Asset Management, 2011. Available at www.jpmorgan.com/pages/jpmorgan/investbk/solutions/research.

in Treasury bonds. And Brazil is followed by another three emerging countries, Taiwan, Russia and Hong Kong, all of which are now ahead of Switzerland, Canada and Luxembourg.

The emerging economies themselves are now questioning the leadership of the OECD countries. At the end of 2010, the Chinese rating agency, Dagong, downgraded the rating of the United States (at the beginning of 2011, it would do the same with another OECD country, Japan). Obviously, it might be thought that this agency is biased and it could be asked why China has the same rating as Germany and a higher rating than the United States. However, these ratings can also be seen as a reflection of China's changing vision of the world. The Dagong ratings give us an idea of how China views the world in terms of financial risks and opportunities, and can also be considered political signs.

Viewed in this manner, it is still striking, for example, that according to Dagong a country such as Chile enjoys a better outlook than the United States. Both have the same rating (A+), yet for Chile the perspective for the future is 'stable', whereas it is 'negative' for America. The United States is now hardly one step up from emerging economies such as Russia and South Africa, both of which have become major strategic economic partners of Beijing. Moreover, Latin American countries such as Brazil enjoy top ratings and have dethroned the USA and other OECD countries.

While the physical geography of nations remains the same, the financial and economic geography is changing. We are now witnessing a world where the most solid certainties of yesterday are being questioned. What appears to be certain is that the world of tomorrow will be very different from the world of yesterday. When Stefan Zweig settled in Brazil in the mid 1940s, he wrote that Brazil was the country of the future. Without question, the emerging countries are the countries of the future. However, they have now become countries of the present: China, Brazil and India have become industrial, economic and financial players.[11] The OECD countries, with the United States in the lead, will continue to play a major role, but they will see how they

---

[11] This enthusiasm for emerging markets is a repetition of economic history: at the end of the nineteenth century and until the First World War, in what was the first major economic and financial globalisation, Europeans went as far as to have 60% of their investments in emerging markets. See Rui Pedro Esteves, 'The Belle Epoque of International Finance. French Capital Exports,

are no longer the world epicentres and the absolute references against which everything is measured.

Investments in the emerging countries

We have seen that the emerging countries are less affected by the crisis than their counterparts in the OECD. As a result, these economies are attracting the respect of international investors. Moreover, and as a sign of the changing times, these investors are now being added to investors from the same emerging countries who have become capital generators at a global level.

The emerging countries have become increasingly attractive throughout the decade 2000–10, as reflected by the foreign direct investment (FDI) statistics. Asia, China and India have become important receivers of foreign investment. In Latin America, Brazil and Mexico, as well as Chile and Colombia, received growing amounts of FDI. The economic reforms undertaken, the political stabilisation achieved,[12] as well as the growth and expansion of the middle classes over that decade, have created a growing investor interest in emerging markets.

In 2010, for the first time in modern history, the emerging economies accumulated more foreign direct investment entries than the OECD countries. As recorded in various reports by international organisations such as the World Bank or the OECD,[13] we are witnessing the emergence of a multipolar world. Investments are moving towards emerging

1880–1914', University of Oxford, Department of Economics, Discussion Paper Series 534, February 2011. Available at www.economics.ox.ac.uk/research/WP/pdf/paper534.pdf; and Marc Flandreau, Juan Flores, Nicolas Gaillard and Sebastián Nieto-Parra, 'The End of Gatekeeping: Underwriters and the Quality of Sovereign Bond Markets, 1815–2007', NBER Working Paper 15128, 2009, 15128.

[12] On the impact of the political stability and institutions in the flows of FDI, see Laura Alfaro, Sebnem Kalemli-Ozcan and Vadym Volosovch, 'Capital Flows in a Globalized World: The Role of Policies and Institutions,' in Sebastian Edwards (ed.), *Capital Controls and Capital Flows in Emerging Economies: Policies, Practices and Consequences*, National Bureau of Economic Research, University of Chicago Press, May 2007, pp. 19–72. For more about the determining factors of FDI, see Elif Arbatli, 'Economic Policies and FDI Inflows in Emerging Markets', IMF Working Paper, August 2011. Available at www.imf.org/external/pubs/ft/wp/2011/wp11192.pdf.

[13] See World Bank, *Multipolarity: The New Global Economy. Global Development Horizons 2010*, Washington, DC, The World Bank, 2011. Also

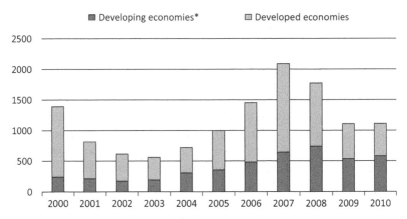

Figure 1.2 Foreign direct investment (entries) in $ billion.
Source: ESADEgeo, 2012 with data from UNCTAD. *Note:* *Includes Russia and other emerging economies.

countries and investment funds are being raised in emerging countries. Throughout the decade of the 2000s, more than 5,000 emerging multinational companies launched operations in other markets in a series of 12,500 greenfield investments that exceeded $1.7 trillion. More than one-third of the investments in emerging countries now come from other emerging countries. In 2010, of the more than 11,100 mergers and acquisitions, about 5,600 – that is, more than half – involved companies from emerging countries, whether as buyers or targets (Figure 1.2).

In the new decade of the 2010s, this attractiveness continues to grow. The emerging markets are the main destinations for investments. From among the large multinational companies surveyed by the consulting firm AT Kearney in its report *2010 Foreign Direct Investment (FDI) Confidence Index*, three emerging countries (China, India and Brazil) are among the top five investment destinations by multinationals (same in the 2012 report) (Figure 1.3).[14]

see OECD, *Perspectives on Global Development: Shift in Wealth*, Paris, OECD Development Centre, 2010; and for an analysis focused on Latin America, see Javier Santiso, *The Shifting Wealth of Nations*, Paris, OECD Development Centre, 2009. Available at www.oecd.org/dataoecd/52/31/41373888.pdf; and another version from 2008 at www.oecd.org/dataoecd/22/8/41125576.pdf.

[14] See AT Kearney, *Investing in a Rebound: The 2010 AT Kearney FDI Confidence Index*, Washington DC, AT Kearney, 2010. Available at www. atkearney.com/images/global/pdf/Investing_in_a_Rebound-FDICI_2010.pdf.

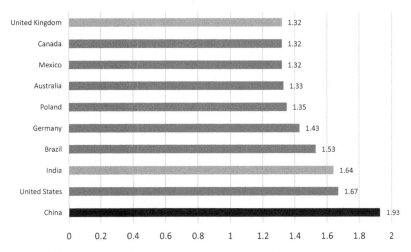

Figure 1.3 Top ten destinations for investment in 2010.
Source: AT Kearney, 2011. *Note:* New entry in the list in black; light grey: position worsens; dark grey: position improves.

Moreover, the current crisis in the OECD countries could be a reason to continue investing in and supporting emerging countries where the bulk of the world's growth over the current decade will be concentrated. The more developed countries will see growth weighed down by debt burdens and pending fiscal adjustments. Therefore, it is not surprising that the three countries with the most positive investment perspectives are the three emerging economies: China, India and Brazil.

In the aforementioned indexes, China, as in the previous year, holds first place, followed by the United States; whereas Brazil is the fourth favourite destination, followed by Germany. Mexico experienced a spectacular leap from 19 to 8 between 2009 and 2010. Two-thirds of the favourite destinations for direct investors for the coming years are now emerging economies. Some of these countries, such as Indonesia, did not even appear on the radar of the top twenty destinations for investment before the crisis in 2007.

In Latin America, Brazil and Mexico continue to stand out as the primary destinations. It is striking that Brazil has risen to fourth place as a favourite destination, ahead of Germany. Brazil even enjoyed the luxury of seeing FDI increase during a year of global crisis, with more than $45 billion invested (Figure 1.4). In 2009, according to UNCTAD, the worldwide decrease in foreign investment was significant, with inflows that hardly reached $23 billion. However,

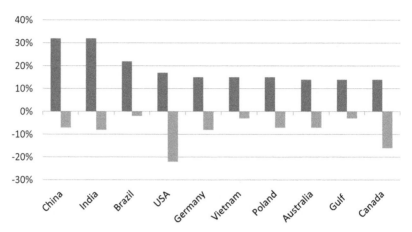

Figure 1.4 Main changes in the perspectives of investors between 2007 and 2010.
Source: AT Kearney, 2010.

investment began to rise again in 2010, when FDI grew 56% and reached $86 billion, with Brazil leading the increase and accounting for more than half of regional investment. Brazil received most of the foreign direct investments, totalling $48.5 billion, followed by Mexico with $17.7 billion.

The region continues to remain attractive. Multinationals such as Walmart and Coca-Cola plan to increase their investments for the 2014 World Cup and the 2016 Olympic Games. With these events in the spotlight, Brazil will most certainly become a favourite destination for investment in sectors such as construction, tourism, infrastructures and services in general.

Mexico, which experienced a strong recession in 2009 – one of the worst recessions since the 1930s – also has a promising future. In 2009, FDI fell sharply ($13 billion after almost $22 billion received in 2008). However, investments are increasing again in 2010–12, with new players such as La Caixa (which bought 20% of the Inbursa Financial Group for $2.2 billion), or the French company Axa (which bought ING Seguros for $1.5 billion). In 2010, Mexico climbed to 18 among the major recipients of foreign direct investment, according to UNCTAD, with a rise of 22% in FDI ($18.7 billion).[15]

---

[15] See UNCTAD, *World Investment Report 2011*, Geneva, UNCTAD, 2011. Available at www.unctad.org/Templates/webflyer.asp?docid=15189& intItemID=6018&lang=1&mode=downloads.

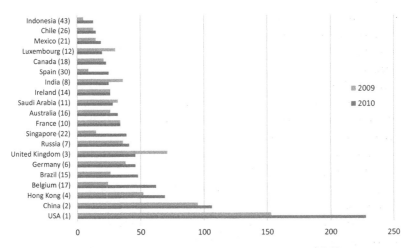

Figure 1.5 World top twenty – economies receiving FDI (in $ billion).
Source: UNCTAD, 2011. *Note:* Ranking for 2009 shown in brackets.

Mexico, along with Brazil and Chile, is therefore in the world's 'top twenty' for FDI, according to UNCTAD (Figure 1.5). It is also noteworthy, and proof of the major shift towards emerging countries, that half of the top twenty now are emerging economies. Asia is in the lead with five countries, followed by Latin America with three.

Without a doubt, the crisis of 2008–12 affected the region, and the flows of FDI fell 42% in 2009 to $77 billion, from a record achieved in 2008 (almost $132 billion). However, in 2010 a recovery in the trend in regional investment was confirmed. This upward trend took place, as we will see, thanks to the emerging multinationals themselves and especially the multilatinas, which have strongly reinitiated investments abroad.

The most remarkable aspect of all of these trends is that we are witnessing significant changes in the flows of FDI on a more global scale. In 2009, nearly half of global FDI (46%) was concentrated in the emerging countries (just twenty years ago they received 15% of total investment worldwide). This same story has repeated itself in 2010–12, according to the results of the surveys mentioned at the beginning of the chapter, and the majority of world growth in the coming years will be in emerging rather than OECD economies.

Investments in star countries like Brazil remain strong, as evidenced by the recent purchase of Tivit by the British Apax Partners for nearly $1 billion. This was a large operation in the technology sector by a company that had not previously made investments in Brazil. In May 2010, Spanish Telefónica continued to invest in Brazil, making an offer of €6.5 billion for control of Vivo, in which Portugal Telecom hold a stake.

The emergence of new investors from emerging markets is another striking trend that the crisis has accelerated. Groups from emerging countries were responsible for nearly 20% of total FDI worldwide in 2008 and 2009 (compared to just 11% in 2000). If we take the data from 2009 for Latin America, the economic powers of the OECD such as the United States and Spain continued to lead investments, with 57% and 9% respectively of the total that arrived in Latin America that year. However, the emerging countries of the region also made major investments in Latin America, representing 10% of the total. Chile and Mexico were at the top of a list that, just as in previous years, was led by Brazil, a trend that was confirmed in 2010 and 2011.

According to UNCTAD, investments by multilatinas in the region also began to recover in 2010. These represented 17% of the total acquisitions made that year in Latin America, exceeding investments in the region by the OECD countries (12% of the total). During the 1995–2002 period, intra-regional FDI (that is, investments made by multilatinas in Latin America) hardly exceeded 5% of the total. This figure rose to more than 36% during the period 2003–10. The most remarkable aspect, however, was the impressive leap made by Asian investors (in particular, China and India), which accounted for 20% of FDI in 2010 in Latin America – totalling more than $20 billion.

Although FDI made by Latin American groups abroad slowed from $43 billion at the peak in 2006 (owing especially to the Vale operation) to somewhat more than $11 billion in 2009, the global crisis did not stop this trend. In 2010, direct investment abroad by multilatinas climbed back to $43 billion. In 2009, Chile became, for the first time, the main Latin American investor, with an investment abroad of $8 billion. However, the other countries of the region, led by Brazil, continued to make substantial investments.

At the beginning of 2010, the Brazilian government-owned energy company Eletrobras disclosed its strategic plans until 2020 and announced that internationalisation in Latin America was among its priorities. A few months later, the Vale mining company took control of a concession in Guinea for $2.5 billion, after having paid another $3.8 billion at the beginning of the year to take over the fertiliser businesses of the North American company Bunge. An increase in investments by Latin American multinationals can be expected, and not just in the region – but also in other markets where they aim to carve out a larger niche for themselves.

Latin America and the Arab countries

The region is also attracting investors from other emerging countries, particularly from the Middle East and Asia.[16] Among the changes that we are witnessing, the intensification of the economic relations between emerging countries is also remarkable. China is obviously at the epicentre of these changes, but new commercial, financial and industrial networks are being built between areas that until recently had few ties. One of these emerging axes is Latin America and the Arab countries.

These ties are not new. Historically, several Middle Eastern diasporas settled in Latin America. Evidence of these migrations are, for example, the business leaders of Syrian or Lebanese origin who have established impressive empires (it is estimated that there are about 20 million Latin Americans of Arab origin in the region, 7 million of them in Brazil). The most spectacular is probably Carlos Slim, the richest man in Latin America, owner of the Carso Group, Telmex and América Móvil, among many other companies. In Chile, the Yarur family arrived from the Middle East at the end of the nineteenth century and founded an empire. The family today owns 50% of the Morandé vineyards, one of the largest vineyards in the country, and are founders and owners of the Credit and Investment Bank, the fourth largest financial institution in Chile. José Said Saffie multiplied the family fortune and is one of the wealthiest men in Chile and Latin America – owning 21% of the Parque Arauco; 16% of the BHIF-BBVA bank; 25% of Embotelladora Andina (a beverage company); 30% of Factorline, the fourth factoring company in the country; 48% of Edelpa, the largest flexible packaging company; and 50% of Reñaca Clinic.

However, until recently, relations with the Arabian Peninsula have been comparatively undeveloped. In the decade of the 2000s, the ties

[16] For more on the relations between Asia and Latin America, one of the best sources of information is the observatory created by Casa Asia, which is available at www.iberoasia.org/.

multiplied at an unprecedented rate, largely due to the Arab sovereign wealth funds.

ADIA (Abu Dhabi Investment Authority) is one of the largest sovereign wealth funds in the world and recently began to invest in Latin America through management funds such as the Southern Cross Group and other global asset management firms. ADIA owns buildings in Río, shares in the São Paulo Stock Exchange (Bovespa), and Brazilian bonds. The Al Qudra holding, in contrast, is involved in Brazilian agro-industrial sectors, while the private equity fund of Abu Dhabi, Mubadala (which has 20% of its investments outside of the United Arab Emirates), also invested heavily in Brazil in 2012. In 2009, a delegation from Abu Dhabi visited fourteen countries in the Western hemisphere, seeking to expand investments.

The emir of Qatar, Sheikh Hamad Al-Thani, visited Argentina, Brazil and Venezuela in January 2010 in search of opportunities. Arab investors, such as the operator of DP World ports, have also participated in the construction of Callao port in Peru. DP World also plans to make an investment of $250 million in Cuba, with the aim of transforming Mariel port into a first-class facility. Others have also made major investments in the same port, nearly $330 million, for example, by Banco Santander in Brazil and Aabar Investments from Abu Dhabi. In October 2010, Qatar Holdings acquired 5% of Santander Brasil for nearly $2 billion. Investors from the Middle East and sovereign funds, such as AIDA, ADIC (now Invest AD), Mubadala, AIC and KIA, are analysing the agriculture and food sectors, oil and gas, commercial real estate, hotels, renewable energies and mining throughout Latin America.

The agro-industrial sector, and everything associated with water (a commodity in short supply on the Arabian Peninsula), is particularly attractive. Companies such as Hassad Food (subsidiary of the Qatar sovereign wealth fund) and Al Dahra Agricultural Company (Abu Dhabi) are also expanding in the region. Cosan, the world's largest producer of sugar cane and ethanol, created a subsidiary specialised in locating and assessing agricultural land called Radar Propriedades Agrícolas, which includes investors from Arab countries among its clients. This interest in the region is not surprising: Latin America concentrates about 30% of all of the world's water reserves, and Brazil alone is home to more than 13% of worldwide reserves. 'Blue gold' is becoming as precious as black gold. However, Arab funds are not the only funds interested in Latin American land and property.

The Latin American presence in the Middle East is not as prominent. Only two Latin American banks – Itaú Bank and Banco do Brazil – have small representative offices in Dubai; and the Brazilian mining giant Vale has established a billion-dollar steel plant in Oman. Emirates Airlines has just started daily flights that connect Dubai and São Paulo, and daily flights on Qatar Airways have connected Doha to São Paulo and Buenos Aires since June 2010. In 2010, the Arab countries became the third main business partner of Brazil, buying more than $10 billion in Brazilian exports, nearly 11% of the total.

To stimulate relations between both regions, several Latin American entrepreneurs created the Gulf Latin American Leaders Council (www.gllc.org). In April 2010, some twenty-five entrepreneurs from the region travelled to the Arab countries. Brazil promoted the first Arab–Latin America Summit in 2005, which was followed up with another summit in Doha, Qatar, in 2009.[17] The third summit, planned to take place in Lima in February 2011, was postponed because of events in North Africa and the Middle East. The magazine *Latin Finance* also began to organise events between both regions, celebrating in Abu Dhabi in 2010 a second Latin America Mid-East Investors Forum, that included the sovereign wealth funds Invest AD and ADIA from Abu Dhabi. Argentina is also making moves and hosted a conference with the United Arab Emirates at the end of 2010. The United Arab Emirates in 2010 announced an expansion of its network of embassies in Latin America, with the opening of an office in Chile. On Kuwait's part, in July, the prime minister embarked on a three-week tour throughout the region in search of investment opportunities.

This show of interest in Latin America is linked to a broader trend. Many sovereign wealth funds now seek to strengthen their investments in other emerging countries as a priority and as an alternative to investing in OECD countries. The Kuwait Investment Authority has rapidly reduced its European and US portfolio from 90% to 70%, in order to strengthen investments in emerging markets (the share of these investments went from 3% to more than 9% of the portfolio).

---

[17] For a historical account of these relations, see www2.mre.gov.br/aspa/history.html.

Relations between emerging countries are becoming stronger and the rate at which they are growing is remarkable in itself. The links between Latin America and the countries of the Arab Peninsula are another illustration of this global trend towards a more decentralised world.

Latin America and Asia

It is also curious how both sides seek to intensify relations with Asia. The most recent example was the offer that Venezuela made to create a $100 billion joint investment fund in the energy sector with India, another country that seeks to ensure its supplies of raw materials in order to continue growing and feeding its huge population.[18]

India and its multinationals are emerging as major investors in Latin America. This is the case, for example, of the Indian multinational Reliance Industries, which invested $500 million in Peru in 2009. The Asian elephant is reaching out boldly towards Latin America, in search of food, minerals and oil to sustain its growth. India is the fourth major importer of oil in the world, hence the interest in assets and fossil fuels from Latin America. Indian multinational oil companies are now starting to invest in the continent. OVL (ONGC Videsh Ltd) initiated operations in Brazil, Venezuela and Cuba after investing more than $2 billion; meanwhile it began operations in Colombia for another $500 million. Bharat Petro Resources invested $280 million in oil exploration in Brazil. Reliance Industries imported in 2010 a quarter of the oil that it consumes from Latin America. At the end of 2009, it signed an agreement with the state company Ecopetrol for oil exploration and production in Colombia. In Peru, Reliance Industries and Jindal Steel are also investing about $700 million in mining and oil projects.

Projects are also multiplying in the agricultural and agro-industry sectors. The Indian Farmers' Cooperative (IIFCO), along with the Canadian cooperative Americas Petrogas, announced in 2011 that it would invest $200 million in the construction of a potassium chloride plant. Its fellow compatriot Shree Renuka Sugars invested nearly

---

[18] For more on the relations between India and Latin America, see http://induslatin.com/.

$410 million in Brazil, buying several local companies in 2009 and 2011 to diversify its supply, and so became one of the five largest Brazilian sugar producers. An Indian consortium, led by Bharat Petroleum Corporation and other private companies such as Rajashree and Godavari, is also looking for opportunities in this sector, as is Bajaj Hindustan. Jindal Steel has already invested more than $3 billion in mining projects in Latin America. In 2011, it announced that it would build a sponge iron plant in Bolivia, investing a total of $600 million. In Bolivia, the firm plans to offer direct employment to more than 5,000 workers, and has promised that 95% of these jobs will go to Bolivians.

Indian investments in Latin America continued to intensify during 2010 and 2011. United Phosphorus Limited (UPL), the largest agrochemical company in India, announced in 2011 that it would buy 50% of Sipcam Isagro Brazil (SIB) for an estimated $600 million. This company, which is based in Mumbai, has already made seven acquisitions throughout Latin America, mainly in Brazil, Argentina, Mexico and Colombia. This fertiliser company needs fertile soil and water, which is something that the region has in abundance. The scheme is also being repeated in Uruguay, where it is planning one of the largest Indian investments in the continent. Aratirí, owner of the Indian multinational Zamín Ferrous, aims to develop a giant open-cast mine on more than 150,000 hectares of land. The project involves an investment of nearly $2 billion, the largest in the history of the country, and would create about 1,500 direct jobs.

However, and this is especially important, Luis Alberto Moreno, president of the Inter-American Bank (which has published a very detailed report about India and Latin America),[19] has explained that India is also making large investments in the continent in areas with considerable added value.

The technology consultancy firms Infosys, Wipro and Tata Consultancy Services already employ more than 17,000 people in Latin America in 2012. Tata, for example, has 7,500 employees in the region, with operations in Uruguay, Argentina, Chile, Mexico and, since 2010, also

---

[19] See Mauricio Mesquita (ed.), *India: Latin America's Next Big Thing?*, Washington, DC, Inter-American Development Bank (IADB), 2010. Available at http://idbdocs.iadb.org/wsdocs/getdocument.aspx?docnum=35239272.

Peru. One of the suppliers to FIFA for the 2014 World Cup in Brazil will be an Indian technology company: Mahindra Satyam. For its part, Tech Mahindra, owned by the English multinational BT Group, plans to buy software companies in the region.

In the pharmaceutical sectors, we are witnessing movements by the generic Indian laboratories Ranbaxy and Strides Acrolab. The latter made a $75 million acquisition in Brazil in 2010. The Indian laboratory Glenmark opened a high-tech pharmaceutical factory in Argentina in 2011. Following an investment of $31 million, this plant will become the global centre for the company's oncology products. The manufacturing company Havells Silvana, which operates in the region from its headquarters in Costa Rica, also plans to expand and has acquired assets in Brazil, Colombia and Costa Rica for $200 million. In the wind power sector, Suzlon Energy Ltd launched itself on the Brazilian market in 2010. In the aluminium sector, Hindalco Industries, which is part of the Aditya Birla Group, announced investments of $300 million in Brazil in 2011.

India has become another major investor (among many) in the Latin American continent. Since 2000, Indian companies have invested about $12 billion in information technologies (IT), pharmaceutical products, agro-chemicals, mining, energy and manufacturing. Moreover, support for the region has been accelerating and proof of this is the growing number of summits between both regions and studies examining this boom.[20]

Other emerging countries are also making a strong breakthrough in the continent. Singapore has signed free trade agreements (FTA) with several countries in Latin America, in particular Chile, Peru and Costa Rica. In 2010, the sovereign wealth fund Temasek of Singapore, which already has teams located in Brazil and Mexico, increased its investments in the region with $400 and $200 million transactions, respectively. PSA International from Singapore operates several ports in Latin America, in particular in Panama and Argentina, and signed a contract in 2011 to manage the container terminal in the Mariel port, which will become the major loading centre in Cuba. The Singaporean company Sembcorp Marine, the second largest builder of offshore

---

[20] See, for example, www.americasquarterly.org/node/2422.

drilling platforms in the world, announced that it would start building a shipyard in Brazil in 2011.

Similarly, South Korea continues to make strong regional investments. In 2011, for instance, the South Korean manufacturer Hyundai Motor announced plans to produce an exclusive model for the Brazilian market at its new $600 million production plant in the state of São Paulo; production started in 2012. The new model will have an engine that can operate on gas or ethanol. Hyundai Heavy Industries, a subsidiary of the same Hyundai group, plans to invest $150 million to build a heavy machinery factory in Río de Janeiro, which will be its first plant outside Asia. Brazil will thus become the fourth largest market for the Korean multinational, following China, Russia and the United States; and Brazilian business will climb from 6% to 20% of Hyundai's total income.

The Korean company SK Energy also announced in 2011 that it is investing $600 million in oil activities in various Colombian blocks over the next three years, as well as more than $480 million in similar activities in Peru. LG International Corp has invested $70 million in an acquisition in Chile, and so becomes the first South Korean company to invest in Chilean oil and gas. Moreover, acquisitions in Chile continue to multiply. One of the most noteworthy was carried out by the Chilean group Errázuriz and the South Korean companies C&T Corporation and Kores. These companies will enter into a joint venture for a potassium and lithium mine in northern Chile – an investment of between $200 and $300 million.

We are also seeing cooperation agreements emerge between Korean and Colombian government-owned companies to invest in other countries. For example, the Colombian oil company Ecopetrol and the Korean National Oil Company (KNOC) announced investments of more than $2.5 billion in Peru over the current decade, which amounts to an estimated $300 million per year.

South Korean and Chinese interest is particularly evident in the lithium market. The Bolivian government signed an agreement in 2011 with the South Korean companies Korea Sources Corporation (Kores) and Posco, to process lithium. Also in 2011, Posco, the largest steel manufacturer in South Korea and fourth largest in the world, announced the signing of a memorandum of understanding to provide technological and financial assistance to the US lithium exploration and mining company Li3 Energy, which will oversee a lithium project in Chile. The agreement includes building a lithium extraction plant in Chile. For its part, the builder, Posco Engineering, a subsidiary of the same South Korean conglomerate, acquired 70% of the Ecuadoran specialist engineering company Santos SMI for $72 million in 2011. Posco also announced an investment of $300 million to expand its steel plant in Mexico in 2011.

Yet the country that stands out the most, apart from the Latin American nations themselves, is undoubtedly China.[21] In 2009, China became Brazil's major business partner for the first time, ahead of the United States; and in 2010 it became the largest direct investor in the country, also ahead of any other Western power. The Asian giant became the third largest investor in the region in 2010: of the $112.6 billion that was invested in 2010, 17% came from the United States, 14% from Holland and 13% from China. The trend was confirmed throughout 2011: between June 2010 and May 2011, in comparison with the same period in the previous year, Chinese investment in Latin America increased 290% and reached approximately $15.6 billion (according to Deloitte). These data confirm the value of Chinese FDI in Latin America, and its share with respect to other regions (until 2009, Latin America had accounted for 12% of overall Chinese FDI).[22]

In the months that followed, announcements of Chinese investments continued, particularly those related to soybeans and banking. The Chinese government-owned company Sanhe Hopeful plans to invest $7.5 billion over the next few years in agriculture and infrastructure in the state of Gioás, in order to guarantee the direct purchase of 6 million tons of soybeans per year, the equivalent to all current local production. This announcement was added to the fact that in April 2011 the Chinese group Chong Qing Grain Group announced plans to invest $2.4 billion in an agricultural complex in north-east Brazil. In August 2011, the first Chinese investment appeared in the banking sector with the purchase by the Industrial and Commercial Bank of

---

[21] See, in particular, the book by Adrian Hearn and José Luis Márquez (eds.), *China Engages Latin America: Tracing the Trajectory*, Boulder, Colo., Lynne Rienner Publishers, 2011.

[22] See Alicia García Herrero, *China's Outward FDI: What Explains Geographical Destination? Some Thoughts for Europe*, Madrid and Hong Kong, BBVA Research, December 2010. Available at www.iberchina.org/frame.htm?images/archivos/ChinaoutwardFDI_agh_bbva.pdf.

China (ICBC) of 80% of the shares of the Argentinean subsidiary of the South African Standard Bank for $600 million.[23] In Argentina, also in 2011, XCMC began the construction of a windfarm park for $200 million, and a urea plant for some $800 million (which will be built by the Chinese-owned company Tierra del Fuego Energía y Química SA).

Chinese investments in the continent are accelerating, as witnessed by the operations carried out by Chinese oil companies CNOOC and Sinochem, which invested, respectively, $3.1 billion and $3 billion in Brazil and Argentina in 2010, for major shares in Bridas and an oilfield in Brazilian waters (formerly owned by the Norwegian company Statoil). In 2010, Brazil became a major receiver of oil industry investment, with more than $17 billion of Chinese investments made last year – an unprecedented total. Nearly half is represented by the takeover of 40% of the Brazilian subsidiary of the Spanish oil company Repsol YPF ($7.1 billion). The flow of Chinese capital for productive activities accounted for one-third of the total of $48.5 billion received from direct investment operations, according to the Central Bank. Other major operations, in addition to the aforementioned investment of Sinopec in Repsol, include the investments of Sinochem ($3 billion), State Grid ($1.7 billion), ECE ($1.2 billion) and Wisco ($400 million), all of which are linked to the energy and raw material sectors.

Peru is also emerging as one of the main destinations of Chinese investment in Latin America. Examples include the investment made by the mining company Chinalco, which bought $703 million of shares in Perú Copper, and the acquisition of Northern Perú Copper by Minmetals/Jiangxi Copper. The application of a free trade agreement on 1 March 2010 between China and Peru only confirms the importance of Asia, and particularly China, in the region. In 2011, Peruvian exports to China already exceeded those to the United States. In 2009, for the first time, Brazil's main business partner was China, ahead of the United States.

A new trend is being profiled in the prototype of Chinese investments in the region. The countries of Latin America are seeking to reverse

[23] For more on Chinese investments, see the regular reports by Deloitte in particular, available at www.deloitte.com/assets/Dcom-China/Local%20Assets/Documents/Services/Global%20Chinese%20Services%20Group/cn_CSG_MMChinaOutboundMA_301110.pdf.

an asymmetrical relationship with China by encouraging the creation of added value through these Chinese investments. It is hoped in this way to overcome part of the threat that China represents (namely, that of cornering Latin American nations into low added value production and an ever narrowing business fabric).[24] As we shall see, this trend also includes technology sectors.

An example of this strategy of widening the relationship with China can even be seen in traditional areas such as the agro-industrial sector. In 2011, the Chinese grain group Chong Qing Grain Group announced investments of $2.4 billion in an agricultural complex in north-east Brazil. Interestingly, this is not a typical agreement to export soybeans; rather the investment will also include a soy processing plant, a warehouse terminal and a fertiliser processing plant. Brazil is clearly trying to manage the transformation of these products in order to add value and create local jobs.

We are witnessing a large reconfirmation of the world balances, in terms of both trade and investment flows. The decade 2000–10 ushered in a new era, with a greater role for emerging countries. The decade 2010–20, far from interrupting this trend, is accelerating it. Within this boom of the emerging markets, Latin America has also been a leader. This is largely due to a striking change, a new and virtuous Latin American contagion: that of economies firmly on paths of growth and development. As a result, Latin America has attracted the attention of traditional OECD investors, as well as investors from other emerging countries.

The new Latin American contagion

Latin America has experienced an unprecedented change. A few years ago, I published a book about good revolutionaries and the apostles of ultra-liberalism, an area shaken by economic, structuralist, Maoist, neo-liberal paradigms. These models sometimes impacted violently on

---

[24] For more on this topic, see the analysis by Kevin Gallagher and Roberto Porcekanski, *The Dragon in the Room: China and the Future of Latin American Industrialization*, Stanford University Press, 2010. For a summary, see www.bu.edu/pardee/files/2010/10/18-IIB.pdf; and the presentation on YouTube: www.youtube.com/watch?v=nw3PPRrM1k8; and also Jorge Blázquez and Javier Santiso, '¿Angel o demonio? Los efectos del comercio chino en los países de América Latina', *Revista de CEPAL*, 90, December 2006, pp. 17–43.

the social and economic realities of the continent. I pointed out that some countries – including Chile, Brazil and Mexico – had managed to detach themselves from this tradition of building maximalist economic policies inspired by a purist model. In the intervening years, more nations embraced pragmatic economic policies that combined macroeconomic orthodoxy and social policies (simultaneously supporting free trade and state enterprise). New and committed recruits to this reformist band include Costa Rica, Colombia, Uruguay, Peru, the Dominican Republic and Panama.

It appears that we are facing an unprecedented contagion, a virtuous contagion, in which countries are emulating each other. It is a group that stands out because its pragmatic economic policies transcend the traditional 'left' and 'right' divisions and classifications; and which, especially in Europe, have led to an effort to understand the region. A few years ago, the cliché about Latin America was that Chile was the only 'pretty girl' in the region. Latin America now boasts a world economic leader (with Brazil the seventh economic power in 2010 and ahead of Spain) in terms of nominal GDP. Today there are several 'pretty girls', and some like Mexico and Chile are now members of the OECD (Chile joined the organisation in 2010), while others are doubling their efforts to combine growth and development together with monetary/fiscal economic policies and social spending. All these nations are emulating each other.

Peru is one of the largest and most positive surprises and we will soon see whether the Peruvian trajectory becomes stronger with the new government that was elected in mid 2011. Just two decades ago, Peru was synonymous with Maoist guerrillas, extreme violence, rumours of a coup d'état, bank foreclosures, hyperinflation and debt default. Today this history seems to be in the distant past. Peru has one of the highest growth rates, not just in the region but in the world, and comparable to the Asian champions. Trade in Peru tripled in just a decade. In 2009, in the middle of a fully fledged global crisis, Peru achieved an investment grade rating. Nowadays, the GDP of this country, with a population of 26 million, has reached $140 billion and we are witnessing more than $40 billion in investments over the next ten years, particularly in the raw material clusters.

Regardless of the metric – maximum GDP growth, inflation under control, fiscal cautiousness – the Peruvian data confirm that the country has entered into an era of pragmatism. The individual who perhaps most embodies this transformation is the president himself, Alan García, who, after a disastrous first term in office, reinvented himself and anchored the country with pragmatic economic policies. There are obviously challenges ahead, and not just a few: poverty and inequality have been starkly reduced, but are still high; and fiscal spending (as in the rest of the region) should be more redistributive, especially in education and health. Diversifying the economy in a context of rising raw material prices is not going to be easy. However, Peru has taken giant steps since the mid-2000s, just like its neighbour Colombia, which in 2011 was also awarded investment grade rating and will probably become the third economy in the continent in terms of GDP (it already is in demographic terms, with a population of 46 million).

Economic development is a continuous path. On this route towards a better world, some countries are taking major steps forward. A symbol of this progress and the transformation of Peru was witnessed in 2010 when the Nobel Prize for Literature was (finally) awarded to the Peruvian writer Mario Vargas Llosa. It seems that the present and the future are smiling on Peru. An economic ugly duckling has grown into a swan – just like the rest of the continent.

Multilatinas expanding again

This economic progress of the continent, with the Brazilian growth driver in the front, has meant increasing popularity for the local multinationals: the multilatinas. Local multinationals had emerged strongly in previous decades, with Argentina as the pioneer and followed in the 1990s by Mexico and Brazil. But it was the decade of the 2000s that witnessed an unprecedented progress for multilatinas. These firms have set out to conquer new markets, many of them in Latin America, and with the more daring reaching out to the OECD countries.

In the wake of the crisis of 2008–12, these multilatinas have maintained their expansion. As we are seeing with the new decade of the 2010s, the multinationals of Latin America are once again eager to expand beyond their borders. Although in 2009, like many companies, they experienced a decrease in their international investments, the year 2010 was one of unparalleled growth. Moreover, the multilatinas of Brazil and Mexico are now being joined by others, from Chile, Colombia and even Peru. The geography of the investments is also changing.

Throughout the decade of the 2000s, Brazilian multinationals were particularly active. This internationalisation is still relatively concentrated. The mining company Vale alone accounts for 40% of the international assets of Brazilian companies ($35 billion). The next two companies, Petrobras and Gerdau, possess another $30 billion in international assets (nearly 35% of the holdings of the thirty largest Brazilian companies). The largest Brazilian overseas employer is the agro-industrial giant JBS Friboi, with nearly 80,000 employees, accounting for nearly 45% of all of the employees of Brazilian companies outside of Brazil.

The process of internationalisation by the Brazilian multinationals is still, however, in an initial phase and will progress throughout the decade of the 2010s. At the end of 2009, just nine companies had international assets of more than a billion dollars, and another ten companies had international assets of more than $100 million. The total direct stock of investments abroad by Brazilian multinationals was worth nearly $160 billion at the end of 2009, thus placing Brazil as the seventh largest investor in the emerging foreign market.

Mexican multilatinas have also been very active throughout the past decade. The stock of foreign investments by the twenty major Mexican multilatinas amounted to $117 billion and they have nearly 230,000 employees outside Mexico. The first three Mexican multilatinas – Cemex, América Móvil and Carso Global Telecom – control $86 billion of these assets, that is, nearly 73% of the total. Foreign investments continued in 2009 despite the economic collapse and totalled nearly $7.6 billion. This resilience is partially explained by the activities of two groups (Bimbo and Grupo México) that represent two-thirds of this amount. Investments were back up by 2010. In Latin America alone, Mexican companies invested more than $42.2 billion. Many companies expanded into other emerging countries in the region: Mexico thus invested more than $3.6 billion in Peru, which is more than the total invested in Chile ($3.5 billion). The main destination for Mexican investments in Latin America has been Brazil ($21 billion), followed by Colombia ($5 billion). At the end of 2010, groups such as Bimbo made a strong return to the investors' arena, buying the bread division from the US group Sara Lee for nearly one billion dollars, and in 2012 Bimbo Mexico bought Bimbo Spain (a separate company, subsidiary by then of Sara Lee).

The big news, however, did not come from Brazil or Mexico. Their multilatinas had been actively seeking opportunities for expansion in other countries for decades. The most significant news in the decade of the 2000s, and especially the current decade of the 2010s, has come from Chile, Colombia and Peru, all of which have begun a process of business internationalisation.

The Chilean multilatinas have been particularly active, even in 2009, the year of collapse in the OECD countries. That year, the Chilean multilatinas made $8 billion of acquisitions. In the first three-quarters of 2010, Chilean investment abroad reached nearly $5 billion, bringing the accumulated stock of Chilean FDI to more than $50 billion. The year 2010 witnessed the emergence of a giant in world aviation with the birth of LATAM – a firm that resulted from the merger of LAN (Chile) with TAM (Brazil). Other Chilean companies that started their internationalisation strongly were Sonda, Arauco, Falabella, Ripley, CMPC and Cencosud. Also in 2010, the Chilean retailer Cencosud, owned by entrepreneur Horst Paulmann, took over the Bretas supermarket chain in Brazil. For its part, Sonda, the largest technology company in the region, affiliated with the entrepreneur Andrés Navarro, acquired three companies in 2010 alone, two of them in Brazil (Telsinc and Softeam), as well as the Mexican company NextiraOne México SA.

Peru and Colombia also joined this trend. The Santo Domingo group is now one of the primary shareholders of SAB Miller, of South African origin and one of the largest brewing companies in the world. In Peru, those that stand out above the rest are the Romero, Brescia and Añaños groups. Following these same steps in Colombia are companies such as Cementos Argos, Grupo Nacional de Chocolates (GNC), Organización Terpel and Saludcoop. Colombian companies totalled more than $3 billion in acquisitions in 2010, a figure that is lower than the record year of 2005 ($4.6 billion) but still an indicator of the progress in internationalisation made by the Colombian groups. Other leading businesses include the Bank of Bogotá (which, in 2010, carried out the largest ever purchase made by a Colombian company abroad, in Central America to be specific), as well as Empresas Públicas de Medellín and ISA. In 2011, Grupo de Inversiones Suramericana SA bought pensions, insurance and investment fund operations in Chile, Mexico, Peru, Uruguay and Colombia from the Dutch company ING for nearly $3.8 million. This purchase, which consolidates the Colombian group as the Latin American leader in pensions with a portfolio of

25 million clients, is the largest acquisition yet made by a Colombian company.

The phenomenon of the multilatinas is accelerating. According to the Boston Consulting Group (BCG),[25] multilatinas already total 100 companies in the region, with head offices in eight Latin American countries and combined earnings of at least $500 million. Brazil totals thirty-four companies in this group, ahead of Mexico (twenty-eight) and Chile (twenty-one). Relatively far behind we find Argentina (seven), Colombia (five), and Peru (three). For now, this group of multilatinas concentrates its international activity in the American continent with 110 international representations in the region and fifty-one in the United States. But other continents are now being explored, especially Europe (thirty-three companies) and Asia (twenty-eight). New destinations such as the African continent are also emerging (twelve companies established and mostly propelled by Brazilian groups).

Moreover, some of these multilatinas are now also listed on the New York and Madrid exchanges (in this case, via Latibex), and starting to be listed on Asian exchanges. As a symbol of the changing times and the growing attraction of China, the mining giant Vale was first listed on the Hong Kong stock exchange in 2010. Also in 2010, we witnessed an acceleration of Asian and Arab capital entering the multilatinas. The Singaporean sovereign wealth fund Temasek, bought into the Brazilian group Odebrecht ($400 million), while its counterparts in the United Arab Emirates (ADIA) and China (CIC), along with GIC, also in Singapore, each invested between $200 and $300 million in the Brazilian bank BTG Pactual.

To sum up: we are witnessing a major rebalancing of the wealth of nations towards emerging markets. This rebalancing means that more than ever we need to reset our cognitive maps: there is less and less a centre and a periphery, the West and the Rest, OECD countries at the core of world economics and finance and emerging markets witnessing them. More and more, emerging markets are actors of world economics and finance, trading and investing more between them than with developed countries. The rise of multilatinas is part of this story. It shows also how much Latin America is tying with other regions, Latin American multinationals expanding beyond their frontiers towards

---

[25] See Boston Consulting Group (BCG), *The 2009 BCG Multilatinas*, Boston, BCG, 2009. Available at www.bcg.com/documents/file27236.pdf.

other Latin emerging markets but also towards Asia, the Middle East or Africa. Europe and USA do not disappear from their radar screens. However the boundaries of the world enlarged massively and Western countries are simply one of the (many) options for them.

In order to understand the depth of these trends, it is worth focusing precisely on one of the major actors: the Latin multinationals. Their rise testifies how much the region is transforming, becoming an actor and not only a spectator of the world economic transformations. The progress of the multilatinas, as we have already discussed and will now examine in more detail in the next chapter (2), is clearly led by the major economic power that Brazil has come to represent on the continent throughout the decade of the 2000s. The Brazilian multilatinas stand out in comparison with their peers in other Latin American countries, which is why we have dedicated a special chapter to Brazil (Chapter 3). The Brazilians are already world leaders in various sectors, as demonstrated by Vale in the mining sector, Petrobras in the oil industry, AB InBev, Brasil Foods and JBS Friboi in the agro-industrial sector, and Embraer in aviation. However, Brazil's place in the spotlight does not overshadow another major phenomenon that we are witnessing: the proliferation of multilatinas in more countries in the region (Chapter 4). The traditional multilatinas of Mexico and Argentina have been joined by firms from Chile, Colombia and Peru. These southern and Spanish multilatinas have in fact been the very first movers abroad (in the case of Argentina and Mexico in particular) and, as we will later see, are also writing a new page in the economic and business history of the continent, and helping position Latin America on the world investment map.

2 | *The decade of the multilatinas*

More data and classifications are accumulating on the emerging multi-nationals every year. These data confirm the boom that has emerged from India, China, Russia, Brazil and South Africa. Phenomenal growth – in which the multilatinas are also participating – is being registered in every sector.

The quantitative and qualitative progression of Latin multinationals throughout recent decades is also remarkable. Quantitatively speaking, the number of them is increasing. In 2006, there were eighteen multilatinas highlighted by BGC on its list of emerging multinationals; in 2008 there were twenty-two, and in 2009 there were 100. The sales of these groups are increasing, just like the number of countries where they are operating, as we will soon see. Above all, we are witnessing an extraordinary increase in the number of companies in the region that have turnovers greater than a billion dollars. About a decade ago, there were fewer than 170, and today there are 500 billion-dollar companies in Latin America (Figure 2.1).

Brazil clearly dominates the world of the multilatinas. Out of the 500 Latin American companies with the highest turnovers, 223 are from Brazil, which has a long lead ahead of Mexico with 117. However, we are witnessing a systematisation of the phenomenon of the multilatinas. It is no longer just Brazil, Mexico and Argentina that have international companies. The country that grew the most in 2010 was Chile: sixty-five Chilean companies formed part of the 500 largest in 2010, which is ten times more than the previous year. Peru has also progressed, going from nineteen to twenty-two between 2009 and 2010. Companies from Colombia, Panama, Costa Rica, Guatemala, Ecuador, and Uruguay are also making their way onto the list. A total of thirteen countries currently have companies that rank among the 500 largest in the region (Figure 2.2; Table 2.1).

The primary sector dominates. The semi-government-owned company Petrobras, the Mexican government-owned Pemex and the

Table 2.1 *The top 500 multilatinas by country in 2005–10.*

RK 2010	Country	Number of companies					
		2005	2006	2007	2008	2009	2010
1	Brazil	204	207	211	212	226	223
2	Mexico	138	111	134	126	119	117
3	Chile	54	63	55	60	55	65
4	Argentina	36	41	36	35	33	32
5	Venezuela	11	12	7	7	6	3
6	Colombia	30	35	31	28	30	26
7	Peru	12	18	15	21	19	22
8	Ecuador	5	3	3	3	3	3
9	Costa Rica	4	3	3	3	3	3
10	Bolivia					1	1
11	Uruguay	2	2	2	2	2	2
12	Brazil/Paraguay						1
13	Panama	2	2	2	2	2	2
14	El Salvador	1	1	1	1	1	
15	Guatemala	1	2				

Source: América Economía, 2011.

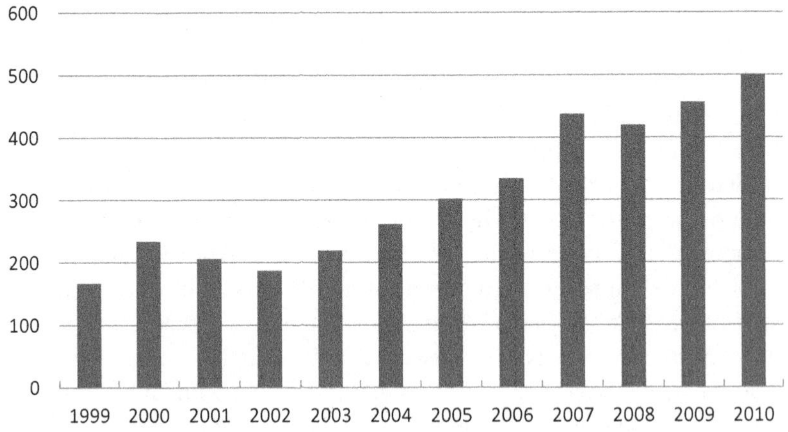

Figure 2.1 Number of companies in Latin America with more than a billion dollars in sales in 2010.
Source: América Economía, 2011.

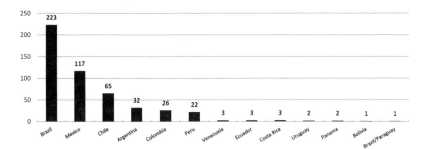

Figure 2.2 Number of multilatinas by country, 2010.
Source: América Economía, 2011.

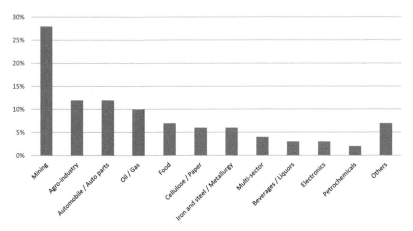

Figure 2.3 Sector analysis of the 500 largest multilatinas, 2010.
Source: América Economía, 2011.

Venezuelan government-owned PDVA are the largest in turnover. Some 28% and 10% of the exports made by the 500 largest companies come from mining and oil, respectively. Agro-industry and foods represent another 19% of the total (Figure 2.3).

However, these government-owned hydrocarbon giants are now being threatened by private companies – such as the mining company Vale or the Mexican *teleco* América Móvil, both with turnovers of about $50 billion that place them right behind. It is not surprising that the oil industry and the mining sector have a large number of companies in the top 500 ranking (thirty-eight and thirty-five, respectively). However, it is remarkable that the sector with the greatest number of companies in the top 500 is commerce (seventy-four), and that sectors such as telecommunications boast a comparable number of firms (thirty-six) (Figure 2.4, Table 2.2).

Table 2.2 *The top 500 multilatinas by sector in 2005–10.*

RK 2010	Sector	Number of companies					
		2005	2006	2007	2008	2009	2010
1	Oil/gas	34	35	32	37	38	38
2	Commerce	71	72	70	74	74	74
3	Telecommunications	45	43	41	37	35	36
4	Electrical energy	45	46	44	43	53	49
5	Automobile/auto parts	29	31	33	33	31	40
6	Mining	27	36	33	32	31	35
7	Iron and steel industry/ metallurgy	42	36	40	36	24	27
8	Multi-sector	25	29	14	15	17	15
9	Agro-industry	15	14	20	19	17	18
10	Beverages/liquors	18	19	15	15	17	16
11	Food	26	24	24	25	23	20
12	Construction	9	9	13	13	20	23
13	Transport/logistics	19	15	17	19	18	18
14	Electronics	14	11	20	20	21	19
15	Petrochemicals	36	13	14	14	12	8
16	Chemicals/ pharmaceuticals	36	16	20	18	21	15
17	Cement	7	8	7	6	6	6
18	Cellulose/paper	11	12	9	10	7	9
19	Basic services	8	3	6	60	6	6
20	Equipment	7	7	6	5	5	5
21	Health services	3	4	6	6	8	5
22	General services		5	2	2	2	2
23	Manufacturing		4	8	8	6	5
24	Textile/shoes	5	4	2	2	4	6
25	Aerospace industry	1	1	1	1	1	1
26	Machines/equipment	3	2	3	4	3	2
27	Software and data						1
28	Graphic industry						1

Source: América Economía, 2011.

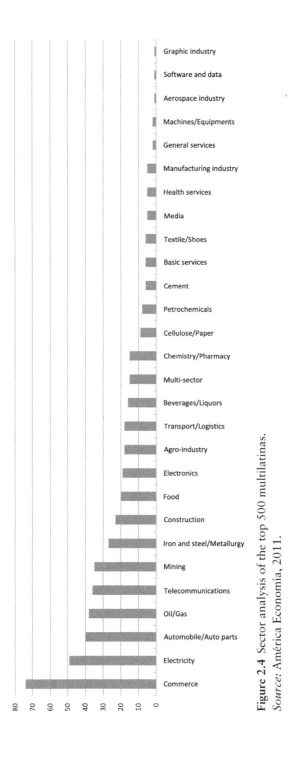

Figure 2.4 Sector analysis of the top 500 multilatinas.
Source: América Economía, 2011.

Although the oil sector leads in terms of aggregate sales (with a reported turnover of $500 billion in 2010), commerce takes the spotlight when it comes to the size of the payroll with 1.5 million employees – maintaining a strong lead ahead of the 'mere' 370,000 employees in the oil industry. In fact, of the five companies that did the most hiring in 2010, three were large Mexican retailers: Walmart (the largest Latin American employer with nearly 220,000 employees), Soriana and Puerto de Liverpool. Other companies that stand out for having the largest payrolls are the Chilean company Cencosud, with nearly 130,000 employees in the region, and the Mexican company Bimbo with 106,000 employees. It is also interesting to note that the second largest regional employer from among the top 500 multilatinas is a telecommunications company. In 2010, América Móvil had more than 150,000 regional employees (Table 2.3).

Multilatinas: emerging multinationals

This surge of multilatinas is noticeable in every classification and is reflected in the prestigious Financial Times 500 ranking.

This ranking classifies the world's top 500 companies, and clearly highlights the tsunami that we are experiencing.[1] Chinese, Indian and Brazilian multinationals have made a huge impact on the ranking (and on many similar rankings). We are also seeing the emergence of multinationals from Taiwan (eight in total). These countries are already forcing those of the OECD to step aside. In the case of Latin America, Brazil has eleven companies in the ranking, surpassing Spain (with seven). In total, there are about 125 emerging multinationals in this classification. It is no surprise that China, India and Brazil lead in number, but there are also multinationals from Indonesia, Malaysia, Taiwan, Korea, Singapore, Turkey, South Africa and Russia, as well as from Latin America, in particular Mexico, Argentina and Chile (Figure 2.5).

This ranking prompts us to make various observations.[2] First of all, it is striking how the emerging multinationals are ousting those

---

[1] www.ft.com/intl/cms/95edc490-9d61-11e0-9a70-00144feabdc0.pdf.
[2] Other rankings of the same type, such as those conducted by Forbes or Fortune, produce identical findings. For a comparison, see www.gfmag.com/tools/ global-database/economic-data/10521-worlds-largest-companies. html#axzz1UETB0Elh.

Table 2.3 *Number of employees in 2010.*

subRK 2010	Multilatina company	Country	Employees	RK América Economía 2010
1	Walmart Mex. and CAM	Mexico	219,767	9
2	América Móvil	Mexico	150,618	5
3	Pemex	Mexico	147,672	2
4	Cencosud	Chile	127,000	29
5	Odebrecht	Brazil	118,701	8
6	FEMSA	Mexico	108,572	26
7	Correios e Telégrafos	Brazil	107,992	72
8	Grupo Bimbo	Mexico	106,545	48
9	CBD – Grupo Pâo de Açúcar	Brazil	96,662	14
10	Norberto Odebrecht	Brazil	92,128	45
11	Construtora Norberto Odebrecht	Brazil	92,128	156
12	Marfrig	Brazil	90,625	46
13	Walmart – Bod. y Tien. Descuentos	Mexico	86,777	40
14	Falabella	Chile	86,500	55
15	Soriana Organization	Mexico	83,800	69
16	Petrobras	Brazil	80,492	1
17	PDVSA	Venezuela	79,000	3
18	Walmart	Brazil	72,000	34
19	Carso Group	Mexico	70,787	96
20	Vale	Brazil	70,785	4
21	Votorantim Group	Brazil	70,603	18
22	Coppel Group	Mexico	68,960	134
23	Coca-Cola FEMSA	Mexico	68,449	61
24	Carrefour	Brazil	67,000	23
25	Camargo Corrêa Group	Brazil	61,700	42
26	JBS Friboi	Brazil	60,000	7
27	Walmart Hypermarkets	Mexico	58,867	71
28	BRF Foods	Brazil	57,000	27
29	Alfa Group	Mexico	56,332	35
30	Pepsico Group (1)	Mexico	55,000	110
31	Techint	Argentina	54,000	15
32	Salinas Group	Mexico	53,150	90
33	Coca-Cola	Brazil	53,000	43
34	Teléfonos de México	Mexico	52,062	52

(*cont.*)

Table 2.3 *(cont.)*

subRK 2010	Multilatina company	Country	Employees	RK América Economía 2010
35	Casas Bahia	Brazil	51,891	137
36	Cemex	Mexico	46,523	24
37	Gerdau	Brazil	45,000	16
38	Ambev	Brazil	44,900	22
39	Bal Group (1)	Mexico	40,320	54
40	Elektra Group	Mexico	39,429	145
41	Comercial Mexicana	Mexico	38,930	114
42	Walmart Chile	Chile	37,500	106
43	Modelo Group	Mexico	36,566	78
44	Cosan	Brazil	35,351	39
45	El Puerto de Liverpool	Mexico	35,254	122
46	Grupo Industrial Lala (1)	Mexico	34,400	97
47	Grupo Chedraui	Mexico	33,018	121
48	Extra	Brazil	30,000	53
49	Eletrobrás	Brazil	29,708	17
50	Empresas ICA	Mexico	29,674	186

Source: América Economía, 2011.

from the OECD in every sector. This is unsurprising in the area of raw materials, for example, given that many of these materials are located in emerging countries. Accordingly, Chinese and Brazilian oil companies, Petrochina and Petrobras respectively, rise to second and fifth place worldwide, just behind Exxon Mobil, the US company that continues to be the world's largest oil and gas company. However, the FT classification, by focusing on companies listed on the stock market, overlooks many government-owned companies, particularly Aramco in Saudi Arabia, Pemex in Mexico and PDVSA in Venezuela, all of which are leaders in their respective sectors. Nevertheless, the FT ranking clearly shows the eruption of the emerging multinationals during this decade. We can witness the same phenomenon in the Fortune 500. Each year more companies from emerging countries join the list, displacing US and European companies. China went from thirty-seven companies in 2009 to forty-six in 2010 and sixty-one in 2011 (sixty-nine if we include Taiwan). India and Brazil maintain the same

Figure 2.5 Largest multinational companies in the world (FT 500).
Source: ESADEgeo, 2012; based on Financial Times data.

number of companies as in 2010, eight and seven respectively, while Korea adds about fourteen multinationals.

Petrochina and Petrobras, with mammoth stock market capitalisations (more than $325 billion and nearly $250 billion respectively) could theoretically buy out several oil companies, such as the French Total (with just under $145 billion of capitalisation) and the Spanish Repsol YPF (with just under $75 billion of capitalisation). The same occurs in the mining sectors: here another Brazilian company, Vale, rises to 23 on the world ranking with a market capitalisation of nearly $170 billion, which places it behind the British-Australian BHP Billiton (sixth in the classification), but already ahead of the other British-Australian company, Río Tinto (31).

The second observation that can be made on this ranking is that there are increasingly more multinationals from emerging countries and that new countries are starting to make their way into the classification. In the top 500 capitalisations worldwide, there are already more than 125 multinationals from emerging countries. As already pointed out, this classification is only partial, as it does not include unlisted government-owned multinationals, which are major companies in many of these countries. Although China, India and Brazil lead in terms of numbers, representation from emerging countries includes multinationals from Indonesia, Malaysia, Taiwan, Korea, Singapore, Qatar, Kuwait, the United Arab Emirates, Saudi Arabia, Turkey, South Africa and Russia. In Latin America, in addition to the Brazilian and Mexican multinationals, there are also listings from Argentina (Tenaris) and Chile (Falabella). It is expected we will soon see Colombian and Peruvian companies added to the ranking.

The third observation is perhaps the most remarkable: that multinationals from emerging nations are climbing into the technology sectors in addition to the traditional sectors, such as raw materials and agro-industry. By leaving unlisted companies out of the classification, we lose relevant information: of particular note here are the Chinese companies Huawei and ZTE, which are ousting the previous world leaders Alcatel-Lucent and Ericsson in the telecommunications industry. Indeed, it is remarkable how many emerging multinationals are making their way in telecommunications. China Mobile (16) already exceeds the US companies AT&T (20) and Verizon (48) and British Vodafone (30) in terms of stock market capitalisation. The Mexican company América Móvil (76) surpasses the Japanese company NTT (106). The

Korean company Samsung is already larger than Nokia, Intel or Cisco. We are also seeing technology companies take prominent positions in this world classification: such as the Taiwanese firms Semiconductor Manufacturing, Hon Hai Precision Industry and HTC; the Chinese Internet company Tencent; the Indian multinational Wipro; and the South African media company Naspers.

The sector of telecommunications, in particular, is full of multinationals from the new world. In addition to the aforementioned Chinese and Mexican multinationals, there are another half dozen, led by Hutchinson Whampoa in Hong Kong, China Unicom in China, SingTel in Singapore, MTN in South Africa, Bharti Airtel in India, Chunghwa Telecom in Taiwan, Emirates Telecoms in the UAE, and Zain in Kuwait. In 2012, these emerging multinationals shocked their European counterparts: nearly the same day (in May 2012) two of them bid for two European telcos: América Móvil, the telecoms group controlled by Mexican tycoon Carlos Slim, offered to buy a stake worth up to 3.2 billion euros ($4.2 billion) in Netherlands-based KPN, seeing it as a base for potential expansion in Europe; at the same moment Chinese Hutchison Whampoa made a €2 billion bid for the bankrupt Irish Eircom Group.

This rise of technological multinationals points towards another massive trend that we will see throughout this decade: a shift of financial and industrial wealth towards the emerging countries and a shift of innovation towards these nations. These countries will progress from just consuming technology (often low cost), to producing technology with increasingly added value. In certain sectors, such as telecommunications, they have already taken top positions; and even in the areas of digital media and Internet, we see how Chinese groups such as Tencent are starting to spearhead the next wave.

Finally, it is worth noting that multinationals also do well in this ranking. We have already mentioned how the Brazilian giants Petrobras and Vale climbed to the top twenty-five in the world. It is worth noting that we have to go down to position 44, for example, to find a Spanish multinational (Telefónica). What is even more remarkable is the growth of the Brazilian banks: Itaú Unibanco (52) is ahead of Santander (55), while Bradesco (93) exceeds BBVA (134). All in all, Brazil places eleven multinationals in the FT Top 500, distancing itself from Spain, which has just seven multinationals. It is striking that, of the Spanish multinationals, most (Telefónica, Santander, BBVA,

Iberdrola, Repsol) largely attribute their inclusion to their presence in emerging markets – and Latin America in particular. However, the 'Latin' presence is not limited to Brazil or Spain, and Mexico also stands out (three multinationals), as well as Chile (two) and Argentina (one) (Table 2.4).

Rankings just tell part of the story and change from one year to the next. However, beyond their limitations, they are an indicator of how the world is turning: like sunflowers that search for the sun, it seems that the world economy is searching for the emerging markets.

The progress of the multilatinas

The progress of the multilatinas was extraordinary throughout the decade 2000–10 and everything indicates that similar growth will be seen during this current decade. A good indicator of this development is the América Economía rankings, which shows that there are growing numbers of multilatinas that are covering ever more sectors and operating in an increasing number of nations.[3]

The term multilatina was coined by América Economía to describe a new emerging reality: that of companies (mostly Argentinean at that time) starting to do business throughout Latin America. Owing to their Latin American expansion, Spanish multinationals can also be included in this category. However, the main phenomenon we will be examining is that of the Latin American multinationals that have been emerging throughout the decade of the 1990s – and above all the decade of 2000–10.[4] The reality of the multilatinas had changed considerably by 2012: from being a phenomenon particular to Argentina to becoming a reality above all in Brazil and Mexico. But we have also seen how many other countries in the region – Chile, Colombia, Peru and Guatemala – also have multilatinas in the ranking. The expansion is now spreading throughout Latin America: of the sixty-six companies that were in this ranking in 2011, fifty-three now operate outside Latin America.

The América Economía rankings are the most comprehensive on the topic of multilatinas and have been published annually since

---

[3] See http://rankings.americaeconomia.com/2011/500/.
[4] See Javier Santiso, 'La emergencia de las multilatinas', *Revista de CEPAL*, 95, August 2008, pp. 7–30.

Table 2.4 *Multilatinas in the FT 500.*

RK 2011	Company	Country	Market value	Sector	Income in $ million	Net income in $ million	Assets in $ million	Employees
5	Petrobras	Brazil	247,417.6	Oil/gas	128,478.4	21,198.2	309,336.9	80,492
23	Vale	Brazil	168,232.1	Mining	50,135.6	18,114.5	127,844.7	70,785
52	Itaú-Unibanco	Brazil	99,719.8	Banking	N/A	8,025.9	439,828.9	108,000
76	AMX	Mexico	81,595.4	Telecommunications	49,187.6	7,349.3	69,568.7	55,627
79	Ambev	Brazil	79,604.2	Beverages	15,200.8	4,555.1	25,053.4	44,900
93	Bradesco	Brazil	71,981.5	Banking	N/A	6,037.2	373,516.9	95,248
140	Walmex	Mexico	53,400.3	Commerce	27,177.6	1,582	15,763.8	219,767
143	Banco Brasil	Brazil	51,965.2	Banking	N/A	8,110.2	488,790.5	109,026
175	Santander Brazil	Brazil	46,256.7	Banking	N/A	4,447.1	217,492.8	54,000
210	Ogx Petroleo	Brazil	39,055.6	Oil/gas	N/A	−74.4	6,017.2	213
255	Itaúsa	Brazil	33,943.5	Financial	N/A	2,661.6	166,090.2	125,000
310	Grupo Mexico	Mexico	29,074.7	Metallurgy	8,314.6	1,759.9	14,822.6	
312	Tenaris	Argentina	29,032.7	Metallurgy	7,820.6	1,143.3	14,153.8	25,422
377	Falabella	Chile	24,340.3	Commerce	9,468	884.6	13,998.9	48,000
378	Siderurgica Nacional	Brazil	24,322.9	Metallurgy	8,705.1	1,515.9	21,813.4	19,000
406	Copec	Chile	22,724	Oil/gas	13,265.6	1,106.9	19,270.7	
439	Eletrobras	Brazil	21,481.6	Electricity	14,949.9	97.8	76,289.4	25,809

Source: Author – based on Financial Times, 2012.

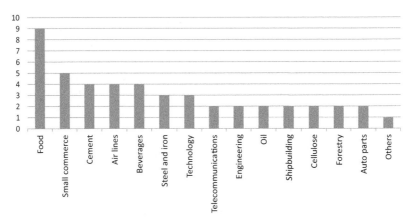

Figure 2.6 Sector distribution of the multilatinas in the multilatinas (AE) ranking.
Source: ESADEgeo, 2012; with data from América Economía.

2006 – and so enable an analysis of evolutions and trends. This ranking seeks to measure accurately to what extent the multilatinas are multinationals, and how much they have expanded internationally. There are nuances in this measurement; a presence in five countries within the same region, such as Latin America for instance, gives a lower rating than having operations in five countries spread across more than one continent. In addition to the international presence in terms of plants, offices or representations, the methodology also measures internationalisation in terms of assets, investments and human resources.

The first point that stands out is that the number of multinationals is growing. In addition, since the ranking in 2006, the sectors where the multilatinas are active have expanded considerably. Traditionally, they arose from sectors related to raw materials and agro-industry. The largest multilatinas, in terms of stock market capitalisation, continue to be companies in the raw material sector, such as the Brazilians Petrobras and Vale. But even this fact has started to be overtaken by recent trends: technology and telecommunication companies such as the Mexican América Móvil are now emerging with stock market capitalisations that are near those of the oil and mining sectors. Thus, in 2011–12, we saw how food, commerce, cement, airlines and even technology and telecommunications claim positions ahead of the traditionally dominant oil sector (Figure 2.6).

If we look at the more globalised multilatinas, namely, the ten firms with the highest percentage of investments abroad, this diversity stands out: in the lead is a pharmaceutical supplier (Bagó from Argentina), followed by a supplier for the oil industry (Tenaris, also from Argentina), and firms in other sectors such as cement (Cemex from Mexico), an agro-industrial group (JBS Friboi from Brazil), and even a technology company (Brightstar). The latter has its headquarters in Miami, but was created and founded by a Latin American, Marcelo Claure from Bolivia (which is why it appears as a Bolivian company in the ranking). With 3,600 employees and a turnover of nearly $10 billion in 2012, it is the most internationalised of the multilatinas.

The inclusion of a technology company such as Brightstar is the most interesting development in the 2010 ranking. This company also leads the ranking of the most global multilatinas because it trades in more countries (sixty-one) and regions (eight) than any other. It even exceeds the Brazilian company JBS Friboi and the Mexican company Cemex, both in eight regions, but in 'only' twenty-one and thirty-five countries respectively. Brightstar also exceeds the mining company Vale, which trades in nine regions, but 'only' thirty-eight countries. Brightstar's rate of globalisation is the highest in the whole region, with 84% of its employees abroad, 76% of its investments also abroad, and more than 60% of its sales in international markets (Figure 2.7).

In Table 2.5, we reproduce the top twenty multinationals exactly as they appear in the ranking. Once again, we highlight the diversity of the sector and country of origin of the multilatinas: beverages, foods and mining, but also telecommunications, pharmaceuticals and retail.

In terms of sales abroad, the oil company PDVSA is in the lead, both in terms of volume exported as well as in percentage of the total produced. The diversity is striking: PDVSA is followed by Telmex (a telecom operator), Sudamericana de Vapor (shipping) and Embraer (aviation), companies that all sell more than 90% of their production abroad (Figure 2.8).

If we analyse the ranking, not just by sectors but also by countries, we see a certain concentration. Brazil, with twenty-seven of the sixty-six multilatinas, has a very dominant presence, ahead of Mexico (fifteen) and Chile (eleven). If we make rankings by sales volumes or number of employees, the Brazilian multilatinas also stand out. Petrobras, with $128 billion in sales in 2010, is the highest selling multilatina, ahead of another oil company, the Venezuelan PDVSA, with $95 billion in sales. The agro-industrial companies JBS Friboi and Brasil Foods, with

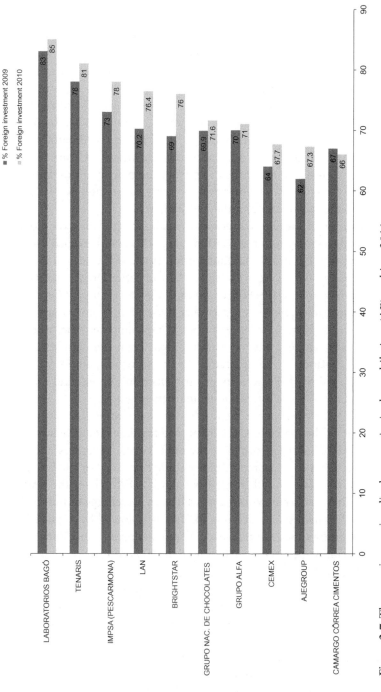

Figure 2.7 The most internationalised companies in the multilatinas (AE) ranking, 2011.
Source: América Economía, 2011.

Table 2.5 Globalisation of the multilatinas in 2011.

RK 2011	Company	Country of origin	Sector	Number of countries	Areas/ Regions	% Sales	% Investments	% Employees	Index of globalisation
1	Brightstar	Bolivia	Telecom.	61	8	60	76	84	**82.3**
2	JBS Group (Friboi)	Brazil	Food	21	8	89.2	65.5	64.0	**78.2**
3	Cemex	Mexico	Cement	35	8	75.6	67.7	65.8	77.7
4	Tenaris	Argentina	Iron and steel industry	11	5	80.4	81.0	71.7	77.0
5	LAN	Chile	Airlines	19	7	78.0	76.4	43.0	**73.2**
6	Telmex	Mexico	Telecom.	9	3	94.9	50.2	92.2	**70.0**
7	Alfa Group	Mexico	Auto parts/ Petrochemicals	17	6	54.0	71.0	51.5	69.8
8	IMPSA (Pescarmona)	Argentina	Energy	11	3	84.0	78.0	65.0	69.0
9	Vale	Brazil	Mining	38	9	33.6	49.8	27.1	**67.2**
10	Const. Norberto Odebrecht	Brazil	Engineering	34	7	70.5	56.0	48.6	**66.3**
11	Gerdau	Brazil	Iron and steel industry	14	6	38.9	59.9	48.0	**65.1**
12	Ajegroup	Peru	Beverages	16	4	78.0	67.3	74.0	**64.0**

(cont.)

Table 2.5 (cont.)

RK 2011	Company	Country of origin	Sector	Number of countries	Areas/ Regions	% Sales	% Investments	% Employees	Index of globalisation
13	Grupo Bimbo	Mexico	Food	18	6	55.0	60.1	52.7	63.8
14	Petrobras	Brazil	Oil	28	8	34.5	31.0	19.9	61.3
15	Avianca – Taca	El Salvador	Airlines	23	4	82.0	22.0	77.0	61.3
16	Laboratorios Bagó	Argentina	Pharmaceuticals	18	4	23.1	85.0	69.0	60.3
17	América Móvil	Mexico	Telecom	18	4	36.0	33.0	70.0	60.2
18	Grupo Nac. de Chocolates	Colombia	Food	11	4	38.0	71.6	19.5	59.1
19	Grupo Casa Saba (Fasa)	Mexico	Retail trade	4	2	73.0	53.0	70.0	58.8
20	Marfrig	Brazil	Food	22	6	54.9	31.6	41.7	57.0

Source: América Economía, 2011.

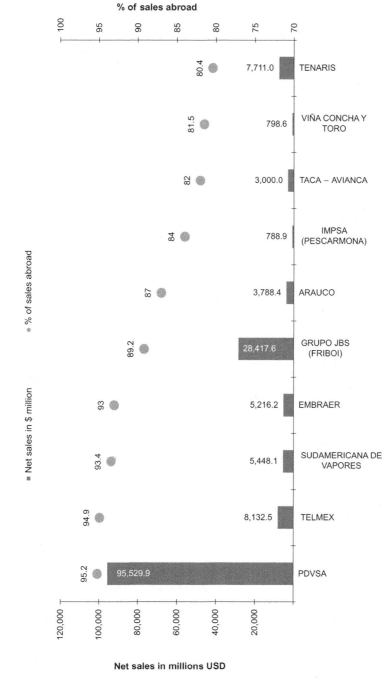

Figure 2.8 The ten companies with the largest percentage of foreign sales. *Source:* América Economía, 2011.

Table 2.6 *Top twenty multilatinas by sales volume in 2010 (in $ million).*

RK 2011	Company	Country	Sector	Sales 2010
14	Petrobras	Brazil	Oil	128,000
9	Vale	Brazil	Mining	49,949
17	América Móvil	Mexico	Telecommunications	49,221
2	JBS Group (Friboi)	Brazil	Food	28,418
11	Gerdau	Brazil	Iron and steel industry	18,841
3	Cemex	Mexico	Cement	14,435
7	Alfa Group	Mexico	Auto parts/ petrochemicals	11,045
13	Grupo Bimbo	Mexico	Food	9,487
6	Telmex	Mexico	Telecom	8,133
20	Marfrig	Brazil	Food	7,788
4	Tenaris	Argentina	Iron and steel industry	7,711
1	Brightstar	Bolivia	Telecom	6,400
10	Const. Norberto Odebrecht	Brazil	Engineering	5,500
5	LAN	Chile	Airlines	4,387
19	Grupo Casa Saba (Fasa)	Mexico	Retail trade	4,100
15	Avianca-Taca	El Salvador	Airlines	3,000
18	Grupo Nac. de Chocolates	Colombia	Food	2,225
12	AJE Group	Peru	Beverages	1,127
8	Impsa (Pescarmona)	Argentina	Energy	789
16	Laboratorios Bagó	Argentina	Pharmaceuticals	655

Source: América Economía, 2011.

124,000 and 120,000 employees respectively, lead the classification by payroll. Regardless of the standard of measurement, the Brazilian multilatinas dominate (Figure 2.9, Tables 2.6 and 2.7).

The evolution of the ranking also illustrates the pace at which the multilatinas are moving. Just a year ago, the Brazilian technology companies Bematech and Totvs did not even appear in the ranking, but in 2010 they catapulted to positions 59 and 63, further illustrating the technology sector push in this classification. The most spectacular

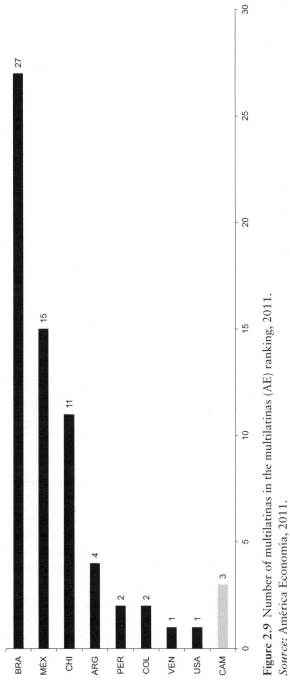

Figure 2.9 Number of multilatinas in the multilatinas (AE) ranking, 2011.
Source: América Economía, 2011.

Table 2.7 *Top twenty multilatinas by number of employees in 2010.*

RK 2011	Company	Country of origin	Sector	Employees 2010
2	JBS Group (Friboi)	Brazil	Food	123,936
13	Grupo Bimbo	Mexico	Food	102,000
10	Const. Norberto Odebrecht	Brazil	Engineering	87,662
14	Petrobras	Brazil	Oil	76,919
6	Telmex	Mexico	Telecom	74,769
9	Vale	Brazil	Mining	60,036
17	América móvil	Mexico	Telecom	55,000
7	Alfa Group	Mexico	Auto parts/ petrochemicals	52,000
3	Cemex	Mexico	Cement	46,500
18	Grupo Nac. de Chocolates	Colombia	Food	28,200
4	Tenaris	Argentina	Iron and steel industry	22,591
5	LAN	Chile	Airlines	17,000
19	Grupo Casa Saba (Fasa)	Mexico	Retail trade	11,922
12	AJE Group	Peru	Beverages	9,800
15	Avianca-Taca	El Salvador	Airlines	6,700
16	Laboratorios Bagó	Argentina	Pharmaceuticals	6,500
1	Brightstar	Bolivia	Telecom	3,600.0
8	IMPSA (Pescarmona)	Argentina	Energy	1,500

Source: América Economía, 2011.

inclusion is indeed that of the pharmaceutical laboratory Bagó, an Argentinean multilatina that appears at 16 for the first time, as well as IMPSA, another Argentinean multilatina of the Pescarmona group, which jumps to 8 in the classification. However, it is the Colombian multilatinas that lead the way in terms of progress: the Avianca group climbed from 31 in 2009 to 15 in 2010; and the cement company Argos appears for the first time at 40.

The jump of ten positions for the Colombian airline Avianca is explained by an M&A operation, namely the absorption of its Central American rival Taca to form the Avianca-Taca group (in 2010, it was present in twenty-three countries). With a fleet of 160 planes and 16,000 employees, it is today one of the world's leading airlines. Its turnover reached $3 billion in 2010, and it flies to 110 cities on the

American continent, in addition to serving other international destinations. The airline operates in twenty-three countries and four of the regions as segmented by América Economía.

Other mergers and acquisitions that pushed multilatinas into the classification were those of the Mexican firm Grupo Casa Saba, which jumped twenty-six positions after buying the Chilean pharmacy chain Farmacias Ahumada in 2010 (for nearly $640 million), and the Chilean company Concha y Toro, which climbed ten positions. This latter company began its trajectory as a family business, and was first listed on the stock market in 1933 when it began exporting to Europe. In 1994, it was the first wine producer to be listed on the New York Stock Exchange. Three years later, it signed an agreement with Baron Philippe de Rothschild jointly to produce a wine called Almaviva. In 2011, the Chilean vineyard confirmed the purchase of the US company Fetzer Vineyards for $234 million – one of the top ten wine brands in the United States. With this operation, Concha y Toro became the fifth largest wine producer in the world and its distribution is strengthened in the United States, its second export market, after Britain. Concha y Toro now has a presence worldwide in more than 130 countries, and the Chilean market scarcely represents 17% of its sales.

Following the acquisition in 2011 of the Latin American pension assets of ING, the Colombian insurance and financial group Suramericana jumped into the 2012 classification, just like the Chilean company LAN and the Brazilian company TAM which merged to create one of the largest airlines in the world (LATAM). These two multilatinas illustrate something that is becoming more apparent year after year: although Brazil dominates the number of multilatinas, 'new' countries are also emerging, Chile in particular, which in 2010 already had eleven multilatinas in the América Economía ranking, and Colombia, which only has two to date but will very likely see its presence increase in the coming years and pass Argentina (four).

To these companies, we must add Petrobras, Vale, JBS Friboi and América Móvil because, as América Economía points out, these firms show the most potential for international growth with respect to their track history and investment capacities. After the purchase of Tamco in the United States in 2010 for $165 million, the Brazilian company Gerdau also appears in the top ten for the greatest growth potential. The Brazilian petrochemical company Braskem will also appear in a higher position after buying several plants in the USA and Germany from the US giant Dow Chemical in 2011 for $323 million. For its part, the Mexican industrial conglomerate Alfa will also see itself positively affected by a new acquisition made in the United States in mid 2011 (for $185 million) (Figure 2.10).

New multilatinas and new frontiers

When América Economía began systematically to trace the phenomenon of the multilatinas in 2006, the vast majority still had a perimeter of internationalisation that was focused on the continent, hence the term 'multilatinas'. This focus has changed over the years, and these multilatinas have become increasingly 'global latinas',[5] expanding to and making acquisitions in the United States, Europe and Asia. Some have built exclusively Latin American companies, such as the Mexican FEMSA, for example. The Chilean, Colombian and Peruvian companies have developed, above all, an Andean internationalisation, although, as we have already seen, some are expanding broadly throughout the whole continent (Suramericana, for example) or to the United States (Concha y Toro). Mexican companies first expanded towards the United States, whereas Brazilian companies started to expand in Latin America, and then later looked towards the United States, Europe, Asia and even Africa.

Asia is among the favourite destinations preferred by these multinationals, with thirty-four companies of different nationalities out of a total of sixty-six starting operations in recent years. Some Latin American companies already have cooperation agreements with Indian counterparts, as is the case of the Brazilian company Marcopolo, which produces buses with Tata Motors in India, or the Brazilian steel company Gerdau, which has invested $70 million with local partners. Marcopolo had more than 20,000 employees and a turnover of $1.9 billion in 2010 – and is also active in China.

Quantitative and complete information about the investments of multilatinas in Asia is limited. The official statistics about FDI in Latin

---

[5] This term was recently coined by Lourdes Casanova of INSEAD. See Lourdes Casanova, *Global Latinas: Emerging Multinationals from Latin America*, London, Palgrave Macmillan, 2009; and also an article by Lourdes Casanova, 'El ascenso de las multilatinas en la economía mundial', *Revista ICE*, 859, March–April 2011, pp. 21–31. Available at www.revistasice.com/CachePDF/ICE_859_21-32__AB6E846F8E555C313551E3D3F54FCE10.pdf.

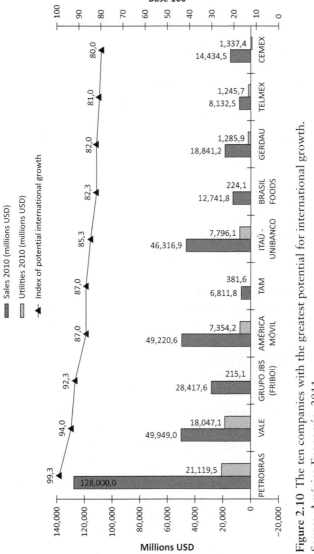

Figure 2.10 The ten companies with the greatest potential for international growth.
Source: América Economía, 2011.

America show very low participations; however, these must be taken with caution, given that FDI often passes through tax havens that are not the final destinations. It is very probable that the official statistics show figures that underestimate the breadth of the Latin investment phenomenon in Asia. A research study conducted by the Economic Observatory of the Mercosur Network[6] shows a somewhat different reality, calculating information based on data from the companies, as well as estimates from the web and the press.

Brazil leads investment activity in Asia and has the greatest number of companies investing in Asia. However, several Mexican, Chilean and Argentinean companies are also active. China is the country where most seek to operate (thirty-five in total), ahead of Japan (thirteen), the United Arab Emirates (ten), India (seven), Singapore (six), Malaysia and Hong Kong (five each) and Thailand (four). The sectors are varied – with food and beverages followed by engineering and construction, steel and metallurgy, auto parts and transport vehicles, and oil and mining.

A country that still has very few investment relations with Asia is Mexico. The total volume of Chinese investments in Mexico in the early 2000s was just $500 million, and there are relatively few Mexican investments in China (just $65 million invested in the last decade). Chinese investments amounted to more than $15 billion in Latin America in 2010, according to CEPAL. Mexico, however, missed out on this investment wave and only received $5 million, compared with the $9.5 *billion* that Brazil received.

This seems to be changing. In 2008, Mexico began to offer direct flights from Mexico to Shanghai, and then in 2010 from Mexico to Beijing. The Chinese company Minth invested $16 million in 2010 to establish a plant in Aguascalientes, where it produces door frames, mouldings and automobile interiors. Mexican investors such as Nemak, Gruma, Bimbo and Corona have set up bases in China. For example, in 2010, the auto parts subsidiary of Grupo Alfa, Nemak, expanded its plant in China, where it hopes to more than quadruple current production by 2014, when China is expected to pass the United States as the world's largest car market (Table 2.8).

Mexican multilatinas are starting to develop in India. The Mexican company Cinepolis, the fourth largest cinema chain in the world, with

[6] See http://oered.org/.

Table 2.8 *Multilatinas in Asia.*

Country	Company	Sector	Centres of production	Technical/commercial assistance and representation
Argentina	Techint	Steel	China, Japan, Indonesia, Saudi Arabia, India, Korea, Qatar, Kazakhstan, UAE	Singapore
	IMPSA	Metallurgy	China, Malaysia, Philippines, Vietnam	India, Hong Kong, Indonesia, Singapore
	Bagó	Pharmacy	Pakistan	
	Arcor	Food/beverages	China	China
	Chemicals	Pharmacy		
Brazil	Vale	Mining	China, Indonesia, Japan, Korea, Oman, Kazakhstan, Philippines, Malaysia, Mongolia, Hong Kong	Singapore
	Petrobras	Oil	China, India, Japan	Iran, Singapore
	Votorantim	Mining/metallurgy		China
	Embraer	Aviation	China	Singapore
	Odebrecht	Engineering/construction	UAE	China
	Sadia	Food/beverages		UAE, China, Japan
	Perdigão	Food/beverages		UAE
	Vicunha	Textile	China	
	Marfrig	Food/beverages	China, Korea, Thailand, Malaysia	

(cont.)

Table 2.8 (cont.)

Country	Company	Sector	Centres of production	Technical/commercial assistance and representation
	Gerdau	Steel	India	
	Weg	Equipment	China, India	Korea, EAU, Japan, Singapore, Thailand
	Banco do Brasil	Financial		China, Japan, Hong Kong, Korea, UAE
	Bradesco	Financial		Japan
	Itaú	Financial		China, Japan, Hong Kong, UAE
	Sabó	Auto parts	China, Japan	
	Marcopolo	Transport vehicles	India, China	
	Randon	Trucks/auto parts	China	UAE
	Caixa Economica Federal	Financial		Japan
	Iochpe	Auto parts/railway	China	
	Andrade Gutierrez	Engineering	UAE, Saudi Arabia, Qatar, Iran, China	
Chile	Sociedad Química y Minera de Chile	Chemical/mining	China, India, Thailand	Japan
	Molymet	Chemicals		China
	Banco de Chile	Financial		China
	BCI	Financial		Hong Kong

	Company	Sector	Countries
	ENAP	Oil	Iran, Kuwait
	Antofagasta	Mining	Pakistan
	Viña Montes	Catering	Japan
	Luksic	Wines	China
Mexico	Cemex	Cement	Philippines, China, Bangladesh, UAE, Israel, Malaysia, Thailand
	Grupo Televisa	Entertainment	China
	Grupo Bimbo	Food/beverages	China
	Gruma	Food/beverages	China, Malaysia
	Alfa	Auto parts	China
	Modelo Group	Food/beverages	Japan
	Carso Group	Auto parts/equipment	China

Source: ESADEgeo, 2012; based on Economic Observatory for the Mercosur Network, 2011.

operations throughout Latin America, expanded to India in 2009 and plans to invest $160 million. Today it has 15,000 employees spread across ten countries. Founded in Michoacán, this company has cinemas in Mexico, Guatemala, El Salvador, Costa Rica, Colombia, Panama, Brazil, Peru, Honduras and India. The company also launched operations in the United States in 2011.

Nemak, a subsidiary of the Mexican conglomerate Alfa, decided at the end of 2010 to expand its operations in Asia, investing $15 million in an automobile plant in India. The company operates in thirteen countries with twenty-seven industrial plants, including operations in India. Another Mexican group that has made its way to China is Gruma. In addition to China, Gruma has operations in Mexico, the USA, Britain, Italy, Holland, Guatemala, Costa Rica, El Salvador, Venezuela, Ukraine and Australia. To help propel its growth, the company also aims to make further acquisitions in Europe, the Middle East and the USA.

Other regions in the emerging world where Latin America is weaving relations and diversifying investments include Africa and the Middle East.[7] Investments are still limited in the Middle East, although trade flows between both regions have grown. In Egypt and the United Arab Emirates, Chilean investments reached $130 million. For its part, the bank Itaú has opened offices in Dubai and Abu Dhabi in order to take advantage of the growing trade flow between Brazil and the Middle East. The Mexican company AHMSA has invested more than $100 million in Israeli mining explorations.

Although commercial relations have boomed with the Middle East, Brazil only invests in four countries: the UAE, Bahrain, Lebanon and Libya. The Brazilian company with the longest history in the Arab world is the leading food group Sadia, present in the Middle East since the 1970s and exporting $550 million a year to the region. In 2009, before the merger with Perdigão created Brasil Foods, nearly 25% of Sadia's exports were aimed at the Arab market. In 2001 it became the second largest brand in the regional frozen food market, with

---

[7] For more on the growing relations between Latin America and the Middle East, see a report by SELA [Latin America and the Caribbean Economic System]: www.sela.org/attach/258/EDOCS/SRed/2011/03/T023600004688-0-Relaciones_de_ALC_con_el_Medio_Oriente.pdf; and on relations with Peru, see also the study available at www.idei.pucp.edu.pe/docs/2011-paises-arabes-jaime-garcia.pdf.

a 25% market share. For its part, Petrobras developed projects and agreements with Libya, Algeria and Saudi Arabia. Embraer has been entering the Arab aviation market with private jets and commercial planes. Odebrecht participated in various construction projects in the metropolitan area of Dubai, Djibouti and Abu Dhabi.

The proliferation of investments and economic relations worldwide is still an incipient phenomenon, but points towards a globalisation of the multilatinas in the current and previous decades. Brazilian multilatinas have expanded throughout the continent, from North to South America, and have explored investments in Europe, Asia, the Middle East and even Africa – a continent we will talk about in the next chapter. As pointed out in this chapter, multilatinas are no longer limited to a Latin American expansion but are becoming more global. We are therefore witnessing a major change: the rise of emerging global multinationals from the region. Some like Antofagasta, Tenaris and AB InBev have gone even further, with their global headquarters respectively in the United Kingdom, Luxembourg and Belgium.

3 | The expansion of Brazilian multilatinas

The Brazilian multilatinas experienced phenomenal progress over the decade 2000–10. In 2000, only a handful of Brazilian multilatinas had a significant international presence. Few people expected that these multilatinas would soon be rubbing elbows with the world's major corporations.

However, this is exactly what has happened in sectors such as oil with Petrobras,[1] mining with Vale, agro-industry with JBS Friboi, and aviation with Embraer (which now rivals the Canadian company Bombardier for first place in its segment worldwide). In the banking sector, giants such as Bradesco, Itaú Unibanco and Banco do Brasil are now moving onto the international stage, and this investment wave has still not finished.[2]

The capitalisations of all these groups exceeded in 2010 those of their respective Spanish rivals. For instance, Petrobras exceeds Repsol; Vale and Embraer do not have an equivalent in Spain; JBS Friboi far exceeds Campofrío and Ebro Foods; and the Brazilian banks exceed the Spanish BBVA in terms of stock market capitalisation. Brazil, previously a country with a bright future ahead of it, has now become a world power, and Brazilian multilatinas continue to grow strongly.

These firms represent only the tip of this tropical iceberg. Currently, there are 223 Brazilian companies whose sales exceed a billion dollars a year. More than 800 firms have an annual turnover of more than $120 million a year, and already represent 46% of the country's GDP.

---

[1] For more on the trajectory of Petrobras, see the article by Andrea Goldstein, 'The Emergence of Multilatinas: The Petrobras Experience', *Universia Business Review*, 2010, pp. 98–111. Also see by this author an essay on emerging multinationals, *Multinational Companies from Emerging Economies: Composition, Conceptualization and Direction in the Global Economy*, London, Palgrave Macmillan, 2007.

[2] For case studies on Vale, Embraer and Petrobras, see the articles included in BID, *From Multilatinas to Global Latinas, 2010: The New Latin American Multinationals (Compilation Case Studies)*, Washington, DC, IADB, 2010.

The internationalisation of Brazilian economy can be measured by the presence of foreign multinationals (São Paulo is already one of the main focuses of production for German companies, for example), as well as by the international trajectory of Brazilian multinationals.

As we will see in this chapter, this progress corresponds, above all, to that of a country and an economy which has projected itself strongly onto the international scene with a combination of natural and human resources – and sufficient technology and capital to compete in the major leagues. Brazilian companies have become spearheads in the more regional phenomenon of multilatinas.

Brazil: a present power

One of the most common clichés about Brazil is that it is a country of the future. This cliché goes back to the 1940s, when the novelist Stefan Zweig published what was his last book, dedicated to Brazil. Nevertheless, we are now witnessing something unprecedented: the emergence of Brazil as a present power and not just an eternal promise for the future.

Today, Brazil is one of the major emerging countries, which along with China and India are changing the course of the world.[3] In 2011, Brazil became the seventh economic power in the world (and in 2012 the sixth), with a nominal GDP of more than $2 trillion. The economy is larger than Spain's, and ten times larger than Chile's. In the various international arenas, such as the G20 or the IMF, its role has become more prominent. On issues of climate change or international commerce, the position of Brazil matters.

Brazilian president Lula was declared to be one of the most influential leaders in the world in 2011. The economic pragmatism of the country (combining monetary and fiscal orthodoxy with major social programmes) has become a reference for many emerging economies, including those in Latin America. Above all, one of the great achievements of the Lula years has been establishing this combination successfully, when few people believed it possible in 2002. The nation

---

[3] See Javier Santiso, *Brazil and the Shifting Wealth of Nations: The Re-balancing of the World towards Emerging Markets*, Madrid, ESADE Business School, Conference at the Fundación Juan March, 25 January 2011. Available at www.march.es/Recursos_Web/Culturales/Documentos/conferencias/PP2714.pdf.

has also managed to reduce endemic poverty and inequality through growth and targeted programmes. The middle class in Brazil is growing quickly and in 2010 represented nearly 45% of the total population (a growth of 10 percentage points in less than five years).

Economic progress has remained visible, with great successes reaped at the beginning of 2010 when it was announced that Brazil would host the World Cup in 2014, and, for the first time in its history, the 2016 Olympic Games. An agricultural superpower, Brazil is becoming a first-rate international player in the oil market, as shown by oil discoveries off the coast of Río. But let us not fool ourselves and fall into yet another cliché: Brazil does not just export soybeans, oil and minerals; it also exports high-tech products, as evidenced by the performance of its national champions in aviation, technological services or cosmetic products. As we will see, Brazilian multilatinas operate in very diverse sectors – including agro-industrial, mining and aviation.

The Olympics and the World Cup ultimately symbolise the massive change in the world economic balance that we are witnessing; and Brazil, along with China and India, is one of the main actors in this change. The case of Brazil is symbolic. In the middle of the 2008–12 global crisis, the country received record foreign direct investments ($45 billion). This record was exceeded in 2010, with $48.5 billion of FDI. Yet even more symbolic is the fact that Brazil has also become a strong overseas investor (Figure 3.1).

Bradesco was predicted a new record for 2011 with nearly $60 billion of FDI in Brazil.[4] The annual sums between 2007 and 2011 (including the global crisis of 2008) defy any historical comparison, with averages that were well above the five-year period (1997–2001) when major investments were also made. It was expected that China, after investing about $12.6 billion in Brazil in 2010, would exceed this amount in 2011, with $13 billion in FDI[5] (Figure 3.2).

At the same time as this foreign investment tsunami was taking place, Brazil also experienced an unprecedented increase in foreign investments made by its companies abroad. The progress of Brazil

---

[4] See the report by the chief economist of Bradesco, Octavio de Barros, one of the best specialists on capital flow dynamics: www.fiesp.com.br/irs/cosec/pdf/ transparencias_reuniao_cosec_13_06_11_-_octavio_de_barros_-_distribuicao_ final.pdf.

[5] For more information by Bradesco on the Brazilian economy, see www. economiaemdia.com.br/.

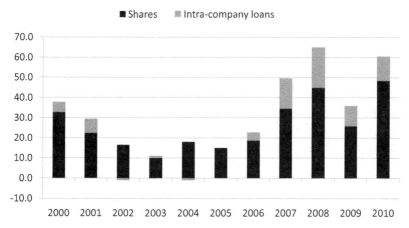

Figure 3.1 FDI flows in Brazil, 2000–10 (in $ billion).
Source: UNCTAD and Banco do Brasil, 2011.

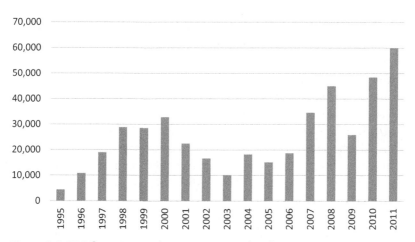

Figure 3.2 FDI flows in Brazil, 1995–2011 (in $ million).
Source: Bradesco, 2011.

and its financial markets has widened all the financial metrics of these multilatinas. The decade 2000–10 witnessed the emergence of multinationals whose stock market capitalisations are now comparable to those of their counterparts in OECD countries. That of the bank Itaú-Unibanco, for example, exceeds many of its European rivals, including the Spanish bank BBVA; the mining company Vale is comparable with the Anglo-Australian mining company Río Tinto; and the oil giant Petrobras surpasses its European competitors, capitalising more than the Spanish oil company Repsol or the French oil company Total.

The Brazilian miracle

In the oil sector, with the recent discoveries in Río de Janeiro, Brazil is becoming one of the world's largest producers and exporters of crude. Petrobras, the largest company on the continent in terms of stock market capitalisation, is already one of the largest in the sector and an innovative player, with offshore technological capacity. The company encourages diversification towards bio-fuels, and ethanol in particular. This will also become an important axis of diversification, given that the government insists that Petrobras is supplied 65% locally. This will enable the company to build its own oil freighters and platforms and provide services. Norway followed a similar strategy with its national champion Statoil – and the company has become a very powerful rival for diversifying towards high-technology clusters.

Perhaps the Brazilian miracle is to be found in this unique combination of pragmatism in terms of both macro- and microeconomic policies. When most advisors (international organisations and economists from Ivy League universities) recommended privatising all the banks, Brazil remained calm and encouraged diversity: some banks were privatised, some were bought by foreign companies, some remained public, and others remained in the hands of private national investors. This unique combination has enabled the country to weather the global crisis of 2008–12 more easily than others, as it could turn to diverse channels of bank financing.

The same is happening in other sectors where the Brazilians were repeatedly told that they should change course, and abandon their obsession with national champions, especially in the high-technology sectors. Once again (and rightly so), the Brazilians did not heed the advice of international experts and wise men, and today the multilatina Embraer rivals the Canadian Bombardier and the French Dassault as the largest aviation company in its market segment.

However, there is another sector where the Brazilian miracle has been stunning: agro-industry. Within a couple of decades, Brazil managed to launch various agro-industrial multinationals that now dominate their sectors. The most recent is Brasil Foods, founded in 2009 after the merger of Sadia and Perdigão. The company has more than 113,000 employees and operates in 116 countries. Exports represented slightly more than 40% of its income in 2010 and it has three industrial plants outside Brazil: in Argentina, Britain and Holland. JBS Friboi was founded in 1953 and has 125,000 employees in 110 countries. It is now the largest animal protein processing company in the world. Today, this multilatina has production platforms and offices in Brazil, Argentina, Italy, Australia, the United States, Uruguay, Paraguay, Mexico, China and Russia. The majority of its income (65%) comes from the United States, followed by Brazil (16%) and Australia (12%). The Brazilian state (through the Brazilian Development Bank, BNDES) still holds 30% of the capital.

Following these two giants is Marfrig, the third largest agro-industrial company in the country. It has 90,000 employees and branches in twenty-two countries, and it exports its products to 140 countries. The company has made purchases in Argentina (Quick-food, bought in 2007 for $140 million), Britain (Moy Park, bought in 2008 for $680 million), the USA (Keystone Foods, bought in 2010 for approximately $1.3 billion). Another major acquisition in 2010 was Seara Alimentos Ltda from Cargill Inc. ($900 million). Another company that stands out is Cosan, a Brazilian conglomerate and leader in bioethanol, sugar and energy. Founded in 1936, the company had 45,000 employees in 2011 and has joined with Shell to develop one of the largest bioethanol projects to date.

To these Brazilian multilatinas, we must add ABInBev, the largest brewing company in the world, and resulting from the merger of various brewing companies in Brazil, Belgium and the United States. It originated as the Brazilian company Ambev – the largest private consumable goods firm in Brazil and the largest brewing company in Latin America – which merged with the Belgian beer company Interbrew, and went on to be called InBev. In 2008, the Belgo-Brazilian company InBev acquired the US firm Anheuser-Busch for nearly €33 billion, and formed Anheuser-Busch InBev – the largest brewing company in the world. The headquarters of this multinational is now in Belgium, but more than half of its management board, including its CEO and CFO, are Brazilian.

Not only are international groups such as Brasil Foods, ABInBev, Cosan and JBS Friboi rising, but an innovation-based green revolution has taken place after repeated efforts since 1990. In just thirty-two years, Brazil has gone from being an importer of foods to becoming one of the world's top agricultural powers, competing with the traditional 'big five' in this sector: the United States, Canada, Australia, Argentina and the European Union. It is also the first country in the tropical belt successfully to make such a leap, as all the other major players are in temperate zones in the northern and southern hemispheres.

The boom in productivity by Brazilian farms has been spectacular. Between 1996 and 2006, the country's crops grew more than 360%; meat exports multiplied tenfold, exceeding those of Australia (now the world's second largest meat exporter). Today, Brazil is the world's largest exporter of sugarcane and ethanol, and one-third of the world's soy exports are from Brazil. These triumphs have been achieved as a result of innovation and productivity. To grasp the miracle that has taken place, we must remember that Brazil today provides a quarter of the soy sold worldwide, and that only 6% of the country's total arable land is under cultivation. In addition, all of this has been achieved despite the clichés that continue to be associated with the country, namely, without subsidies or state intervention. According to the OECD, government subsidies granted to farmers total less than 6% of farm income; whereas they exceed 12% in the United States, and 26% on average in other OECD countries (29% in the European Union). Industry best practices are now found in the emerging countries, in Brazil, and not in OECD countries.

Despite another lingering cliché, this miracle was not achieved by destroying the rainforests. The expansion of the farms took place more than 1,000 kilometres away from the area of the Amazon, in the acid lands of the Cerrado region. In these lands, a government agency called EMBRAPA (Brazilian Enterprise for Agricultural Research) started importing plant and animals species from 1973 onwards, and the agency found a way to adapt soy from Asia to the climates and lands of Brazil. This achievement was based on genetic research, as well as trial and error, and it took several years to arrive at the miracle of productivity that is now the envy of the entire world. Based on innovation in the processes and products, EMBRAPA managed to shorten the production cycle of soy so that two crops can be harvested each year. And soy was not the only area where the country made unexpected leaps. Brazil is now the world's largest exporter of orange juice, chickens, coffee, meat and sugar; the world's second largest exporter of soy and corn; and the fourth largest exporter of cotton and pork.

The potential for development in the agro-industrial sector is enormous: the world population will climb from 7 billion to more than 9 billion by 2050. Brazil has the world's largest expanse of unused arable land. According to the FAO, it still has more available land than the USA and Russia combined; and once again, all of this land is far from the Amazon and in the region known as the Cerrado (where 70% of the total production in Brazil is already concentrated). To this, we must add that Brazil has access to more than 8 trillion cubic meters of water per year: Brazil alone (with 190 million inhabitants) has more renewable drinking water than all of Asia (with 4 billion inhabitants).

The Brazilian miracle is both democratic and economic. Other tropical countries now seek to import the Brazilian innovations, but what is striking is that there were no shortcuts. EMBRAPA achieved its breakthroughs not overnight, but as a result of dedication, trial and error, daring initiatives, and some luck – that is, by innovation and entrepreneurship. With more than 8,000 employees, EMBRAPA has also begun to develop international cooperation by exporting Brazilian technology around the world, including Africa. In terms of international cooperation, the company maintains sixty-eight bilateral technical cooperation agreements with thirty-seven countries and a total of sixty-four institutions. In addition to laboratories in the United States, France and the Netherlands, EMBRAPA also has a regional office in Ghana to share scientific and technological knowledge with Africa.

The investment path of the Brazilian multilatinas is still important. Although many of the investments are concentrated in Latin America, even in this region there is scope for an increased presence.[6] The case of Peru is illustrative: the total stock of Brazilian FDI hardly exceeded a billion dollars in 2010. Since 2005, it has been growing at an annual rate of 30%, concentrated in mining, hydrocarbons, industry and services. However, despite this recent growth, Brazil has less of a presence than other countries in the region, such as Chile for example, which invests 30% more in Peru than Brazilian firms.

It is very likely that the investment relationship will continue to experience exponential growth over the coming years, as indicated by data from 2011. In the first half of the year alone, Brazil announced

[6] For more on investment by Brazilian multilatinas, see Alfonso Fleury and Maria Teresa Leme Fleury, *Brazilian Multinationals: Competences for Internationalization*, Cambridge University Press, 2011.

Table 3.1 *Main investments by Brazilian multinationals.*

Sector	Company	Project	Investment ($ million)	State
Oil	Petrobras	Modernisation of a refinery in Talara	700 (est.)	Announced/ approval of the International Energy Agency (IEA)
Oil	Petrobras	Exploration and drilling of Block 58 (Cuzco)	130	Announced
Oil	Kuntur (Odebrecht)	South-Andean pipeline	3,000	Announced/ approval of the International Energy Agency (IEA)
Oil	Odebrecht/ Petrobras	Petrochemical industry in southern Peru (Ilo/Matarani)	2,000	Announced
Mining	Vale do Río Doce	Bayóvar (phosphates)	450 (est.)	Started
Mining	Votorantim	Modernisation of a refinery in Cajamarquilla (zinc)	300	Started
Iron and steel	Gerdau	Modernisation of Siderperú	120 (est.)	Started
Agro-industry and energy	Odebrecht	Chavimochic	852	Started
Energy	Eletrobras	Concession of five hydroelectric plants (total power generated: 6.7 GW)	15,000 (est.)	Announced
Infrastructures	Odebrecht/ Andrade Gutiérrez/GyM Consortium	South Interoceanic Highway	800	Started
Infrastructures	IIRSA-North Consortium	North Interoceanic Highway	500	Started

Source: BBVA, 2011.

investment projects in Peru worth more than $24 billion, according to estimates by BBVA.[7] The builders Odebrecht and Andrade Gutiérrez are managing several highway projects. Petrobras and Odebrecht are involved in a macro gas project managed by Camisea. The most significant project, however, is in the hydroelectric sector, where the Brazilian giant Eletrobras is building several plants in Peru that could represent an investment of $15 billion (Table 3.1).

Brazilian multilatinas are searching for new investment frontiers

Brazilian multilatinas are also intensifying their search for new markets and countries where they can invest. They are raising their horizons beyond Latin America, the United States and Europe, and focusing on new frontiers in Africa, the Middle East and Asia.

Relations have blossomed quickly over the decade 2000–10 with Africa. This has been generally true for BRIC nations and not only for Brazil: trade with the African continent increased from $22 billion to more than $166 billion between 2000 and 2008. Standard Bank estimates that by 2015 this trade will triple and reach $530 billion. Africa represents 6.3% of Brazilian trade. Back in 2001, Europe accounted for more than half of exports to Africa, and the United States was ahead of China. But by the end of the decade, Europeans and Americans had lost position, whereas China had made remarkable progress and Brazil accounted for 2.6% of total exports to Africa, compared to less than 1.8% at the beginning of the decade. The majority of Brazilian exports to Africa go to just two countries – Angola and South Africa – which together account for 75% of the regional total (Figure 3.3).

FDI in Africa is mainly led by South Africa and China, followed by India, Taiwan, Korea, Turkey and Brazil. In the 2000s, China and India have invested $29 and $25 billion in the African continent, and Brazil has also made a major impact with more than $10 billion invested, exceeding Russia ($9 billion).[8] In 2009, the stock of FDI of the BRIC

---

[7] See the BBVA study on the relations between Peru and Brazil: http://serviciodeestudios.bbva.com/KETD/fbin/mult/110726_EconomicWatch_Peru-Brazil_tcm348-264701.pdf?ts=882011.

[8] On the progress of BRIC in Africa and Brazil in particular, see a report issued by Standard Bank, *BRIC and Africa: Tectonic Shifts Tie BRIC and Africa's Economic Destinies*, Standard Bank, October 2009. Available at http://ws9.standardbank.co.za/sbrp/LatestResearch.do.

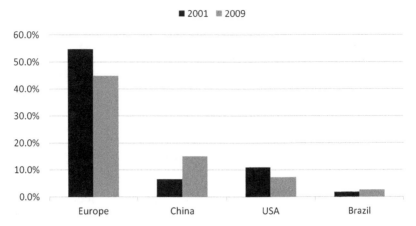

Figure 3.3 Progress of Chinese and Brazilian exports to Africa, 2001–9 (as percentage of the total exported).
Source: BNDES (Brazilian Development Bank) based on UNComtrade, 2011.

countries in Africa represented about $60 billion, and this is projected to more than double by 2015 and reach $150 billion.[9] By then, China and India will continue to lead BRIC investments in Africa, with $70 and $40 billion, respectively. However, Brazil ($25 billion) will have set itself apart from Russia ($15 billion). These amounts, as the IMF pointed out, are low estimates given that total FDI is expected to be higher.[10]

A prime example of the growing Brazilian interest in Africa is the multinational Vale. This Brazilian mining giant has an investment plan for $9 billion in several countries until 2014. These countries are located (not surprisingly) in North and South America, with major investments planned in Argentina, Peru and Canada. However, the plan also includes African countries such as Guinea, Zambia and

---

[9] See Standard Bank, *BRIC-Africa in 2015: Tectonic Shifts Continue Apace,* Standard Bank, November 2010. Available at http://ws9.standardbank.co.za/ sbrp/search.do.

[10] See Montfort Mlachila and Misa Takebe, 'FDI from BRIC to LICs: Emerging Growth Driver?', IMF Working Paper, 11–178, July 2011. Available at www.imf.org/external/pubs/ft/wp/2011/wp11178.pdf. See also Era Dabla-Norris, Jiro Honda, Amina Lahreche and Geneviève Verdier, 'FDI Flows to Low-Income Countries: Global Drivers and Growth Implications', IMF Working Paper 10/132, 2010.

Mozambique, as well as Asia and the Middle East (Oman, Indonesia and Malaysia). In Argentina, Vale projects include a potassium mine ($1.2 billion), one of the firm's largest developments planned.

In Mozambique, Vale is working with the Brazilian construction company Odebrecht in the development of coal reserves, the construction of an energy plant, and rail and port infrastructures for coal exports. These initial investments are estimated at more than $1.3 billion. In Mozambique, the oil company Petrobras and the iron and steel company CSN are also active.

For its part, Odebrecht has become the largest company in the Angolan private sector, with activities that range from food production to ethanol production, construction and retailing. Cement construction company Camargo Corrêa has further investments planned after recently investing $8 billion mainly in production units in Angola and Mozambique. Brazilian banks Bradesco and Banco do Brasil are also seeking opportunities in these two nations.

The presence of Brazilian multilatinas in Africa illustrates something that we pointed out in the introduction to the book: the world is becoming increasingly decentralised. Direct investments made by Brazil in Africa total about $10 billion. In 2010, more than half of international trade in Africa will be carried out with other emerging countries and not with OECD members. Since 2008, this South–South trade (including that trade with Brazil) represented more than 50% of the total trade of the African continent.[11] During his last term in office, Lula visited about twenty-seven African countries (during his first term, he visited the continent six times), and doubled the number of Brazilian embassies on the continent. Meanwhile, trade jumped from $3 billion to nearly $30 billion between 2000 and 2010. BNDES (the Brazilian Development Bank) started a process of internationalisation with credit lines of $2 billion available for operations in Africa. In addition to the interest in African countries, there has also been an increase in relations with Arab countries. As we have seen in the previous chapter, this progress also reflects the growing South–South trend. Brasil Foods announced in 2011 an investment of $120 million in the United Arab Emirates where it plans to open an industrial plant.

---

[11] See McKinsey, *Lions on the Move: The Progress and Potential of African Economies*, Boston, McKinsey Global Institute, June 2010. Available at www.mckinsey.com/mgi/publications/progress_and_potential_of_african_economies/index.asp.

Brazilian multinationals are just the tip of the iceberg. Their expansion abroad is the largest and the most spectacular one from Latin multinationals. However, as we will see in the following chapter, they are not alone. The pioneers in fact have been Spanish-speaking multinationals, namely from Argentina and Mexico. Later some from Colombia, Chile and Peru also joined the pack. Brazil became a significant source of outward foreign direct investment (OFDI) only in the 2000s. As we have seen in this chapter, Brazilian multinationals' outward FDI is concentrated in the secondary and tertiary sectors. The investments are going mostly to neighbouring economies, the USA and Europe, even if more recently we have seen an increasing interest for new geographies like Asia, the Middle East and Africa. During the decade 2000–10, Brazilian OFDI continued to show a high level of concentration particularly in North America, Latin America and the Caribbean, which together accounted, on average, for 79% of all FDI stock from Brazil between 2001 and 2008, followed by Europe (21%); Asia, Africa and Oceania together accounted for the remaining 1%.[12]

In less than a decade the stock jumped from $52 billion in 2000 to $181 billion in 2010, recovering in 2010 ($12 billion of OFDI). This growth has been spectacular in comparison not only with other Latin American countries but also with other BRIC emerging countries. By 2008, Brazil had a larger stock of OFDI than all of the other large emerging economies considered, except for Russia. Only in 2009 did China surpass Brazil. The internationalisation of Brazilian multinationals is an impressive phenomenon, comparable to other BRIC countries. It should not however mask what is going on throughout the continent. In fact, as we will see, the expansion of Spanish-speaking multinationals was also impressive. These multinationals also went abroad before the Brazilian ones, pioneering the Latin American multinationals boom.

In 2011, underlying the diversity of the multilatinas phenomenon, Brazilian multilatinas focused more on the domestic market (which explained why overall outward FDI from Latin America went down from $45 billion to $22 billion between 2010 and 2011). Chile had

---

[12] See Milton de Abreu Campanario, Eva Stal and Marcello Muniz da Silva, 'Outward FDI from Brazil and its policy context', Vale Columbia Center FDI Profiles, May 2012. Available at www.vcc.columbia.edu/files/vale/documents/Profile-_Brazil_OFDI_10_May_2012_-_FINAL.pdf.

the most outward FDI with $12 billion. Mexico invested outside $10 billion, and Colombia $8 billion.[13] As we will now see, it looks as though, beyond Brazil, Andean multinationals are intensifying their internationalisation, while the Mexican ones are experiencing a revival.

[13] In fact in 2011 Brazil recorded a negative FDI position of $9.3 billion, essentially because of loans that foreign subsidiaries of Brazilian firms made to their parent companies. See ECLAC, *Foreign Direct Investment in Latin America and the Caribbean 2011*, Santiago de Chile, ECLAC, 2012. Available at www.cepal.org/publicaciones/xml/2/46572/2012-182-LIEI-WEB.pdf.

4 | The expansion of Spanish-speaking multilatinas

América Economía points out that Brazil is the undisputed leader with the largest number of multilatinas in the region – but there are other multilatinas. The consultancy firm BCG predicted in a recent report on multilatinas that, of the top 100, thirty-four would come from Brazil, followed by Mexico (twenty-eight), Chile (twenty-one), Argentina (seven), Colombia (five), Peru (three), Venezuela and El Salvador (one each). This last ranking also points towards a trend that has been confirmed over the years: more countries in the region are producing multilatinas. Another way of looking at the BCG ranking is that sixty-six of the 100 top multilatinas – or two-thirds – will soon be non-Brazilian.

The majority of the multilatinas – Brazilian or otherwise – are dominated by private investors (97%) and most are controlled by families (77%).[1] This contrasts with Russian and Chinese multilatinas that are mostly controlled by the state and public investors: 33% in the case of Russia and 69% in the case of China. In terms of international expansion, the multilatinas are still concentrated on the continent: of the top 100 identified by BCG in 2009, 53% are active in Argentina, 49% in the United States and 42% in Peru. The Brazilian multilatinas, as we have seen, are generally more focused on South America, and the Mexican multilatinas are more focused on North America. However, as we will see, new trends have emerged between 2009 and 2011, and the most noteworthy is the multiplication of investor destinations beyond the Americas.

The development of the capital markets has been significant for multilatinas. The prosperity of the local capital markets has facilitated their expansion throughout the decade of the 2000s. During this period, the equity stock and debt of the emerging markets was growing at a rate

---

[1] Boston Consulting Group (BCG), *The 2009 BCG Multilatinas*, Boston, BCG, 2009. Available at www.bcg.com/documents/file27236.pdf.

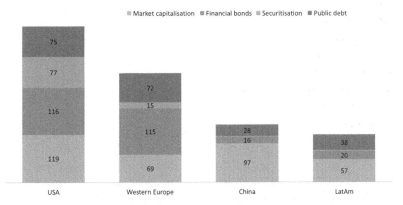

Figure 4.1 Depth of the financial markets in 2010 (as percentage of GDP). *Source:* McKinsey Global Institute, 2011.

of more than 18% a year, compared to 5% for the OECD countries. The consequence is that the financial markets of the emerging countries, although still smaller than those of the developed countries, are rapidly transforming. The total value of financial stock in the emerging countries is still less than 200% of GDP in comparison with 430% of GDP in the OECD countries. The trend, however, is changing. Share values reached nearly 150% of the regional GDP in Latin America in 2010[2] (Figure 4.1).

These share values have grown in size, with increasingly larger institutional investments (in particular, the local pension funds, but also international investments earmarked for emerging markets). At the same time, the cost of capital, as both corporate debt as well as equity, has been falling for the multilatinas throughout the decade 2000–10.[3]

---

[2] See McKinsey, *Mapping Global Capital Markets 2011*, Boston and Washington, DC, McKinsey Global Institute, August 2011. Available at www.mckinsey.com/mgi/reports/freepass_pdfs/Mapping_global_capital_markets/Capital_markets_update_email.pdf.

[3] See Martín Grandes, Demian Panigo and Ricardo Pasquini, 'The Cost of Corporate Bond Financing in Latin America', Center for Financial Stability, Working Paper, 20 July 2007. Available at www.cefargentina.org/files_publicaciones/16-36wp20-cob-grandes-panigo-pasquini-julio-2007.pdf; and Martín Grandes, Demian Panigo and Ricardo Pasquini, 'The Cost of Equity beyond CAPM: Evidence from Latin American Stock Markets 1986–2004', Center for Financial Stability, Working Paper, 17 March 2007. Available at www.cefargentina.org/files_publicaciones/16-33wp17-coe2-jan-2007.pdf.

Seventy-seven percent of the multilatinas analysed by BCG took advantage of local financial markets to fund themselves in better conditions and at comparable or often lower costs than their OECD competitors. This alignment of financial conditions has enabled Latin American investors to compete with their OECD rivals. This has been particularly true for Brazilian and Chilean multilatinas, which have made intense use of local financial markets: 79% and 100%, respectively.

Multilatinas have often relied on mergers and acquisitions for expansion: between 1998 and 2008, more than 310 M&A operations were made by multilatinas outside of their country (153 by Mexican multilatinas and ninety-eight by Brazilian multilatinas). This investment activism has enabled the multilatinas broadly to expand their perimeter of investment. While they still concentrate most of their operations on the American continent (fifty-one of the 100 analysed are present in North America; eighty-six in South America), we are witnessing an increase in activity towards other geographical areas: thirty-three are already present in Europe, but above all we are seeing how they are beginning to operate in Asia (twenty-two), and even Africa (twelve).

Thus, two phenomena are combined: an increasing number of countries in the region are producing multilatinas, and more of these companies are searching for new investment frontiers beyond Latin America. We can be sure that these trends are not going to slow down. One of the consequences of the global shift is that more capital is available in and for the emerging markets. Goldman Sachs estimates that in 2030 these markets will represent 55% of the global stock market capitalisation, compared to the current 31%. By then, institutional managers in the OECD countries will have significantly raised their investments in these countries, from 6% exposure to emerging markets in their variable income portfolios to more than 18% in 2030. This means that they will spend more than $4 trillion in shares in emerging multinationals. By then, the stock market capitalisation of China will be the largest in the world (28% of the total), followed by the United States (23%). Brazil, with 3% of the world total, will exceed Spain with 1%, and will equal Japan and Britain; Mexico and Chile, on the other hand, will hold 1%, which is comparable to Spain.[4]

---

[4] Goldman Sachs, *Emerging Markets Equity in Two Decades: A Changing Landscape*, New York and London, Goldman Sachs Global Economics Papers 24, September 2010.

Table 4.1 *The 'Brookings Graduation Scorecard' ranking in 2011.*

RK 2011	Country	RK 2011	Country	RK 2011	Country
1	Singapore	12	South Africa	23	Estonia
2	Taiwan	13	Bulgaria	24	Argentina
3	Chile	14	Malaysia	25	Hungary
4	Israel	15	Indonesia	26	Turkey
5	China	16	Thailand	27	Russia
6	Korea	17	Peru	28	Romania
7	Brazil	18	Vietnam	29	Lithuania
8	Uruguay	19	Egypt	30	Latvia
9	Poland	20	Colombia	31	Venezuela
10	Czech Republic	21	Philippines	32	Ecuador
11	India	22	Mexico	33	Ukraine

Source: Brookings Institution, 2011.

Obviously, these forecasts – while questionable in some ways – point towards a more decentralised world that favours emerging markets and their multinationals. This new world can already be glimpsed: multi-latinas are no longer just a Brazilian phenomenon. We will now see how Chilean, Colombian, Peruvian, Mexican and Argentinean companies are an ever larger presence around the world and are dethroning the traditional OECD multinationals.

This progress reflects the economic development of a whole region. Chile is no longer the only 'pretty girl' in the neighbourhood and is being joined by Brazil, Mexico, Colombia, Uruguay and Peru. All of these Latin American countries are now profiled as open economies that rival their Asian counterparts, as shown by the Brookings Graduation Scorecard (BGS). While this scorecard still shows Singapore and Taiwan as the leaders, Chile is just behind them and ahead of China, while Brazil and Uruguay are ahead of India and Indonesia[5] (Table 4.1).

---

[5] This index combines eleven variables around four central criteria: macroeconomic growth, quality of the policy, financial resistance and indicators of economic development. See Mauricio Cárdenas and Eduardo Levy-Yeyati (eds.), *Latin America Economic Perspectives: Shifting Gears in an Age of Heightened Expectations*, Washington, DC, Brookings Institution, 2011. Available at www.brookings.edu/~/media/Files/rc/reports/2011/0408_blep_cardenas/04_blep_cardenas_yeyati.pdf.

Mexico

Mexican multilatinas were the first to embark on international adventures, even before many of the Brazilian companies mentioned in the previous chapter. The most symbolic case is that of the cement company Cemex. In 2007, Cemex bought the Australian company Rinker for $14.6 billion, one of the largest investments ever made by a multilatina abroad.

Most of the Mexican multilatina investments were concentrated in North and South America. With respect to Brazil, the main difference is probably the volume of investments in the USA. FDI data, as well as trading data, reflect the strong dependence of Mexico on the United States. Mexican economic cycles show a perfect correlation with the USA – especially industrial cycles.[6]

Mexico (as well as Central America) is strongly linked to the United States. In 2009, the 'Mexican cluster' exported just 9% to the emerging markets, while the 'Brazilian cluster' exported 56% of its total to emerging markets. As a result the Brazilian cluster was less exposed to the crisis in the OECD countries, especially the one that unfolded in the United States in 2008. Mexico is one of the major regional economies most exposed to the United States and the advanced OECD economies: exports to these countries represent more than 28% of Mexican GDP, compared to less than 5.5% for Brazil (the country least exposed to advanced economies in commercial terms)[7] (Figures 4.2 and 4.3).

This asymmetry between Mexico and Brazil also largely explains the differing performances of both economies when the 2008 crisis struck. Whereas Mexican GDP plummeted, the Brazilian economy grew. The Mexican multilatinas, which were the most prosperous in the region, became trapped in an adverse cycle, with their main international market collapsing (the United States). As their domestic markets

---

[6] For more about this interrelationship of the economic cycles of both countries, see Diego Comin, Norman Loayza, Farooq Pasha and Luis Servén, 'Medium Term Business Cycles in Developing Countries', Harvard Business School, Working Paper 10–029, September 2010. Available at www.hbs.edu/research/pdf/10-029.pdf.

[7] See Alejandro Izquierdo and Ernesto Talvi, *One Region, Two Speeds? Challenges of the New Global Economic Order for Latin America and the Caribbean*, Washington, DC, IADB, 2011. Report available at http://idbdocs.iadb.org/wsdocs/getdocument.aspx?docnum=35816781.

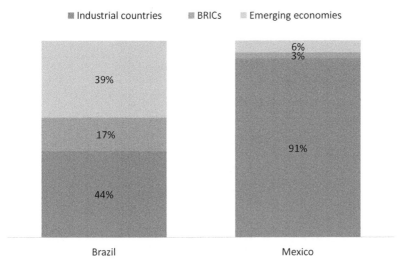

Figure 4.2 Exports by destination in 2011 (as percentage of total exports).
Source: BID, 2011.

suffered, the financial costs of these often heavily indebted companies skyrocketed.

Mexican multilatinas saw their income drop 45% in 2008 and they then had to face unsustainable debts. Cemex, the most global of the Mexicans, was very exposed to the United States and Mexico and had to make major divestments to lighten its debt load. It was the third largest cement company in the world and had been leading the process of globalisation by Mexican multinationals by making leveraged purchases over the previous fifteen years. In 2009, it sold operations in Australia and assets bought for $1.9 billion from Swiss competitor Holcim. Company debt, which amounted to $14.5 billion in 2010, was renegotiated. Its last major acquisition was the purchase of the Australian company Rinker (strongly anchored in the United States) for $14.2 billion in 2007 – which was a milestone at the time. In 2010, after restoring its balances, Cemex embarked on another international expansion, investing $100 million to build a cement plant in Peru through a venture capital investment fund.

In the case of FDI, the pattern is similar: for the 'Mexican cluster' 93% of FDI in 2009 came from the advanced economies (above all the United States in the case of Mexico); whereas for the 'Brazilian cluster',

Figure 4.3 Export of goods and services to advanced economies, 2009 (as percentage of GDP).
Source: BID, 2011. *Note:* the 'Brazilian cluster' is shown in dark grey, and the 'Mexican cluster' in light grey.

88% came from advanced economies (with a greater presence of European FDI). The origin of the FDI in both cases is not a discriminating factor, unlike the final destination of the products made by the investor companies, especially in the manufacturing and industrial sectors. In the case of Mexico, much of the FDI points towards the domestic and US markets, in contrast to Brazil. As a result, investment and capital flows were redirected more generally towards Mexico, particularly in 2008 and 2009.

To a certain extent, there was 'decoupling' of the emerging markets and the OECD countries; however, the Mexican trajectory shows that this phenomenon was incomplete and did not affect all of the emerging economies. Moreover, if there was decoupling of the *real* economy for some emerging economies (such as Brazil), this was not the case from the *financial* standpoint.[8] For many emerging markets such as Brazil, the increasing South–South relations with other emerging markets softened the recessive impacts. Nevertheless, all the multilatinas were affected by the financial changes and the restructuring of investor portfolios, as becomes obvious in the crisis that lashed Europe in 2011 (Figure 4.4).

The crisis of 2008 nearly stopped Mexican FDI abroad, interrupting the investment cycle of the Mexican multilatinas (that year Mexican FDI outside of the country hardly reached $1.1 billion). However, this was only temporary. By the year 2010 another milestone in the history of the Mexican multilatinas had been achieved. Mexican businesses invested $14.3 billion in productive assets abroad, according to official data from Mexican authorities ($12.7 billion according to the *CEPAL Review*). This record amount reflected a clear geographical and sector diversification. By 2010 Mexican multilatinas had exceeded the peak reached in 2007 (when they doubled the figures for 2006)[9] before the global crisis struck them in 2008 and caused a drastic reduction in the investment activity that year. In 2010, Mexican multilatinas achieved

---

[8] For more on this point, see the analysis by Eduardo Levy-Yeyati, 'Emerging Economies in the 2000s: Real Decoupling and Financial Decoupling', Universidad Torcuato di Tella, Working Paper (not published), June 2010. Available at www.bde.es/webbde/GAP/Secciones/SalaPrensa/Agenda/Eventos/10/Jul/04.Levy-Yeyati.pdf.

[9] For details of FDI inside and outside of Mexico, see www.economia.gob.mx/swb/es/economia/p_Direccion_General_Inversion_Extranjera.

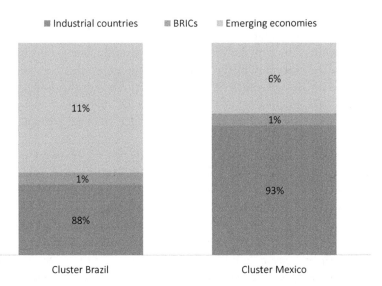

Figure 4.4 FDI towards the Brazilian and Mexican clusters, 2009 (as percentage of the total).
Source: BID, 2011. *Note:* Brazil cluster (Argentina, Brazil, Chile, Colombia, Peru); Mexico cluster (Costa Rica, Dominican Republic, El Salvador, Honduras, Mexico); Emerging economies and industrial countries as defined in the World Economic Outlook (IMF).

an 80% recovery with respect to 2009, as Mexican FDI outside of the country rebounded to $7 billion (Figure 4.5).

The most outstanding investment was achieved by Casa Saba, which acquired the Chilean company Fasa, a pharmacy chain operator, for $637 million. In another noteworthy transaction, Mexichem bought the fluoride division of the British company Ineos Group, which includes assets in the United States, Canada, Britain, Taiwan and Japan, for $354 million. Mexichem plans to expand to Brazil (with investments of more than $100 million), a country where Cinepólis also had ambitious plans (intending to build 290 cinemas for $276 million between 2010 and 2012).

Also in 2010, Grupo Televisa signed an agreement for $1.2 billion to acquire a share in Univision. That same year, we also witnessed the agreement of Grupo Bimbo with Sara Lee Corporation to buy its bread business in the United States for a billion dollars. Also in the United States, Sigma Alimentos (Grupo Alfa) took over the US company Bar-S

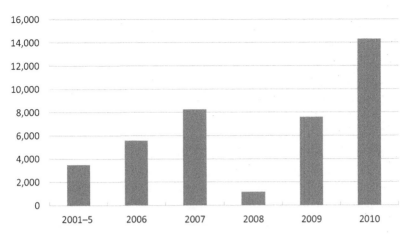

Figure 4.5 Foreign investment of Mexican multilatinas, 2001–10 (in $ billion). *Source:* ESADEgeo, 2012; based on the CEPAL Review and the Central Bank of Mexico, 2011.

Foods for $575 million. Grupo México, which has the third largest copper reserves in the world and operates the largest railway network in the country, has mines in Mexico and Peru through its unit Southern Copper. In the United States, the recently reincorporated Asarco (for which it paid more than $2.9 billion in 2009) served as another counter-cyclical example of Mexican multilatina business activity.

These operations highlight the tendency of Mexican multilatinas to concentrate acquisitions in the American continent – where the USA is a particularly important destination. In 2010, the USA accounted for 56% of the total, followed by South America (27%) and Europe (15%). This picture confirms a previous trend where the major operations were carried out in North American or related markets. Among these investments were those of Vitro (glass packaging and related industries) and Cementos Mexicanos (Cemex), two groups that have spearheaded Mexican expansion abroad.

However, new destinations are appearing, particularly in Latin America and Europe. In Latin America, in addition to the operations mentioned in Chile, there are also notable investments in the Andean countries. For instance, Mexican investments in Ecuador reached about $2 billion in 2010, with the announcement of the purchase of 75% of the shares of the Ecuadoran Coca-Cola bottler by the

Mexican company Arco. Asia also appears on the investor radar. In 2011, for example, Mexichem announced investments of $150 million in Japan and Korea to install refrigerant and hydrofluoric acid plants. In Europe, Bimbo announced its interest in bidding for the assets of Sara Lee in Spain (Bimbo España). The year before, FEMSA announced that its board of directors had reached an agreement to exchange its beer operations for a 20% share in Heineken, in a transaction valued at $7.4 billion. FEMSA therefore focused its business as a Coca-Cola bottler with a presence in Mexico, Guatemala, Nicaragua, Costa Rica, Panama, Colombia and Argentina.

In 2010, along with the United States, Brazil was one of the main destinations of Mexican FDI, with a total of $3.6 billion invested. According to the Mexican secretary for foreign relations, Brazil is now the main destination for Mexican investments worldwide, and Mexico has a combined investment of $17 billion in Brazil. The main Mexican companies that have invested in Brazil are América Móvil, Telmex, Coca-Cola FEMSA, Dako Electrodomésticos Mabe, Nemak, Grupo Posadas, Bimbo, Softtek and Mexichem. Bimbo, for example, entered Brazil in 2001 with the Pullman, Nutrella and Ana María brands, and has seven plants in the country – its third market worldwide after Mexico and the USA. Other Mexican companies that expanded in Brazil in 2010 were the white goods manufacturer Mabe, the bottling company Coca-Cola FEMSA and the Carso Group, owned by the magnate Carlos Slim, in the telecommunications sector. Coca-Cola FEMSA, the Mexican bottling company and the largest in Latin America, spent $150 million in 2011 on a new plant in the Minas Gerais region of Brazil.

Among the most internationalised groups are Gruma, a multilatina founded in 1949 in the city of Monterrey. Today Gruma is one of the largest producers of corn flour and tortillas in the world, operating mainly in the United States, Mexico, Venezuela, Central America, Europe, Asia and Australia, and exporting to 105 countries worldwide. The firm has approximately 20,000 employees and ninety-five industrial plants. As proof of its appetite, in 2011 it carried out acquisitions, particularly in the United States, for $9 million, and set roots in Russia with another purchase for $7 million. In 2011, it demonstrated its recovery from the crisis in the USA by posting earnings of nearly $360 million, 50% more than in 2010. A sale of shares in the bank Banorte enabled it to unload 50% of its debt.

Another Mexican investment paradigm is that of América Móvil and Teléfonos de México – both owned by Carlos Slim – which have built an empire across the continent. With a presence in nineteen countries and more than 200 million users, they are among the world's largest telecommunications companies. In 2011, it was announced that the companies would invest $8.3 billion internationally, some $3.7 billion of which would be in Mexico and $2.5 billion in Brazil (nearly 75% of the total).

In 2012, América Móvil committed to two major operations in Europe, buying a controlling equity stake in Dutch telecom operator KNP and another controlling stake in Telekom Austria, both giving complete access to continental Europe, from the Netherlands to Austria and Eastern Europe.

Argentina

For many years Argentina boasted some of the most important multilatinas. Groups such as Techint, Arcor and Bagó were pioneer multilatinas, and among the first Latin conglomerates to internationalise. These multilatinas continue to be major references today, despite the relative decline of Argentinean multilatinas. While Chile, Colombia and even Peru have watched their multinationals grow in importance and number, Argentina has gone down the opposite path.

Argentinean companies currently have a stock of FDI outside of the country of just $30 billion, less than half of Chile's investments abroad. Colombia, which had a late start in the race of the multilatinas, is already close to matching the figures for Argentina. At the end of the decade of the 2000s, the top nineteen Argentinean multilatinas totalled $20 billion in assets abroad, and had 42,000 employees outside of the country, and about 315 subsidiaries spread across forty-two countries worldwide.[10] These firms are spread in a wide array of sectors, including pharmaceuticals, electronics and computation, civil engineering, chemicals, hydrocarbons and services, and oil.

It is also worth noting that Argentina has been creating technology-based multilatinas over the decade 2000–10 – such as Globant, and

[10] See ProsperAr Invest in Argentina, *Primer Ranking de las Multinacionales Argentinas*, Buenos Aires and New York, ProsperAr and Vale Centre, Columbia University, 2009. Available at www.prosperar.gov.ar/es/descargas/Publicaciones/Primer-Ranking-de-empresas-multinacionales-argentinas/.

Mercadolibre which has been listed on NASDAQ since 2007. We will examine these in the chapter on Multilatinas 2.0. These companies point to the potential of Argentina (and the regional potential) in the Internet. Globant has a total turnover of $90 million, mainly in the United States and Britain (93% of the total) and is searching to gain ground in Brazil and expand worldwide.

Another company that stands out in the sector of technology is Assa, an Argentinean multilatina in the sector of consulting and outsourcing. The company was founded in 1992 and has operations in Brazil, Chile, the United States and Mexico. In 2010, the private investment fund HSBC Latin American Partners and the investment arm of the World Bank, the International Finance Corporation (IFC), invested $20 million in the company. With this capital injection, Assa plans to accelerate its international expansion, including to Europe. In 2010, it was announced as one of the 100 best IT service companies in the world, sharing the podium with another ten companies from the continent.

The Latin American IT companies considered among the best in the world are (in alphabetical order): CPM Braxis based in San Pablo, Brazil; DBA Engenharia de Sistemas Limited in Río de Janeiro, Brazil; Globant, Grupo ASSA, Grupo Prominente and Hexacta in Buenos Aires, Argentina; Hildebrando in Mexico City, Mexico; the Mexican company Neoris, based in Florida, United States; Stefanini IT Solutions in San Pablo, Brazil; Synapsis in Santiago, Chile; and Transactel in Guatemala. The regional IT industry is growing and went from just 5% of the total of the top 100 in 2009 to 11% in 2010.

Grupo Assa, with central offices in Buenos Aires, has operations in the Americas and Europe. Today the company employs more than 1,000 consultants and plans to more than double this number over the next few years. Its international presence is concentrated in Latin America, although some firms, such as Tenaris, Arcor, IMPSA and Bagó are present in Asia, and, in the case of Arcor, present in the Middle East. Many are developing major activities in Europe. It is worth mentioning the cases of Tenaris and Ternium, from the Techint group, given that these multilatinas have decided to move their headquarters to Europe (Luxembourg). Arcor, Bagó, Molinos Río de la Plata, Tecna, Iecsa and Assa are also active in Europe. The majority of these are present in the United States, as shown in Table 4.2, which reveals the index of regionalisation (calculated as the

Table 4.2 *Index of regionalisation of Argentinean multilatinas.*

Company	South America	North America	Europe	Central America	Asia	Middle East and Africa	Southeast Asia and Oceania
Grupo Techint	29	45	14	10	1	–	–
Arcor SAIC	67	15	11	–	4	4	–
IMPSA	45	9	–	–	27	–	18
Grupo Bagó	50	8	4	31	8	–	–
Molinos Río de la Plata SA	60	13	27	–	–	–	–
Grupo Los Grobo	100	–	–	–	–	–	–
Cresud	80	20	–	–	–	–	–
Roemmers	100	–	–	–	–	–	–
TECNA	67	22	11	–	–	–	–
Lecsa SA	70	–	20	10	–	–	–
SA San Miguel AGICI	67	–	–	–	–	33	–
BGH	100	–	–	–	–	–	–
CLISA	100	–	–	–	–	–	–
Petroquímica Río Tercero SA	100	–	–	–	–	–	–
Grupo Assa	40	40	20	–	–	–	–
Grupo Plastar	–	100	–	–	–	–	–
Sancor Coop. Unidas Ltda	100	–	–	–	–	–	–
Havanna	94	–	1	5	–	–	–
Bio Sidus	–	100	–	–	–	–	–

Source: ProsperAr Survey, Vale Center Columbia University, 2011.

quotient of the number of subsidiaries in a specific region divided by the number of its subsidiaries, and multiplying the result by 100) (Table 4.2).

The top nineteen Argentinean multilatinas have 222 subsidiaries in South and Central America, and fifty-five in North America. They also have nine in Asia and the Middle East and twenty-five in Europe. The majority of their foreign assets are in North and South America. The Techint Group has the most assets abroad, representing 91% of the assets held abroad by the top nineteen Argentinean multilatinas. Arcor took second place, with 3% of the total assets abroad. The foreign assets of these nineteen companies represented 68% of the $28 billion of foreign assets held by all Argentinean companies at the end of the decade of the 2000s.

Many of the Argentinean multilatinas have become case studies in business schools. For instance, the veterans Arcor and Tenaris are studied at Stanford and Harvard.[11] These companies, along with others from the country, were pioneers in foreign investment, with examples that go back to the end of the nineteenth and beginning of the twentieth century. The early experience of companies such as Alpargatas, Bunge & Born, Siam Di Tella, Quilmes and Aguila-Saint opened the road for other Argentinean multinationals such as Techint, YPF (the government-owned oil company), Pérez Companc, Bagó and Arcor. The regional integration of Mercosur prompted many of these groups to respond with increases in productivity and technological intensity[12] (Figure 4.6).

However, many of the Argentinean groups such as Loma Negra (the cement company owned by Amalia Lacroze de Fortabat) went on to be controlled by Brazilian multilatinas (in this case Camargo Correa, for more than a billion dollars in 2005). Many Brazilian companies took advantage of the 2001 crisis in Argentina to buy assets: among others, Pérez Companc was bought by Petrobras, and the brewing company

---

[11] See for Arcor: https://gsbapps.stanford.edu/cases/detail1.asp?Document_ID= 2876; and for Tenaris: https://gsbapps.stanford.edu/cases/detail1.asp? Document_ID=2603.

[12] See Paula Bustos, 'Trade Liberalization, Exports, and Technology Upgrading: Evidence on the Impact of MERCOSUR on Argentinian Firms', *American Economic Review*, 101(1), 2011, pp. 304–40. Available at www.crei.cat/ people/bustos/Trade_Skill_PBustos.pdf.

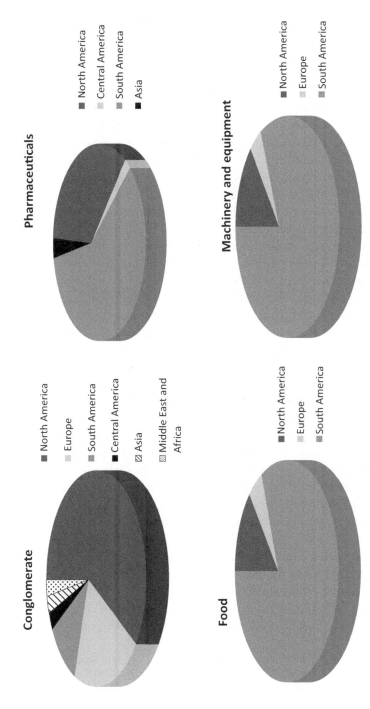

Figure 4.6 International assets of Argentinean multilatinas: geographic distribution (percentage of subsidiaries abroad).
Source: ProsperAr, 2010.

Quilmes and textile company Alpargatas were also bought by Brazilian rivals.[13]

Many of the other historic multilatinas, such as YPF and Pérez Companc, were also eventually sold to foreign groups. Aguila-Saint was sold to an Argentinean multilatina (Arcor) and Siam Di Tella closed its operations. Bunge & Born underwent a major process of restructuring during the 1990s, and no longer exists as such. It is now an international company located in the United States, with its headquarters in New York. Other Argentinean firms, with some exceptions, have remained lagging somewhat behind their counterparts in Latin America or other emerging countries. With the exception of the Techint Group, no Argentinean multinational exceeds $10 billion in foreign assets or has more than 20,000 employees. In contrast, many Brazilian firms are larger (Table 4.3).

One of the main Argentinean multilatinas is the Techint Group, which consists of six companies (Tenaris, Ternium, Tenova, Tecpetrol, Humanitas and Techint Engineering & Construction). Founded in 1945 by the Rocca family, it is a multinational based in Luxembourg, with operations mainly in Argentina, Bolivia, Brazil, Canada, Colombia, Ecuador, United States, Guatemala, Indonesia, Italy, Japan, Mexico, Peru, Romania and Venezuela. In 2010, the group posted a turnover of $20 billion and had more than 55,000 employees.

Tenaris is one of the spearheads of the group. It has been listed on the New York Stock Exchange, and in 2002 became a holding company in Luxembourg. In addition to Buenos Aires and New York, it is also listed in Milan and Mexico City. During the decade of the 2000s, this structure enabled it to have access to international capital and make acquisitions, particularly in Romania, the United States, Canada, Colombia and Mexico, and to open commercial offices in China and Saudi Arabia. Its industrial presence is distributed in fifteen countries and it has trading arrangements and direct operations in a total of twenty-five countries. In 2010, 43% of its sales were in North America, followed by South America (25%), the Middle East and Africa (16%), Europe (10%) and Asia (6%). Tenaris accounts for more

---

[13] To read more about this phenomenon, see Andrés Niembro, Daniela Ramos and Cecilia Simkievich, 'El papel del Mercosur en la llegada de la IED a Brasil y la internacionalización de empresas brasileñas', Fundación CENIT, Working Paper, May 2009. Available at www.fund-cenit.org.ar/investigaciones/dt33.pdf.

Table 4.3 *Ranking of Argentinean multilatinas (foreign assets in $ million).*

Position	Company	Sector	Foreign assets
1	Grupo Techint	Conglomerate	17,406
2	Arcor SAIC	Food	491
3	IMPSA	Machinery and equipment	300
4	Grupo Bagó	Pharmaceuticals	192
5	Molinos Río de la Plata SA	Food	190
6	Grupo Los Grobo	Agricultural production	175
7	Cresud	Agricultural production	68
8	Roemmers	Pharmaceuticals	58
9	TECNA	Construction	50
10	Iecsa SA	Civil engineering	50
11	SA San Miguel AGICI	Food/beverages	23
12	BGH	Electronics	15
13	CLISA	Waste	8
14	Petroquímica Río Tercero SA	Chemicals	8
15	Grupo Assa	IT services	7
16	Grupo Plastar	Plastic and rubber	5
17	Sancor Coop. Unidas Ltda	Food	3
18	Havanna	Related services food	2
19	Bio Sidus	Scientific research	1

Source: ProsperAr, 2010.

than one-third of the group's total sales and has more than 25,000 employees. Ternium is the second gem of the Techint empire, with 15,500 employees distributed between Argentina, Mexico, Colombia, the United States and Guatemala.

Another very successful Argentinean multilatina was Pérez Companc, which Petrobras bought in the 2000s. From this empire remains the food company Molinos Río de la Plata, of which the Pérez Companc family, the wealthiest in the country, owns 73%. Molinos Río de la Plata SA is an Argentinean multilatina operating in 190 countries and founded by Bunge & Born. It was acquired in 1999 by the Pérez Companc group, then leaders in the food industry in South America, active in more than fifty countries worldwide, and the largest company in Argentina in its sector. Its sales in 2010 exceeded $2.6 billion – of which 67% were exports.

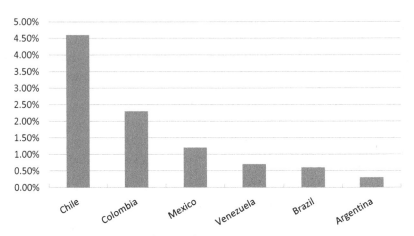

Figure 4.7 Latin America: foreign direct investment in 2010 (net outputs as percentage of GDP).
Source: ESADEgeo, 2012; with data from ECLAC.

Chile

Despite the global crisis, Chilean multilatinas surprised everyone in 2009 and 2010 by making a record number of investments abroad. These totalled $4.9 billion in 2009, and another $4.8 billion was added a year later. Chile led the regional ranking in 2010 in terms of investment relative to GDP with external investments reaching a record of 4.6% of GDP. This was followed by Colombia (2.3%) (Figure 4.7).

Chilean foreign direct investment totalled $57 billion between 1990 and 2010, and was made in more than twenty countries in the Americas, Europe, Asia, Oceania and Africa.[14] In the first half of 2011, Chilean FDI reached $3.5 billion, which means that the total amount invested abroad by Chile since 1990 exceeded $60 billion.

During the 1990–2010 period, Argentina continued to be the main receiver of Chilean FDI, despite a decreasing trend in more recent years (just $56 million in 2010). The combined Chilean FDI in Argentina totalled nearly $16 billion. Throughout this same period, Chilean direct investments showed a rising curve in Brazil. In 2009, Brazil

---

[14] See Ministerio de Relaciones Exteriores, *La inversión directa de capitales chilenos en el mundo, 1990–2010*, Santiago de Chile, Ministry of Foreign Affairs, Directorate-General of International Economic Relations, 2011. Available at www.direcon.gob.cl/bibliotecas/scategorias/list/1937.

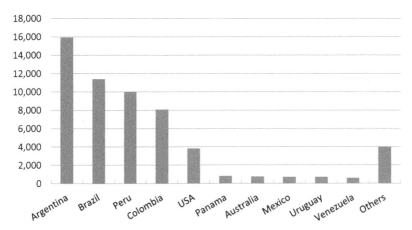

Figure 4.8 Foreign investment by Chilean multilatinas, 1990–2010 (in $ million).
Source: Chilean Ministry of Foreign Relations, 2011.

was the main receiver of Chilean capital, and in 2010, despite occupying third place behind Peru and Colombia, it received $1.2 billion in Chilean investments. In total, Chilean FDI in Brazil totalled more than $11 billion, which is one-fifth of the total Chilean FDI during the period 1990–2010 (Figure 4.8).

Chile has concentrated investment over the decade of the 2000s and until recently in neighbouring Peru. In 2010, Peru captured more than 40% of the foreign investment made by Chile, which was a record of $1.8 billion. Colombia occupied second place with $1.7 billion. In these two Andean countries, Chile has invested $10 and $8 billion respectively. In total, ten countries, all on the American continent except for one, concentrate nearly 95% of the total FDI made by Chile over the period 2000–10.

Interestingly, we can also observe how Chilean FDI began to diversify geographically since 2010. While most FDI was poured into the American continent, there were one Asian country (China) and two European countries (Belgium and Italy) among the top ten destinations in 2010. The amounts are still modest, but indicate that Chile is widening its horizons in the same way as Brazil (but with a time lag). During the 2000s, Chilean companies have started to invest in the Middle East, with $130 million in the UAE and Egypt. In Europe, Chilean FDI at the end of 2010 reached $870 million, or 1.5% of the

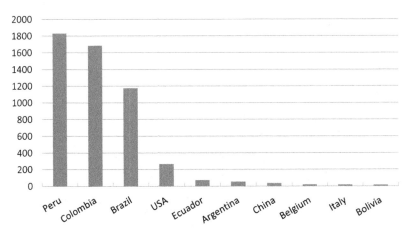

Figure 4.9 Foreign investment by Chilean multilatinas, 2010.
Source: Chilean Ministry of Foreign Relations, 2011.

total invested abroad. Half of these investments were made in Spain and another quarter in France. However, these amounts are small when compared to that invested in the United States ($3.8 billion for the period 1990–2010, which is slightly less than 7% of the total) (Figure 4.9).

In terms of sectors, Chilean capital over that period has been mainly directed towards services (40%), energy (28.8%) and industry (23.1%). In some sectors, Chile is beginning to position itself as a regional and international leader. The country is the leading world exporter of copper, and as such is backed by top-level groups in this sector, beginning with the government-owned Codelco or the privately owned Luksic group (which oddly has established the headquarters of its main mining company, Antofagasta, in London).

Chilean multilatinas are also gaining ground in other sectors: the country is already the third retail operator in Latin America; it is among the top ten producers of sawn timber in the world; its multilatinas are fourth worldwide in the production of cellulose and boric acid. Chilean multilatinas account for 30% of world production of lithium and derivatives, 33% of the world's sodium, 35% of the world's molybdenum and 47% of the world's specialty vegetable nutrition. With the merger of LAN and TAM, this Chilean-Brazilian multilatina will

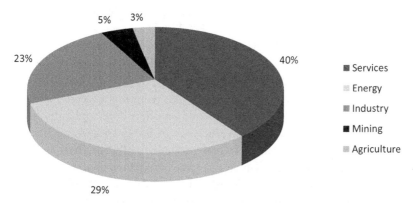

5%   3%

23%   40%

                                                ■ Services
                                                ▨ Energy
                                                ■ Industry
                                                ■ Mining
                                                ▨ Agriculture

29%

Figure 4.10 Foreign investment by Chilean multilatinas by sectors, 1990–2010.
Source: Chilean Ministry of Foreign Relations, 2011.

handle 37% of the Latin American airline load and 0.6% of world air traffic, and earn 10% of airline income worldwide (Figure 4.10).

Throughout the 2000s, many Chilean multinationals were expanding – especially retail companies. Cencosud, the third largest company in Chile after Codelco and Enersis, is in Argentina, Brazil, Colombia, Chile and Peru; Falabella is present in Argentina, Colombia and Peru; and Ripley and Parque Arauco are in Peru. The retailer Cencosud, owned by entrepreneur Horst Paulmann, bought the Bretas chain of supermarkets in Brazil in 2010. Today, Cencosud, active in Argentina, Brazil, Chile, Peru and Colombia, employs more than 100,000. In 2011, Copec, one of the largest conglomerates in the country, operating in the forestry and energy sectors, pursued international expansion with a $76 million purchase and investment in Colombia. Copec controls the cellulose production company Arauco, which is among the top five world exporters, with operations in Brazil (where it bought a local business for $230 million in 2009), Argentina and Uruguay.

Also worth mentioning is the recent operation carried out by Mall Plaza, a shopping centre construction and management firm. The company owns and operates eleven shopping centres in Chile and two in Peru, and aims to convert these centres into a single entity to serve as a reference point for the company's regional expansion. Mall Plaza invested $75 million in 2011 to build the first shopping centre in Colombia – in Cartagena.

In regional terms, the Mercosur countries dominate (nearly 50% of the total FDI invested between 1990 and 2010), followed by the Andean region, and NAFTA (8%). Europe (1.5%) and Asia/Oceania (2%) are still marginal. But we are now seeing investments in other regions of the world. Cencosud opened an office in Shanghai in 2008 with the aim of improving the efficiency of its Asian and specifically Chinese supply. A remarkable case is the broadly internationalised multinational Soquimich which operates in eighteen countries world-wide – including the United States, Europe and Asia. From its European offices in Belgium, it leads operations in various African countries and the Middle East. It also has a direct presence in Turkey, South Africa, the United Arab Emirates, India, China, Japan and Thailand. In Europe, it is present in Belgium, Germany, Italy, Portugal and Spain. For its part, the shipping company Compañía Sudamericana de Vapores (CSAV), founded in Valparaíso at the end of the nineteenth century, is the oldest and largest in Latin America. In 2011, the group Luksic bought an almost 20% share in the shipping company for more than $240 million (through Quiñenco, the financial and industrial arm of Luksic) with the aim of re-energising the business.

The Luksic group controls 65% of the Antofagasta mining company, 50% of Banco de Chile, the second financial institution in the country, and 48% of Madeco. It has activities on every continent. In 2006, the Banco de Chile opened a branch in Beijing, making it the first Latin American banking representation in the Chinese capital. Madeco, a diversified group of companies that processes copper, aluminium, PVC and flexible container products, has twelve production plants in Chile, Peru and Argentina. It entered into the capital of the French company Nexans in 2008 in exchange for a cable business and took a 20% share of the French multinational three years later.

Chilean investments in Asia are still small, but indicate a growing mutual interest. In the first half of 2011, the Chilean foreign investment committee received applications for investments amounting to $417 million from Asian countries, well exceeding the $300 million requested during the whole of 2010.

China, in particular, has its eyes set on Chile, which produces 35% of the world's copper. Despite the robust trade between both countries, which in 2010 exceeded $25 billion, Chinese investment represents only 0.11% of the foreign investment received between 1974 and 2010: totalling just $85 million. However, trends may soon change. The Chinese sovereign wealth fund CIC, which manages more than $300 billion, equivalent to 1.5 times the Chilean GDP, announced in 2011 its interest in investing in the country, particularly in mining and infrastructure projects.[15] Chilean investment in China only amounts to $212 million, which represents 0.4% of the total invested abroad by Chilean firms. In 2010, Chilean investment in China reached nearly $70 million. In addition to the Banco de Chile, Cencosud and Soquimich, the Chilean firms Falabella, D&S and Celulosa Arauco have also started operations in China. In 2011, Codelco and China Minmetals Corp signed a strategic investment alliance. The two government-owned banks Banco del Estado (Chile) and the China Development Bank have also signed similar agreements.

Colombia

Like Chile, Colombia has experienced remarkable changes over the last few years, both from a macro- and a microeconomic standpoint. Like Chile, which was one of the first countries in the region to obtain an investment grade rating, Colombia was awarded an investment grade rating in June 2011, thus recognising a decade of effort to stabilise the economy and put it onto a path to sustainable growth.

Macroeconomic progress has been accompanied by microeconomic progress, with the international expansion of the Colombian multilatinas. Like Chile (which became a member of the OECD at the beginning of 2010), Colombia also started a process of incorporation at the end of 2010 (which will be extended several years, in the same way as Chile) and its candidacy was well received with an initial economic report on the country.[16]

Not only has Colombia received a major boost in FDI (more than 3.5% and 4% of GDP in 2010 and in 2011, respectively), but it also became a direct investor. For the period 2001–10, Colombia achieved a combined investment (stock) of nearly $60 billion. In 2010, FDI in Colombia reached $6.8 billion, which was in line with the previous

---

[15] See www.inversionextranjera.cl/.
[16] See OECD, *Colombia Economic Assessment*, Paris, OECD, 2010. Available at www.oecd.org/dataoecd/38/14/46797800.pdf.

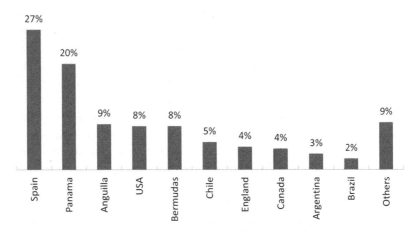

Figure 4.11 FDI by Colombia, 2010 (in $ million).
Source: Central Bank of Colombia, 2011.

year.[17] FDI in Colombia in 2010 grew by 113% and reached a record of $14.4 billion, according to UNCTAD, the United Nations Conference on Trade and Development. It grew again by more than 26% in the first six months of 2012 compared to the same period last year.[18]

Oil and mines account for nearly 70% of the total. In the first half of 2011, this figure was exceeded with $7.4 billion invested in the country. It is difficult to use official statistics to discover the origin of investment as nearly 50% of FDI enters Colombia through tax havens such as Panama, Anguilla, Bermuda and the Cayman Islands. However, it is striking that Brazil only represents 2% of the FDI.

We are seeing an unprecedented progress in Colombian FDI. During the year 2010, it reached $6.7 billion, a growth of more than 110% on the previous year. This represents nearly one-third of all FDI during the period 2001–10 (about $20.5 billion of combined FDI), which indicates a net acceleration in the foreign investment activity of Colombian multilatinas. More than twenty Colombian companies can be considered multilatinas; that is, they have substantial operations abroad (Figure 4.11).

[17] See the detailed report on FDI in Colombia by Proexport Colombia: www. inviertaencolombia.com.co/Adjuntos/246_Reporte%20de%20Inversion.pdf.
[18] See the economic report published by the Banco de Bogotá, one of the largest banks in the country: https://pbit.bancodebogota.com.co/Investigaciones/PresentacionPDF.aspx?PDF=42.

Avianca-Taca, Sudamericana, Aval and Cementos Argos are some of the most active in terms of foreign acquisitions. In 2010, the financial company the Aval Group drew attention with the purchase of BAC Credomatic in Central America, for more than $1.9 billion. In 2011, Sudamericana stood out when it bought assets from the pension funds in Latin America of the Dutch company ING for $3.7 billion. Taking advantage of the movements of integration in the Andean capital markets, the Colombian brokerage firms also went in search of business abroad. Many operate in the United States, and InterBolsa, for example, already has a major presence in Brazil and Panama. Also active in the Panamanian market are Corredores Asociados, Correval and Valores Bancolombia. This last firm is also setting up a brokerage in Peru.

The Colombian industrial multilatinas are also making waves. ISA has spread itself widely in the region in various lines of business. In energy, it operates in Brazil, Peru, Panama and Bolivia; in telecommunications in Peru, Chile, Ecuador, Venezuela, Argentina and Brazil; and in road infrastructures in Chile. Over the years, ISA has become one of the largest transporters of energy in Latin America, with more than 36,000 kilometres of high voltage lines. ISA has strengthened itself as a multilatina through half a dozen acquisitions, namely in Peru, Bolivia and Brazil. In 2010, it bought $300 million in assets from the Spanish railway company Ferrovial in Chile. ISA's strategy for growth projects $3.5 billion in income by 2016, 80% of which will be generated outside Colombia.

Also in the energy sector, Empresas Públicas de Medellín (a public services company) has found opportunities in Panama and El Salvador, and the Empresa de Energía de Bogotá (utilities company) has set up branches in Guatemala and Peru, where it supplies electricity. Another noteworthy company is Cementos Argos, which has operations in Panama, the Dominican Republic, Haiti and the United States. Founded in 1934, Argos is today the fifth largest producer of cement in Latin America. In 2009, its annual sales were near $2 billion, 44% of which was from Colombia, and with a notable 34% from the United States, 9% from other Latin American countries, and another 13% coming from businesses unrelated to cement. In May 2011, Argos, following its strategy of international expansion, bought more than $760 billion in assets from its French rival Lafarge in the United States.

In the agro-industrial sector, Alpina, a food supply company active in Ecuador and Venezuela, is building a plant to supply the US market. The Mundial Group, which supplies chemicals and paints, among other products, is present in almost all of South America and Mexico. A Colombian agro-industrial multilatina with a special talent for internationalisation is Nacional de Chocolates, which belongs to the Grupo Empresarial Antioqueño (Antioquia Business Group). Like many Colombian groups, this company began its expansion in the nearest regional markets. In the 1990s, it launched operations in Ecuador and Venezuela. However, in the decade of the 2000s it took a great leap overseas and graduated as a multilatina, making its way to twelve countries with its own operation, branches, and exports to seventy nations. Between 2000 and 2009, the group's international sales rose from just $45 million to more than $700 million. The number of employees outside the country also increased from 400 to more than 5,600 at the end of the 2000s – out of a total of 28,000. In 2011, it had eight production plants in six countries: Colombia, Costa Rica, Mexico, Panama, Peru and Venezuela (all in Latin America). The company grew through a dozen acquisitions. The last major acquisition was the purchase in 2009 of the Mexican company Nutresa, a chocolate sweets producer.

Colombia has several important conglomerates. The Carvajal Organization is one of the oldest, founded in 1904, and now formed of twelve companies with 23,000 employees. It has operations in more than sixteen countries, including Mexico, Peru, Ecuador, Argentina, Venezuela and Panama, and exports to more than fifty countries. In 2010, 45% of its income came from overseas. It is also present in Spain, and has interests in the United States and Asia. Recently, Carvajal agreed to purchase the Mexican group Convermex, the world's third largest producer of polystyrene glass, for about $180 million.

In the more traditional sectors of hydrocarbons, another important company is Terpel, which sells combustibles. The company has a 40% market share in Colombia, and also has assets in Chile, Panama and Ecuador. The oil company Ecopetrol also deserves special mention. It is not only benefiting from the boom in the oil market in Colombia, but is expanding internationally through an aggressive strategy of drilling and acquisition in Brazil, Peru and Mexico. In 2011, together with Talisman, it bought the Colombian operations of the British company

BP for nearly $1.9 billion. It also made an acquisition in Peru with the Korea National Oil Corporation for nearly $900 million.

For now, the Colombian groups are graduating as multilatinas just like those of Chile, through internationalisation across the Americas. They are also following the path of the Brazilian multinationals, and it is expected that throughout the current decade we will see investments in other continents. But only time will tell; for now, the records of Colombian investment in China, for example, carried out by the Central Bank, show a very conservative flow of just $800,000 between 1994 and 2000.

Peru

The journey through the world of the multilatinas contains yet another surprise. As well as those in the countries already mentioned (Brazil, Mexico, Argentina, Chile and Colombia) there are multilatinas in other countries in the region that are also following this trend.

Even in Peru, we are seeing groups sprout up with major international ambitions, like AJE Group, founded by the Añaños family, with a presence in the Americas, Europe and Asia. One of these firms is Gloria, which, in 2010, took over an Argentinean company that it had merged with in 2006, after investing $19 million. This operation followed another acquisition for $40 million in Bolivia, with which it financed the first steps of its international expansion, focused initially on neighbouring countries. In addition to these countries, the Peruvian group owns milk product suppliers in Colombia, Ecuador and Puerto Rico.

Also in the sector of food and services, Alicorp, the crowning glory of the Romero group, bought its first company in Argentina in 2008, which was the third largest supplier of personal care products in that country, for $65 million. Shortly thereafter, it sealed the purchase of a Colombian company for nearly $7.5 million. After waiting out the crisis, Alicorp acquired 100% of an Argentinean company that produces cookies in 2010, followed by the purchase of a pasta producer in mid 2011. Founded in 1954, Alicorp was the largest agro-industrial group in the country in 2011, with operations in South America, Central America and North America. The beverage company rose two positions after being at 13 in the 2009 América Economía ranking, and announced sales of $1.1 billion in 2010.

In 2010, the brothers Pedro and Mario Brescia acquired the mining company Sierra de Madeira, in Brazil, for more than $470 million. With this purchase, they initiated an internationalisation that gained strength in 2009 with the purchase of the largest cement company in Chile (assets of the French company Lafarge).

For its part, in 2007, the group Interbank opened a branch office in China, and a year and a half later, conscious of the growing traffic between the two countries, the bank launched an import and export (trading) company. Interbank set up a commercial representative office in Shanghai, and has signed cooperation agreements with the Bank of China to establish a platform for services to Chinese investors in Peru. In 2011, it received a loan for $30 million from the China Development Bank (CDB) to fund projects and businesses that encourage commercial trade and investment between both countries. Today, the Interbank Group (IFH Perú), founded by Carlos Rodríguez-Pastor, is one of the most important groups in the country, with a reported turnover of a billion dollars and a presence in banking and insurance, restaurants and hotels, retail, real estate, administration and cinemas. At the beginning of 2011, it acquired the fast-food restaurant chain Bembos, which operates in Peru, Panama, Nicaragua and India.

The most symbolic case of the Peruvian business boom is undoubtedly Gastón Acurio, who founded an empire of thirty-four restaurants in fourteen countries, which he was running through his 'gastrogrupo' Inversiones La Macha (47% owned by Los Robles, the firm led by Andrés Belfus, former manager of the Chilean retail company Ripley). Its assets include the restaurant franchise Astrid y Gastón, which began in 1994, and currently has franchisees in Peru, Chile, Colombia, Ecuador, Venezuela, Panama, Spain, Mexico, Argentina, the United States and Britain. Acurio also developed other franchises and products including: a designer chain of pastry and delicatessen products; the 'La Mar Cebichería' seafood restaurants; and the restaurant-bistro-pastry shop Tanta, which now operates in Peru, Chile, Bolivia, Spain and the United States. Gastón Acurio plans to open a brand of hotels called 'Nativa' and continue expanding the restaurants towards Asia, once the United States and Europe are consolidated. In 2011, he opened a new restaurant in New York, investing $15 million. With an estimated turnover in the range of $100 million in 2010, Acurio invests in creating wealth and also in his school in Pachacutec, one of the poorest areas of Lima.

Above all, Gastón Acurio has led a movement that has put Peruvian cuisine on the international map, making it a tool for creating wealth, and forming a significant part of the nation's 'branding'. Behind Acurio, many other Peruvian chefs have emerged, such as Javier Wong, Christian Bravo, Iván Kisic and Rafael Osterling. Today, Peruvian cuisine produces 11.25% of the Peruvian GDP, is exported all over the world, and has boosted the self-esteem of the Peruvians. Gastón Acurio has landed in position 42 on the prestigious 'Restaurant' list of the world's best chefs. Making it on the list is testimony to a major transformation that is taking place in Latin America, and Peru in particular, with the emergence of a great cuisine that shows that innovation, business creativity and scalable economy are the keys to success.

The success of Gastón Acurio has ceased to be a local event. His restaurants can now be found on the streets of New York, San Francisco, London, Barcelona and Madrid – as well as Lima or Bogotá. Beyond the culinary success, there is also the economic and business success, with nearly 3,000 direct employees and many more indirect employees, and a national 'branding' that has changed profoundly. In addition, tourists to Peru now come to do more than just visit the ruins of Machu Picchu and the streets of Cuzco, and enjoy the many top gourmet restaurants in the capital that have followed in the steps of 'Astrid y Gastón'.

Exploring new areas

Beyond the specific characteristics of each of the countries mentioned, our attention is drawn to the fact that in this current decade of the 2010s the multilatinas are exploring new areas for investment. The previous case of Gastón Acurio and his restaurants shows that many of these multilatinas operate in the United States and Europe – as well as Latin America. Meanwhile, the new investment frontiers for these multinationals are profiled as Asia, Africa and the Middle East.

In Asia, we are seeing growing numbers of Latin American projects. The industrial chemical conglomerate Mexichem, one of the largest in Mexico, announced in 2011 that it plans to invest $150 million building plants for refrigerants in Japan and fluorhydric acid in Korea. The world's largest producer of potassium nitrate, the Chilean company SQM, set up an industrial plant in China in a 50–50 joint venture with local company Migao Corporation and endowed it with a $20 million investment.

Argentina has been particularly active in repositioning its relationship with China. The Argentinean company ProntoWash, an ecological car washing company, reached an agreement with the Chinese company Guangzhou Eco-EnvironTech in 2011 to develop this concept in the cities of Guangzhou, Beijing and Shanghai, among others, with an initial investment of $4 million. Another Argentinean company that is reaching out to China is the Chemo Group. This Argentinean pharmaceutical company signed an agreement in 2011 with the Chinese company FOSUM Pharma, in which both companies will make a combined investment of $73 million to research, develop, produce and distribute generic medicines to the Chinese markets, and build a plant in Shanghai. Banco de la Nación, owned by Argentinean capital, announced the opening of a commercial office in Peking, in addition to the offices that the organisation already has in the United States, Spain, Panama, Venezuela, Brazil, Bolivia, Paraguay, Chile and Uruguay. The main objective is to take advantage of the commercial trade between both countries, whose bilateral flows reached more than $13 billion in 2010, up 60% on the previous year, and turning China into Argentina's second largest business partner.

Interest in Asia is also stimulating Latin American countries to embark on joint ventures. The best example is the agreement made between Colombia and Chile in March 2011, with the aim of strengthening their presence in Asia and attracting investment in these countries. The agreement enables the Colombian promotion service Proexport to use the facilities of ProChile in China, Japan and South Korea. In addition, Peru will be included in a proposal to create a tourist package for Asians to visit Cartagena de Indias (Colombia), Machu Picchu (Peru) and Torres del Paine (Chile). These countries also aim to strengthen their relations with Asia by opening new embassies. To illustrate this, in 2011 Colombia opened an embassy in Indonesia (along with others in Turkey and the United Arab Emirates), thus confirming the intensified search for new investment frontiers.

This Asian connection sometimes has a Spanish side. In 2009, the Chilean multilatina Compañía Sudamericana de Vapores (CSAV), the largest shipping company in Latin America, connected the port of Barcelona with the Indian port of Nhava Sheva through a new weekly service running a thirteen-day route that will be covered by six ships. With this service, Barcelona will thus be linked to the geographic areas covered by CSAV, which are South America, the Pacific, the Caribbean and the Mexican Gulf. In 2011, Singapore Airlines started operating a Singapore–Barcelona–São Paulo route, which flies non-stop between Barcelona and the Brazilian city three times a week. It is expected that there will be a high demand for seats due to events such as the 2014 World Cup and the Olympic Games in 2016.

As stressed in this chapter, the phenomenon of multilatinas goes well beyond Brazilian ones. Spanish-speaking multilatinas from Argentina and Mexico have in fact been the pioneers. Later Brazil entered into the game along with Andean country based multinationals from Chile, Colombia and Peru. Also interestingly, all these multinationals once focused on Latin America, and, from time to time trespassing towards the USA (mostly the Mexican ones) or Europe (mostly the Argentinean ones), are now exploring new geographies, looking towards Asia and the Middle East in particular. The boom of Andean multinationals (Chile, Colombia and Peru) is a new phenomenon. Another emerging trend, as we shall see in the next chapter, is the rise throughout the whole continent of another type of multinationals – Multilatinas 2.0 – more technologically orientated, IT providers and startups, some even listed in the NASDAQ.

5 | *Multilatinas 2.0*

As we have seen, the rise of the multilatinas spans many sectors and nations. It is not an isolated phenomenon and follows a broader movement in which several emerging Asian, Arab and even African countries are participating. This commercial rise also extends to the innovation and technology sectors.

The decade 2000–10 saw a radical change in the world's focus towards emerging markets from a commercial and financial standpoint. In the decade 2010–12 we are seeing a dramatic change towards emerging markets from the standpoint of innovation. We have already seen this in 2012: The major supplier to the telecommunications industry is no longer an American, French or Swedish multinational; it is now Chinese. From Shenzhen, Huawei has conquered the world (specifically via Latin America, hand in hand with Telefónica, who granted the company one of its first global contracts). Also, the major provider of personal computers has finally ceased to be the US giant HP but its Chinese rival Lenovo. China in 2012 surpassed Europe as the second largest venture hub globally.[1] From Moscow, the venture capital fund Digital Sky Technologies (DST) is revolutionising the industry. Another Chinese multinational, Tencent, has achieved the third largest internet capitalisation in the world. In 2011 it raised a startup investment fund of $760 million, one of the largest in the world. This amount was topped by DST in Russia, and both cases were outside Silicon Valley. Even what seems to be a purely Western technology, such as Apple's iPad, incorporates emerging market technology. Nearly 20% of iPad's value originates in Korea, Taiwan and China.[2]

As we will see, Latin America is not excluded from this dynamic. The acquisition by Indra in mid 2011 of Brazilian Politec shows that

[1] See Ernst & Young, Globalizing venture capital, Ernst & Young, 2012. Available at www.ey.com/FR/fr/Newsroom/News-releases/Communique-de-presse – Global-venture-capital-investment-trends-report-2012.
[2] See http://pcic.merage.uci.edu/papers/2011/Value_iPad_iPhone.pdf.

the continent is also a target for technology investors. Indra wagered on the future of Brazil and reached an agreement to buy 100% of Politec, one of the main Brazilian information technology companies, for $145 million. This purchase shows how the continent is changing the profile of Spanish technology companies. With this transaction, Indra's international sales will increase from 40% to 47% of total sales. As such, Brazil will be the second largest national market for Indra with 10% of sales, making Latin America the largest regional market for Indra and representing 22% of sales. The same is happening with Telefónica, which acquired Brazil's Vivo in 2010 for €7.5 billion. Telefónica's Latin American operations, headed by Brazil, represented 46% of the group total and included more than 190 million customers in 2011. Brazil's contribution to income exceeded 23% of the total in 2011 and is expected to continue growing in the years ahead. Brazil may soon become Telefónica's main market. (Spain currently provides 30% of its worldwide revenue.)

These transactions show, above all, the technology boom in Brazil and other countries on the continent. The most spectacular case is the Mexican company América Móvil, which has become one of the largest telecommunications operators in the world, and has entered into the world's top ten by market capitalisation. Chilean multinational Sonda, with 9,000 employees, already has a presence in nine of the region's countries and multiplied its acquisitions in 2010, particularly in Argentina, Mexico and Brazil to consolidate its position as a technology leader. The company offered Chilean rival Quintec some $70 million in 2011 to consolidate itself as a leader in the region, also acquiring its international operations (Table 5.1).

Brazilian Tivit, founded in 2005 with the merger of three of the country's technology companies and with 26,000 employees, benefited from the entry of British venture capital fund Apax Partners – bringing its value to nearly a billion dollars. We are also seeing the emergence of a local software industry. In addition to Sonda and Tivit, Mexico's Softtek, Argentina's Globant, and Brazil's TOTVS and Stefanini also stand out.

Softtek, for example, has more than 6,000 employees, and thirty global offices in North America, Latin America, Europe and Asia (the fact that a woman, Blanca Treviño, is CEO also makes the company noticeable). Former Spanish government minister Francisco Álvarez-Cascos has been named president of Softtek España in Spain – where

Table 5.1 *International expansion of Sonda.*

Year	Company acquired	Acquiring company	Value (in $ million)
2010	CEITECH SA, Argentina	Sonda SA	6.3
2010	Sonda Procwork SA-Business, Brazil	Capgemini SA	–
2010	Kaizen Consultoria e Serviços em Informática Ltda., Brazil	Sonda Procwork SA	6.7
2010	NextiraOne México SA de CV	Sonda Mexico SA de CV	29
2010	Soft Team Consultoria, Brazil	Sonda Procwork SA	8.64
2010	Soft Team Sistemas, Brazil	Sonda SA	8.68
2010	Telsinc Informática SA, Brazil	Sonda SA	37.58
2008	Red Colombia SA	Sonda de Colombia SA	13.6
2007	Procwork, Brazil	Sonda SA	118.1
2006	Qualita-Technical Support, Mexico	Sonda SA	–

Source: ECLAC, 2011.

the company has a global service centre (in Coruña), in addition to offices in Madrid and Barcelona (there is another European office in London). Neoris, the technology subsidiary of Mexico's Cemex, is another important technology company in Latin America. It generates more than $300 million in revenue, has 3,000 employees worldwide, and has eighteen offices in nine countries. It is a multinational with a multicultural leadership. Its chief executive is Argentinean, the marketing director is Brazilian, and its president for Europe, Africa and the Middle East is Spanish.

Another company that stands out is Stefanini IT Solutions, a Brazilian multinational that specialises in information technology and provides business process outsourcing (BPO). Among the services it offers are consulting, integration, development of solutions and infrastructure. It has nearly 13,000 employees and a presence in twenty-seven countries. The company reached $750 million in revenue in 2011, of which 40% came from its international operations. Brazilian TOTVS in turn operates in Latin America and has more than 15,000 employees in forty offices in Argentina, Brazil, Chile, Mexico, Paraguay and Uruguay. It has also opened software development centres in Europe (Lisbon), with Portugal its European base for expansion. It is also present in the United States and Africa (Angola and Mozambique). By

Table 5.2 *Growth of TOTVS SA.*

Year	Company acquired	Acquiring company	Value (in $ million)
2010	Soft Team Consultoria	Sonda Procwork	8.64
2010	Soft Team Sistemas	Sonda SA	8.68
2010	Midbyte Informática SA	TOTVS SA	–
2009	Hery Software Ltda	TOTVS SA	7.06
2009	Tools Arquitetura Financeira	TOTVS SA	0.8
2009	YMF Arquitetura Financeira	TOTVS SA	10.22
2009	RO Resultados em Outsourcing	TOTVS SA	1.69
2008	Datasul SA	TOTVS SA	375.47
2008	Setware Informática Ltda	TOTVS SA	2
2007	BCS Engenheiros Associados	TOTVS SA	–
2007	HBA Informática Ltda	TOTVS SA	–
2007	BCS Flex Comércio E Serviços	TOTVS SA	–
2007	BCS Comércio E Serviços	TOTVS SA	27.27
2007	TQTVD Software Ltda	TOTVS SA	–
2007	Inteligência Organizacional	TOTVS SA	1.96
2007	Midbyte Informática SA	TOTVS SA	3.29
2007	TOTVS BMI Consultoria	TOTVS SA	–

Source: ECLAC, 2011.

2011 TOTVS was the largest application software company with headquarters in an emerging country, and was the sixth largest company in the world in its sector.

Other multilatinas in Brazil are included in the Bloomberg Businessweek's Tech 100 list of the top 100 technology companies in the world. In addition to the already mentioned TOTVS, these include: Redecard (information technology services); Vivo (telecom subsidiary now 100% owned by Telefónica); B2W Varejo (internet services); CA Technologies (software); and Positivo (computer and peripherals). Combined they invoiced more than a billion dollars, putting them in a similar league with Indra in Spain, for example (with sales of $3 billion), the second largest technology firm in Spain after Telefónica (Table 5.2).

Argentina startup Mercadolibre has been listed on the NASDAQ since 2007 with a market value of around $3.8 billion in 2011, making it the largest technology company on the continent to be listed on this

Table 5.3 *Four giant Latin multinational technology companies.*

Company	Origin	Estimated earnings (in $ million)	Estimated number of employees
Globant	Argentina	65 (2009)	2,000
Softtek	Mexico	234 (2007)	6,000
Sonda	Chile	952 (2010)	10,000
TOTVS	Brazil	682 (2010)	15,000

Source: ECLAC, 2011.

platform. Founded by Marcos Galperín and Hernán Kazah in 1999, during their MBA programmes at Stanford, this startup has become the largest e-commerce company in Latin America. Mercadolibre is the portal leader in twelve Latin American countries and recently began operations in Portugal. This company has become one of the most successful firms studied by the University of Stanford and the Davos World Economic Forum.[3] (Among those studied were various Latin American startups such as the Argentineans Globant and Technisys, and Colombian Refinancia, along with startups from India, China, Turkey, South Africa and Russia – in addition to several from the United States and Europe) (Table 5.3).

Another Argentine company, Globant, with more than 2,000 employees in eight countries in Latin America and commercial offices in the United States and Europe, has been a case study at the Harvard Business School and the World Economic Forum, along with European and American startups such as Skype and eBay.[4] Globant (with commercial offices in Boston, San Francisco and London) already has 90% of its projects originating outside Latin America. American venture capital funds are investing in this technology company and Riverwood Capital invested $15 million in 2011. In 2010 its revenue topped $60 million, making it another of the continent's successful startups and an emerging multilatina. In August 2011, Globant bought Nextive to increase its presence in the United States. This acquisition will enable it

---

[3] See Stanford University and World Economic Forum, *Global Entrepreneurship and Successful Growth Strategies of Early Stage Companies*, Stanford and Geneva, World Economic Forum, 2011. Available at www3.weforum.org/docs/WEF_Entrepreneurship_Report_2011.pdf.

[4] See www.weforum.org/issues/global-entrepreneurship.

to expand its portfolio of solutions for mobile devices and add another 130 professionals to its team.

We are thus seeing the emergence of Multilatinas 2.0, companies that come out of the continent with regional and international ambitions and put Latin America on the radar for the second wave of major global change for emerging markets: that of innovation. The following companies already appear in the rankings of the world's most innovative companies: Brazilian Natura Cosmetics is in eighth place, just behind Google in Forbes' 2011 list of the world's most innovative companies (a top ten that also includes China's Tencent and India's Bharat). As an innovative company, it is the object of a case study by Stanford and Harvard universities.[5] Boston Consulting Group also includes in fourth place (just before Google) Mexican América Móvil in their top ten of the most innovative, value-creating companies.[6] The top ten is led by emerging multinational internet company Chinese Tencent, and also includes Taiwanese companies Mediatek, China Mobile, Indian companies Bharti Airtel and Infosys, and the South African company MTN. In other words, more than half already come from emerging countries (Tables 5.4 and 5.5).

The world's focus on technology in emerging markets

The decade of 2010–20 belongs to the emerging markets. In the previous decade, these economies emerged as the main catalysts for growth. They now look to be the main players. HSBC, for example, tells us that nineteen of the thirty largest economies in the world in 2050 will be economies that are today classified as emerging.[7] Together they will account for more than the value of the current OECD countries. China will have become the world leader ahead of the United States; India will have surpassed Japan and Brazil; and Mexico will also find itself in the world's top ten, ahead of France and Canada (Table 5.6).

---

[5] See https://gsbapps.stanford.edu/cases/detail1.asp?Document_ID=3354.
[6] See BCG, *The 2010 Value Creators Report. Threading the Needle: Value Creation in a Low Growth Economy*, Boston, BCG, 2010, available at www.bcg.com/documents/file59590.pdf.
[7] See HSBC, *The World in 2050: Quantifying the Shift in the Global Economy*, London and New York, HSBC Global Research, 2011. Available at www.research.hsbc.com/midas/Res/RDV?p=pdf&key=ej73gSSJVj&n=282364.PDF.

Table 5.4 *Top fifteen multinational technology and software companies.*

Company	Country	Net sales (net revenue in dollars)	Employees	Presence in Europe
América Móvil	Mexico	49,100	153,140	Yes
Brightstar	Bolivia/USA	6,400	3,500	Yes
Mercadolibre	Argentina	2,750	52,000	Yes (Portugal)
B2W Varejo	Brazil	2,391	2,375	No
Redecard	Brazil	1,995	1,455	No
Positivo	Brazil	1,300	6,400	Yes (Portugal)
Sonda	Chile	952	10,000	No
TOTVS	Brazil	682	15,000	Yes (Portugal)
Stefanini IT Solutions	Brazil	600	12,000	Yes (Belgium and others)
Neoris	Mexico	300	3,000	Yes (Spain and Hungary)
Softtek	Mexico	257	6,000	Yes (Spain and others)
Bematech	Brazil	192	700	Yes (Germany)
Hildebrando	Mexico	148	1,740	Yes (Spain)
Globant	Argentina	65	2,000	Yes (Britain)
G&L	Argentina	74	500	Yes (Spain)
Assa	Argentina		1,000	No
CPM Braxis Capgemini	Brazil		5,500	Yes (Germany)
Politec	Brazil		5,000	No
Quintec	Chile	170		–
Adexus	Chile			–
Coasin	Chile			–
Tivit	Brazil		26,000	No

Source: ESADEgeo, 2012; based on company data and ECLAC, 2011.

The year 2010 saw dramatic change. While OECD countries continued to collapse, emerging countries grew. As a symbol of the great transformation we are experiencing, China pulled ahead of Japan as the world's second largest economy, while India attracted a record $80 billion in direct investment, twice that of the previous year. In Brazil, petroleum company Petrobras, one of the world's largest, managed to launch the largest share offer in history ($67 billion). In all, in 2010, emerging markets accounted for 40% of the world GDP and, even more remarkable, captured close to 50% of global foreign direct

Table 5.5 *Boston Consulting Group: top ten leading world innovators.*

Company	Country	TSR (%)	Market value (in $ trillion)
Tencent	Hong Kong	106.3	39.5
Apple	USA	45.6	189.6
MediaTek	Taiwan	32	19
América Móvil	Mexico	27.1	75.6
Google	USA	26.3	197
China Mobile	Hong Kong	26	188.5
Bharti Airtel	India	25.6	27.3
MTN Group	South Africa	23.6	29.3
Infosys Technologies	India	21.2	32.6
Hewlett-Packard	USA	20.8	121.8

Source: Boston Consulting Group, 2011.
Note: TSR = total shareholder return.

investment. For the first time, in 2010 six of the top twenty global investors in the world were emerging economies (Table 5.7).

The growth of the middle classes in these economies is increasingly attracting OECD multinationals. For many, emerging markets already represent the bulk of their revenue, ahead of Europe or the USA. In emerging Asia, the middle class already represent 60% of the population (1.9 billion people). In 2010, China, a country where 54 million people are classified as high earners, became the largest car market. The greatest fortune on the planet is no longer in the United States, but in Mexico. The reasons for the growing attraction of the emerging economies are found in these numbers, pointing to high growth, expansion of the middle class, an environment of lower indebtedness and deficit, and controlled inflation.

However, yet another silent revolution is occurring, giving one more reason for OECD nations to bet on emerging markets: the decade of 2010–20 will belong to the emerging economies because in addition to setting the standard for growth, they will increasingly give rise to disruptive innovation. This will also change the profile of OECD multinationals. Two powerful movements are coming together: we are witnessing the rise of emerging multinationals (including those in leading sectors that provide high added value and strong technological contributions); and at the same time, we are seeing more innovation imported from emerging countries by OECD multinationals.

Table 5.6 *Projection of relative worldwide economic importance, 2010–50.*

	Projected percentage without 'structural development'				Projected percentage with maximum 'structural development'			
	2010–20	2020–30	2030–40	2040–50	2010–20	2020–30	2030–40	2040–50
USA	0.5	0.5	0.6	0.6	0.5	1.6	2.3	2.8
Japan	1.2	1.2	1.0	0.9	1.2	2.1	2.7	3.2
China	6.6	5.2	4.2	3.5	6.6	6.0	5.8	5.6
Germany	2.1	1.8	1.5	1.3	2.1	2.8	3.2	3.6
Britain	1.3	1.1	0.9	0.7	1.3	2.1	2.7	3.2
France	1.2	1.0	0.8	0.7	1.2	2.1	2.8	3.4
Italy	2.1	1.7	1.4	1.2	2.1	2.9	3.5	4.0
India	4.1	3.4	3.0	2.6	4.1	5.4	6.5	7.3
Brazil	2.3	1.7	1.4	1.1	2.3	3.5	4.7	5.7
Canada	1.9	1.6	1.3	1.1	1.9	2.5	3.0	3.4
Korea	3.9	2.9	2.4	1.9	3.9	3.7	3.9	4.0
Spain	2.9	2.5	2.0	1.7	2.9	3.4	3.7	4.0
Mexico	3.6	3.0	2.5	2.1	3.6	4.1	4.4	4.7
Australia	1.9	1.5	1.3	1.1	1.9	2.3	2.8	3.1
Holland	1.2	1.1	0.9	0.8	1.2	2.2	2.9	3.4
Argentina	2.5	1.9	1.6	1.3	2.5	3.1	3.6	4.2
Russia	5.1	4.3	3.5	2.9	5.1	5.5	5.7	6.0
Turkey	4.0	3.4	2.9	2.5	4.0	4.4	4.7	4.9
Sweden	0.5	0.5	0.5	0.5	0.5	1.7	2.6	3.2
Switzerland	2.6	2.1	1.7	1.4	2.6	2.6	2.7	2.7
Indonesia	3.1	2.6	2.1	1.8	3.1	4.7	6.2	7.3
Belgium	1.1	1.0	0.8	0.7	1.1	2.1	2.9	3.5
Saudi Arabia	1.9	1.5	1.2	1.0	1.9	2.6	3.3	3.9
Poland	4.1	3.3	2.7	2.2	4.1	4.4	4.8	5.1
Hong Kong	3.0	2.4	1.9	1.6	3.0	3.0	3.1	3.2
Austria	2.7	2.2	1.8	1.5	2.7	3.0	3.2	3.3
Norway	0.4	0.5	0.6	0.6	0.4	1.5	2.3	2.8
South Africa	1.1	0.8	0.6	0.4	1.1	2.9	4.5	5.9
Thailand	3.8	3.1	2.7	2.2	3.8	4.7	5.5	6.1
Denmark	0.6	0.5	0.4	0.4	0.6	1.7	2.6	3.3
Israel	–0.1	0.9	0.8	0.7	–0.1	1.3	2.4	3.3
Singapore	4.2	3.5	3.0	2.5	4.2	3.4	3.0	2.6
Greece	3.0	2.6	2.1	1.7	3.0	3.5	3.8	4.1
Iran	6.2	5.1	4.2	3.4	6.2	6.0	5.9	5.8
Egypt	3.5	4.3	3.8	3.2	3.5	4.5	5.3	6.1
Venezuela	1.4	1.0	0.7	0.5	1.4	2.8	4.1	5.3
Malaysia	5.4	4.3	3.5	2.9	5.4	4.8	4.5	4.2
Finland	1.5	1.3	1.1	0.9	1.5	2.3	2.8	3.3
Colombia	3.0	2.5	2.0	1.7	3.0	4.1	5.0	5.7
Ireland	1.6	1.5	1.3	1.1	1.6	2.3	2.7	2.9

Source: HSBC, 2011.

Table 5.7 *Foreign direct investment, top twenty, 2010.*

RK 2011	Country	FDI (output)	RK 2011	Country	FDI (output)
1	USA	329	11	Netherlands	32
2	Germany	105	12	Sweden	30
3	France	84	13	Australia	26
4	**Hong Kong**	**76**	14	Spain	22
5	**China**	**68**	15	Italy	21
6	Switzerland	58	16	**Singapore**	**20**
7	Japan	56	17	**Korea**	**19**
8	**Russia**	**52**	18	Luxembourg	18
9	Canada	39	19	Ireland	18
10	Belgium	38	20	India	16

Source: UNCTAD, 2011.
Note: Bold indicates emerging countries.

Emerging markets have stopped being low-tech environments. In recent decades we have seen that the spread of technology has been accelerating.[8] In this decade, we will see an increasing number of multinationals from these countries project their innovations towards the world. According to the United Nations, there are nearly 21,500 multinationals located in emerging countries. Some, like Mexican cement-maker Cemex or the Chinese battery maker BYD, are already world leaders in their respective areas. The technology sectors are already noting the push. The main suppliers to the world's telecommunications companies are found in China. In 2008 Huawei from China registered more patents than any other company in the world, and in 2009 it was only outdone by Japanese Panasonic. In 2012 it became the world's largest supplier to the telecommunications industry.

In the telecommunications sector there are already half a dozen multinationals from emerging countries among the top ten in the

---

[8] See Diego Comin and Bart Hobijn, 'Technology Diffusion and Postwar Growth', Federal Reserve Bank of San Francisco, Working Paper 16, June 2010. Available at www.frbsf.org/publications/economics/papers/2010/wp10-16bk.pdf; Diego Comin and Bart Hobijn, 'An Exploration of Technology Diffusion', *American Economic Review*, 100(5), 2010, pp. 2031–59.

world, such as China Mobile, Indian Bharti Airtel, South African MTN and Mexican América Móbil, not to mention the Southeast Asian groups SingTel and Axiata. In the aeronautics industry, Brazilian Embraer revolutionised the sector with a business model that others later copied. Indian group Tata is marketing a car for $3,000, three or four times cheaper than its European competitors. The Tata car is not exactly low-tech and involves no fewer than ninety patents. Chinese Mindray developed medical equipment costing 10% of the price of the competition. From Africa, Safaricom, with its mobile banking system, is revolutionising the market, as have other multinational outsourcers such as TCS, Wipro and Infosys from India.

The digital world will also feel the effects of the wave of multilatinas. Social networking site Facebook could have been Latin. One of its founding partners is Brazilian. Chinese internet group Tencent Holdings is the third in the world in terms of market capitalisation (more than $45 billion in 2011), just behind Google and Amazon. Its largest financial shareholder is another emerging multinational, South African media giant Naspers, which holds 45% of the Chinese multinational (an investment made in 2001 that has since been revalued by 3,100%). Tencent and Naspers have become partners for investing in startups, but unlike Google, their investments focus not on California companies but on emerging countries. In 2010 both invested close to $700 million in Russian Mail.ru. These internet groups are based in Shenzhen, Cape Town and Moscow, and are internationalising quickly.

Naspers, currently in 129 countries with 12,000 employees and revenue of almost $4 million in 2011, made important acquisitions in India and Brazil. In Brazil it bought the internet sales portal Buscapé for $374 million in 2009, one of the largest internet operations in the country. Naspers holds 91% of this Brazilian startup, now expanding throughout Latin America, including Colombia and Argentina. It has more recently invested in the Brazilian and Argentine startups Brandsclub, Grupo Abril, Movile and Dineromail. In 2010 it invested in OLX, a startup active in ninety countries, taking a majority stake for $200 million. In June 2011, the Brandsclub sales portal was bought for $15 million. This injection of venture capital made the transaction very successful, and an initial investment of $6 million in the startup was transformed into $50 million on its sale.

The Russian company Digital Sky Technologies (DST), which owns Mail.ru (a Russian startup that is capitalised for more than $8 billion on the London Stock Exchange) and in which Naspers holds a 10% share, is a shareholder in the main American Internet startups such as Facebook, Zynga and Groupon. At the start of 2011 it raised its holding in Facebook, where it had already invested more than $325 million, and now owns some 10% of the California startup. Other ventures include the $135 million invested in Groupon in 2010 and the $180 million invested in Zynga in 2009, two successful American startups. But DST is also accumulating a portfolio of investments in Internet startups that go beyond the traditional California jewels. For example in 2011 the company wagered some $500 million on the Chinese Internet sales company 360buy.com. Also in 2011, the owner of DST, Yuri Milner, raised a new venture capital fund of more than a billion dollars, DST Global 2.

These emerging multinationals not only produce disruptive innovation, but are also massively frugal, making them lethal competitors. Bharat Biotech, for example, is an Indian pharmaceutical company that sells doses of the hepatitis B vaccine for 20 cents, far below its Western competitors, while its compatriot Ranbaxy does the same with malaria vaccine. Indian Bharti Airtel supplies some of the cheapest telecommunications services in the world with a business model of massive and disruptive externalisation. Chinese BYD has caused a revolution in the world's lithium-based battery market (which will be an important part of electric cars) by lowering innovation and research costs. These multinationals are rapidly climbing the value chains. In 2010 South Korean Samsung entered the list of the world's top ten in terms of investment in R&D, according to the classification established by consulting company Booz & Company.[9] Israel in turn created 4,000 startups, making itself the nation with the second highest number of companies traded on the NASDAQ.

Added to this trend is another: OECD multinationals no longer look at emerging markets as merely places to expand their products and innovations. These countries are already becoming sources of

---

[9] See Booz & Company, *The Global Innovation 1000: How the Top Innovators Keep Winning*, London and New York, Booz & Company, 2010. Available at www.booz.com/media/file/sb61_10408-R.pdf.

innovation and everything indicates that these innovations will become increasingly disruptive. The best-known example of reverse innovation, which has become a case study at the University of Harvard, is that of General Electric (GE). The company produced one of its most disruptive innovations, a cardio prevention kit, in India for less than half of the cost of the product it had previously commercialised.[10] This innovation was later raised to a global level within the company. Siemens did the same with a low-cost X-ray scanner implemented by its Indian engineers. Multinational OECD Fortune 500s already have some 100 research and development centres in emerging countries, mainly in India and China. GE's R&D centre in India is the company's largest. Cisco spent a billion dollars constructing another in India. Microsoft's centre in Beijing is its largest outside the United States. IBM already employs more personnel in India than in the United States; and Germany's Siemens has 12% of all of its 30,000 R&D engineers in emerging Asia.

A UNESCO report in 2010 said that China is about to overtake the US and the EU in the number of researchers.[11] In 2010, 40% of all Chinese university students were studying science and engineering, more than double the proportion in the United States. Emerging markets already account for around 40% of the world's researchers. The global distribution of R&D effort between the North and South is rapidly shifting. In 1990 more than 95% of all R&D took place in developed countries; a decade later this percentage had dropped to 76%. The trend will not shift back. China already spends more than a billion dollars on R&D and plans to triple spending before the end of the decade, which would represent 2.5% of its GDP. (The USA currently spends 2.7% of its GDP.)

The current decade belongs to the emerging markets. This is because we will see the bulk of world growth concentrated in these countries,

---

[10] See Harvard Business School, *How GE Is Disrupting Itself*, Boston, HBS Review, October 2009. Available on http://hbr.org/2009/10/how-ge-is-disrupting-itself/ar/1. The Harvard case study is available at www.gereports.com/reverse-innovation-how-ge-is-disrupting-itself/.

[11] See UNESCO, *Science Report 2010*, Paris, UNESCO, 2010. Available at www.unesco.org/new/en/natural-sciences/science-technology/prospective-studies/unesco-science-report/. On Latin America, see also UNESCO, *National Science, Technology and Innovation Systems in Latin America and the Caribbean*, Paris, UNESCO, 2010, http://unesdoc.unesco.org/images/0018/001898/189823e.pdf.

Table 5.8 *Top ten multilatinas in communications and advertising.*

Company	Country	TSR (%)*	Market value (in $ trillion)
Naspers	South Africa	33.3	15.1
Net Serviços de Comunicaçao	Brazil	30.3	4.7
Modern Times Group	Sweden	17.8	3.3
Shaw Communications	Canada	17.7	9
SES	Luxembourg	13.5	10.7
Grupo Televisa	Mexico	12.8	11.9
Beijing Nehua CATV Network	China	12.5	2.2
Pearson	Britain	11.8	11.4
Cablevision Systems	Britain	10.3	6.4
Zee Entertainment Enterprises	India	9	2.4

Source: Boston Consulting Group, 2011.
Note: TSR = total shareholder return.

and we will see them produce increasingly disruptive and rapid innovation. This decade will reveal a massive shift in the geography of innovation – as well as in the wealth of nations. In its report on the creation of value, BCG highlights that, of the 126 companies analysed, eighty-one, or almost 65% of the total, come from emerging markets. During 2005–9, seven of the top ten telecom companies came from emerging markets (including one from Latin America); moreover, five of the top ten companies, and six of the top ten technology companies, already come from emerging markets such as China, Taiwan, India, Korea, Brazil and Mexico[12] (Table 5.8).

Although Apple and Google are still considered the world's most innovative firms, among the top fifty are companies from Korea (LG Electronics, Samsung), China (BYD, Haier, Lenovo, China Mobile), Brazil (Petrobras) and India (Reliance, Tata).[13]

---

[12] See BCG, *Swimming against the Tide: How Technology, Media, and Telecommunications Companies Can Prosper in the New Economic Reality*, Boston, BCG, 2010. Available at www.bcg.com/documents/file59590.pdf.

[13] See BCG, *Innovation 2010. A Return to Prominence – and the Emergence of a New World Order*, Boston, BCG, April 2010. Available at www.bcg.com/documents/file42620.pdf.

Latin America: the decade of innovation

The first decade of the twenty-first century saw the emerging markets gain a firm footing on the world stage. Between 2000 and 2010, the world underwent a massive shift in financial wealth and industrial flow in favour of emerging economies. The crisis of 2008 in the OECD countries only served to accelerate this trend. In the decade of 2010–20, this first shift will be prolonged by another: the emerging countries will arise as consumer powers and innovators.

As we have seen, the movement is already accelerating. For the first time, in 2012 a non-OECD company became the world's top supplier to the telecommunications industry. The Chinese company Huawei, having unseated American Lucent and French Alcatel (with such unstoppable force that it prompted the two to merge), now has Swedish Ericsson, until now the world leader, in its sights. In the world of telecommunications, multinationals from emerging countries are leading. China Mobile has the largest capitalisation in the sector, and the Mexican company América Móvil is one of the most internationalised and is also in the worldwide top ten in its sector.

In the world of new technologies and the Internet we are also witnessing important structural changes. California startups continue to glow. The focus is on Facebook, YouTube, Zygna, and its neighbours from Chicago, Groupon, and from New York, Foursquare. Apple, Microsoft and Google continue to lead in worldwide capitalisations, but emerging country companies are appearing: Tencent Holdings, the largest Chinese digital company, already has one of the five largest capitalisations in the world in the sector, ahead of many American icons. Latin America is also a player. Silver Lake, one of the largest American capital venture funds, focused its attention on Brazil in 2011, announcing a technology fund of a billion dollars to invest in the country.

Without a doubt, this decade will see these movements accelerate. After having moved its production centres to emerging countries, we are now seeing how OECD multinationals are shifting their largest value added sectors and opening research and development centres in India, China and Brazil. At the same time the multinationals of emerging countries are colonising every technology sector. Korean Samsung has become a technology giant, Brazilian Embraer is launching into the aeronautics sector, and Taiwanese multinationals already dominate segments such as the semiconductor industry.

This structure has many derivatives. Countries like Spain, which are in an intermediate level, without great technology giants, could unfold a strategy of attracting the European corporate headquarters of these multinationals. Tencent, Huawei and Embraer are all in the process of international expansion; and Europe, North Africa and the Middle East are part of this equation. Furthermore, in certain cases, Spain could be a platform for expansion towards Latin America. There are clearly many steps that need to be taken, the first being to increase direct air connections from Madrid or Barcelona to Asia that are similar to those that exist to Latin America (a challenge as Iberia, for example, has almost no direct flights to Asia).

We will also see competition grow between these emerging countries to attract technological investment to their national bases from OECD countries and (ever increasingly) from other emerging countries. The case of Taiwanese Foxconn Technology (a producer of many iPad and iPhone components for Apple) stands out.[14] This company announced in 2011 plans to invest $12 billion in Brazil during the coming decade, diversifying its industrial production towards Latin America and reducing its dependence on Chinese industrial plants in Shenzhen. This is a very significant announcement. If it becomes reality, this investment will be the largest a Taiwanese company has ever made abroad. It is an important announcement for Brazil as well. It puts the country on the international radar of the technology world and means the direct and indirect creation of 100,000 jobs.

---

[14] The work of economists shows how value is broken down to produce an iPod, and challenges traditional views of commerce between countries. See the fascinating work of Jason Dedrick, Kenneth Kraemer and Greg Linden, 'Who Profits from Innovation in Global Value Chains? A Study of the iPod and Notebook PCs', University of California, Irvine, 2008, published in *Industrial and Corporate Change*, 19(1), 2010, pp. 81–116. Available at http://web.mit.edu/is08/pdf/Dedrick_Kraemer_Linden.pdf; also see Clair Brown and Greg Linden's book, *Chips and Change: How Crisis Reshapes the Semiconductor Industry*, Cambridge, Mass., MIT Press, 2009. See http://mitpress.mit.edu/catalog/item/default.asp?ttype=2&tid=12005&mode=toc; and www.irle.berkeley.edu/worktech/greglinden.html. For similar work on the iPad, see Jason Dedrick, Kenneth Kraemer and Greg Linden, 'Who Captures Value in the Apple iPad and iPhone?', University of California, Irvine, July 2011. Available at http://pcic.merage.uci.edu/papers/2011/Value_iPad_iPhone.pdf.

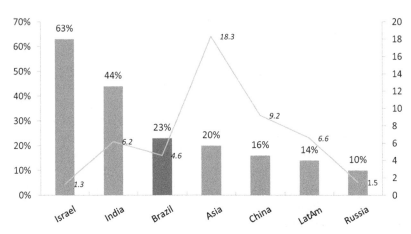

Figure 5.1 Investment in venture capital (left, as percentage of GDP) and amount of investment (right, in $ trillion).
Source: The Economist, using data from EMPEA, 2011.

The decade of 2010–20 will continue to belong to the emerging markets. But in one way it will be different from the previous decade. It is telling that international venture capital, the driver of technology and innovative companies, is placing increasing focus and attention on emerging countries – including Brazil.

Venture capital funds prefer Brazil to all other countries, including China. According to the poll by EMPEA/Coller Capital, published in April 2011, fund managers are thinking about increasing their investments in emerging markets by up to 20% of the total invested in private equity funds. Of all the countries being considered, Brazil stands out, ahead of China and India. The rest of the continent does not come out badly either. Latin America is ahead of India, Turkey and Russia as the preferred destination for investment (Figure 5.1).

Brazil is one of the favourite destinations of international venture capital. The most recent data from the Latin American Venture Capital Association (LAVCA) show the growing attractiveness of the country and the continent. In 2010, venture capital funds raised $8.1 billion in the region, or 120% more than in the previous year.[15] This is a record to date. Southern Cross and Advent International raised unprecedentedly large regional funds, with $1.7 billion of capital committed to

[15] See www.lavca.org/.

each. This situation contrasts with experience in the United States and Europe, where funds raised dropped by 7% and 32% respectively.

The year 2010 was unique for investment. Just over 200 venture capital funds invested $7.2 billion in Latin America, double that of the previous year. Brazil was the object of 46% of operations and received 76% of the total capital invested. World leaders such as Apax Partners, Silver Lake, TPG Capital and Warburg Pincus made their first investments in the country – while others such as Blackstone picked up 40% of Patria, and JP Morgan took all of Gavea, the company created by Arminio Fraga, the ex-governor of the Central Bank of Brazil. New players such as the British 3i also announced their arrival in 2011.

Another interesting trend is the increasing appeal for venture capital (VC). Early stage investments, typical of VC funds, increased by 54% and the average size of investments reached $1.6 million in 2010 (above the average million dollars of the previous year). VC investments reached more than 23% of the total venture capital invested in Latin America. Although Brazil has very few startups that took the leap to the São Paulo Stock Exchange Bovespa (Submarino being one of the exceptions), we are seeing more projects emerging. In the areas of video games, startups such as Mentez, Tutudo and Vostu are emerging, as well as Buscapé and Xangô in e-commerce – to name a few.

Xangô sparked interest in various venture capital funds, such as Redpoint Ventures (based in San Francisco and since 2012 also in Brazil through Redpoint e.ventures), Index Ventures (based in Geneva) and BV Capital (based in Hamburg). Xangô also illustrates a growing trend as the Brazilian diaspora of 'returnees' flock back to the country and so underlines the importance of international connections, as happened with Israel and India. Xangô founder Marco DeMello returned to Brazil after nearly twenty years in the United States, where he worked for companies like Microsoft. Julio Vasconcellos is another expat who created a successful startup – Peixe Urbano – and who worked in New York and Silicon Valley after completing his MBA at Stanford. This American connection helped him find his first investors, Californian Benchmark Capital and Brazilian Monashees, on his return to Brazil.[16] Academic work shows the importance of

---

[16] On the importance of the effects of networks in the world of venture capital, see the work of Isin Guler and Mauro Guillén, 'Knowledge, Institutions and Foreign Entry: The Internationalization of US Venture Firms', *Journal of*

connections among 'venture capitalists' and entrepreneurs. Having shared university lecture-rooms with an investor increases an entrepreneur's probability of receiving investment by almost 60%. Venture capitalists also tend to co-invest 40% more if they share an academic alma mater.[17]

Californian venture funds are focusing their attention on Brazil, and visiting frequently, as in the case of Sequoia and Norwest Venture Partners for example, or even moving operations to the country. Geoffrey Prentice, an executive at Skype who transferred to London-based venture fund Atomico (founded by the creator of Skype), moved to Brazil to start investments in Brazilian startups. Californian funds in turn are increasingly interested in Brazil. In 2011, Redpoint Ventures and General Catalyst Partners invested $19 million in Viajanet, an online travel startup based in São Paulo. In turn, it received $7.6 million from various VC funds led by Ignition Partners and participation from Radar Partners, Andreessen Horowitz, Helion Venture Partners and Redpoint Ventures. Kevin Efrusy, a partner in Accel Partners, one of the most prestigious VC funds in Silicon Valley, increased his visits to Brazil in search of opportunities after leading some $30 million of investments in Vostu, along with General Catalyst, Intel Capital and Tiger Global. Insight Venture Partners invested in KaBuM! and Mentez. Draper Fisher Jurvetson (which formed an association in 2007 with FIR Capital) invested in SambaTech, an online video platform, and Silver Lake invested in Locaweb (with a 20% share estimated at $68 million).

In 2012, the movement speeded up. Sequoia, Flybridge, General Atlantic and Redpont eVentures, four of the largest US-based VC funds, hired teams for Brazil and located them in the country. Also in 2012, General Atlantic completed some of its very first investments

International Business Studies, 41, 2010, pp. 185–205; and Isin Guler and Mauro Guillén, 'Home Country Networks and Foreign Expansion: Evidence from the Venture Capital Industry', *Academy of Management Journal*, 53(2), 2010, pp. 390–410. Also see www.unc.edu/~guleri/Guler%20Guillen% 20AMJ.pdf; also Emilio Castilla, 'Network of Venture Capital Firms in Silicon Valley', *International Journal of Technology Management*, 25($\frac{1}{2}$), 2003, pp. 113–35. Available at www.talentfirstnetwork.org/wiki/images/1/1a/ Networks_of_VC_Firms_in_Silicon_Valley.pdf.

17 Daniel Sunesson, 'Alma Mater Matters: The Value of School Ties in the Venture Capital Industry', April 2009. Available at http://69.175.2.130/ ~finman/Turin/Papers/Alma_mater_matters.pdf.

in the region, betting on Decolar.com, a leading online travel agency in Brazil and across Latin America, and on Aceco TI, a leading company focused on design and maintenance of data centres in Brazil and Latin America. Flybridge invested also in Latin American Internet startups such as the Miami-based English-learning startup Open English and the Brazilian fashion subscription club Shoes4U, which also raised financing from US-based Accel Partners and Redpoint Ventures. Redpoint announced no fewer than four investments – Viajanet, Grupo Xangô, Shoes4U and 55Social – all of them in Brazil. The other big US VCs, already with activity in Brazil and the region, also multiplied the deals. Intel Capital invested in five Brazilian startups in the year 2011 and doubled its team of professionals in the region (since 1999, Intel Capital has invested $75 million in twenty-five Brazilian companies).

Local venture funds are also being developed, although the market is still in its infancy. According to Claudio Furtado, of the Fundacão Getúlio Vargas, fewer than 20% of the total of venture capital investments made between 2005 and 2009 were early-stage transactions, typical of venture capital. His work also shows that of the 144 funds analysed, only a handful correspond to VC funds financing technology startups.[18] The 'dry power', or the capital available for venture capital investments, is reaching notable levels and was estimated to be almost $18 billion at the end of 2009. The levels of investments and capital raised have also stayed high since the record year of 2007 (Figures 5.2 and 5.3).

Among the funds that stand out is the previously mentioned Monashees Capital, co-founded in São Paulo by Eric Archer. This VC fund is one of the largest in the country that specialises in technology companies. It manages some $60 billion and makes two or three investments a year that vary between $500,000 and $5 million. Astella Investimentos (managed by Edson Rigonatti), Ideasnet (co-founded by American Michael Nicklas), Criatec and FIR are other Brazilian venture funds that are starting to invest from Brazil. To these funds we can add global operators who also come from the industry. Among the most prominent is Intel Capital – which has a team based in São Paulo and manages a Brazil and regional fund of around $50 million.

---

[18] See the presentation and study by Claudio Furtado, published in 2011:
www.anbima.com.br/eventos/arqs/eventos_anteriores/6-fundos-1/
workshop2_cfurtado.pdf.

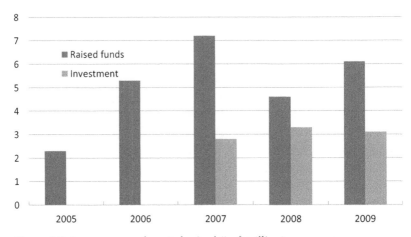

Figure 5.2 Investment and capital raised (in $ trillion).
Source: Claudio Furtado / FGV, 2011.

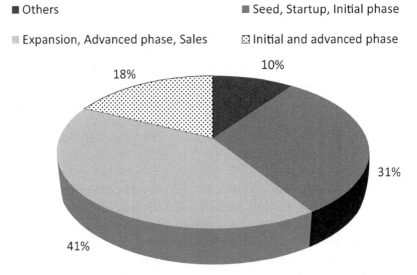

Figure 5.3 Phases of development of investment in venture capital.
Source: Claudio Furtado / FGV, 2011.

Brazil will not become Israel overnight. Israel is the El Dorado of technology startups (with around 4,000, the highest per capita in the world) and venture capital (more than seventy local funds and 220 international funds investing in Israeli startups). We are seeing, nevertheless, success stories emerge of technology companies acquired with international venture capital for amounts of up to a billion dollars. While Brazil still has no companies trading on the NASDAQ (Israel has sixty-four), everything indicates that the current decade will also be one of innovation and technology.

Startups and venture capital funds: searching for Multilatinas 2.0

Beyond Brazil, international venture capital funds are beginning to look towards Latin America. They have traditionally focused their investments on the United States and Europe, and recently on Israel, India and China. Latin America was largely overlooked. This is changing. Although there is a long way to go to reach the levels of a country like Israel, the first steps are being taken.

As already mentioned, we are beginning to see investments by American and European venture capital funds in Latin America. In 2011 the VC fund Atomico made its first Brazilian investments in Restorando.com, an online sales company founded by the creators of Mercadolibre.com. It also invested in a Uruguayan startup, Pedidos Ya! Californian funds Riverwood Capital and FTV Capital wagered $15 million on Globant, an Argentine software company. Also Argentine fnbox, owner of Sonico, one of the largest social networks in the region, raised $6 million in 2008. Among its investors is the VC fund DN Capital Brasil. Silver Lake, another American venture capital fund, did not hesitate to raise a technology fund of one billion dollars for Brazil and invested $68 million in Locaweb in September 2010. In turn, the New York fund Insight Venture Partners bought into Mentez, the country's largest supplier of social internet games (above all, a supplier of games for Orkut and Facebook). From Boston, Flybridge Capital Partners led a round of more than $4.25 million to invest in the startup Open English, based between Miami, Caracas and Bogotá. In turn Intel Capital also invested in 2011 in the Brazilian startup Boo-Box, a software company based in São Paulo (Table 5.9).

Various lessons can be learned from these first Latin American steps in the digital world. The first is that a connection with the Mecca of the world of American venture capital and startups is key. The example of the Brazilian startup Peixe Urbano, a Brazilian version of Groupon, that already employs 300 people, is an illustration. It was founded by the former director of Facebook in Brazil, Julio Vasconcellos. In addition to working for the star American startup at the time, he graduated

Table 5.9 *Transactions of foreign VC funds in multilatina startups.*

VC funds	Year	Investment	Target	Founder	www
Atomico	2011	n/a and 0.5	Restorando.com and PedidosYa.com	Frank Martin and Franco Silvetti (Restorando); Juan Pablo Villani and Ariel Burschtin (PedidosYa)	restorando.com and pedidosya.com
Riverwood Capital	2008	15	Globant	Martín Migoya, Guibert Englebienne, Martín Umaran and Néstor Nocetti	globant.com
FTV Capital	2008	15	Globant	Martín Migoya, Guibert Englebienne, Martín Umaran and Néstor Nocetti	globant.com
DN Capital	2008	4.3	fnbox	Rodrigo Ti	fnbox.com
Silver Lake	2010	68	Locaweb	Gilberto Mautner and Michel Gora	locaweb.com
Insight Venture Partners		4.25	Mentez	Juan Franco and Jaime Roldán	mentez.com
Flybridge Capital Partners		4.25	Open English	Wilmer Sarmiento and Andrés Moreno	openenglish.com
Intel Capital	2011	n/a	Boo-Box	Marco Gomes	boo-box.com
Benchmark Capital	2010	n/a	Peixe Urbano	Alexander Ferraz and Julio Vasconcellos	peixeurbano.com

Source: ESADEgeo, 2012.

from Stanford, cradle of many of California's new enterprises. Among his first investors was a Brazilian venture capital fund (Monashees), and the Californian Benchmark Capital. In the same way as Israel or India, a connection with the USA is important when emulating the achievements of Silicon Valley.

The second lesson is that the role of the state as a driving force and catalyst is vital in every country. It was true in the United States and Israel (in both cases through state contractors and the military), although later the role of the private sector prevailed. State participation is not in itself negative; however, the level of involvement does seem to be a determining factor. In a study by the World Economic

Forum published in 2010, the department chair of the Harvard Business School, Josh Lerner, stresses this point. Based on a sample of more than 28,000 companies receiving VC funds, the direct or moderate support of the government increases the probability of successful investment, compared with purely private financing.[19] However, a major participation in financing by the state and business decisions made by governmental bodies significantly reduces the performance of investments and financed companies.

The challenges that remain in Latin America are important. Private equity is now abundant in many countries. In 2010, according to LAVCA, more than $8 billion was raised by private equity in the region, 2.5% of the world's total, the bulk of which was concentrated in Brazil. Venture capital, which makes investments in the earliest stages (seed and early stage), is in short supply for technology startups. Josh Lerner calculates that enterprise capital investment in Mexico is only 0.0003% of GDP, a tiny part of the private equity that is invested in the country. In contrast, the country that invests the most in enterprise capital is Israel, at 0.42% of GDP, followed by the United States (0.22%).

As we have said, there is a long way yet to go. Until recently, there had only been one technology venture capital fund in Colombia (Promotora; a new one opened in 2012, Axon Capital, that manages one of the Amerigo funds powered by Telefónica), while Peru has none. Chile has several, such as MiFactory ($7 million co-invested by the Said family with the support of Swedish companies Ericsson and Saab); Austral Capital ($36 million); Aurus ($22 million); Equitas Capital or Fondo Copec ($13 million). (In 2013 another Amerigo fund is opening in the country, with the helping hand of Inversur.) However, all are relatively small. Conscious of what still needs to be done, Chile is looking to fuel offer and demand, even promoting the importation of businesses (through the Start Up Chile programme)[20] and the creation of seed capital funds (through a $350 million fund of funds).

Venture capital specialists are increasing their focus on Chile, however, as demonstrated by the relocation in 2011 in Santiago from

[19] Josh Lerner *et al.*, *The Global Economic Impact of Private Equity Report 2010*, Geneva, World Economic Forum, 2009. Available at https://members.weforum.org/pdf/FinancialInstitutions/PrivateEquity_VolIII_WorkingPapers.pdf.

[20] See www.startupchile.org/.

Table 5.10 *Ranking of venture capital attractiveness, 2011.*

Country	RK 2011	Country	RK 2011
USA	1	Colombia	47
India	20	Peru	59
Israel	21	Uruguay	65
Chile	29	Argentina	68
China	30	Ecuador	74
Russia	41	Paraguay	78
Mexico	42	Venezuela	79
Brazil	43		

Source: IESE, 2011 at http://blog.iese.edu/vcpeindex/.

Silicon Valley of the Israeli Arnon Kohavi, founder of Yardeni Venture Capital.[21] Chilean startups are also now attracting the attention of Californian capital venture funds such as Tomorrow Venture,[22] a VC fund founded in 2009 by the then CEO of Google, Eric Schmidt, who invested in Chilean Welcu. We are also seeing acquisition transactions by American startups in Chile, proof of the growing attraction of this market. In 2011 Groupon bought Chilean companies Zappedy and Clandescuento. Chile also led the Latin American IESE ranking on attractiveness of companies for venture capital.[23] This achievement was also approved by LAVCA, which in 2011 named Chile as the most attractive country, according to its annual scoring, and ahead of Brazil[24] (Table 5.10).

In Brazil, BNDES plays an important role in developing the market, sometimes almost completely financing VC funds such as Fundo Criatec (80% of capital). Nevertheless, of almost 150 venture capital funds analysed by Claudio Furtado from Getulio Vargas, there are few that focus on financing technology startups, especially for initial rounds of seed capital and early stage investment. Several local operators exist such as Monashees, FIR, Astella Investments, Criatec and Ideasnet, along with (very few) global operators such as Intel Capital. BlackBerry Partners Fund, a consortium of investors formed by

---

[21] See http://yardenvc.com/about-us/.   [22] See www.tomorrowvc.com/.

[23] See http://blog.iese.edu/vcpeindex/.

[24] See http://lavca.org/wp-content/uploads/2011/07/2011-LAVCA-Scorecard-update.pdf.

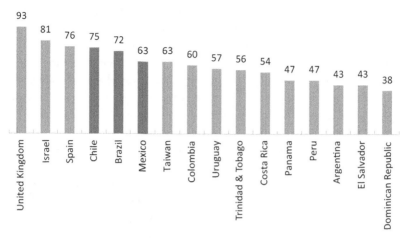

Figure 5.4 LAVCA ranking scorecard 2011.
Source: ESADEgeo, 2012, based on LAVCA data.

Research In Motion, Thomson Reuters and the Royal Bank of Canada, also announced in 2010 a fund of $150 million to invest in the BRICs, including Brazil.

The amounts raised are still small and success stories are needed. There is only one Latin American company (Argentine Mercadolibre) that is traded on NASDAQ. There are still no Latin American technology companies that operate on a global scale. With the exception of the Mexican América Móvil, there are few companies in the region that have revenues of more than a billion dollars (one of them is Chilean Sonda). Paradoxically, Brightstar, a multinational created by a Bolivian but with headquarters in Miami, has one of the highest revenues ($10 billion in 2012). This is another trend. On many occasions Latin American entrepreneurs base their technology startups in the United States where it is easier to raise finance. Being in Silicon Valley implies quality. One of the future challenges is for more Latin American start-ups to emerge – and then operate from Latin America (Figure 5.4).

Latin America and the risk of success mania ('exitomania')

The urgency of this bet on innovation and technology transcends the entire continent. Latin America finds itself at a crossroads in the current decade. The success of the region is such that it is witnessing a tsunami of capital flows, causing appreciations in exchange rates (the other side of the coin), and placing the region on a path that it has already experienced in the past – rapid acceleration and then the potential for an abrupt stop. And if that is not enough, raw materials prices are increasing, propelling a pattern of specialisation already established in the region (more than 50% of regional exports are linked to raw materials). This is not the moment to succumb to success mania or complacency.

Several decades ago, economist Albert Hirschman, an expert on the region, warned of the risks of failure mania ('fracasomania'), the tendency of Latin Americans to repeat failure year after year. It looks as though we are now facing the opposite syndrome. The decade of the 2000s was sweet for the region, with high levels of growth, stable monetary and fiscal policies, and reduced poverty and inequality. Of course, not every nation took this road but many have now embarked on this economic *posibilismo*,[25] beginning with Chile, Brazil and Mexico, and now also Peru, Colombia and Uruguay to mention a few. These nations are pulling away from the maximalist and ideological traditions of regional policy in economic and political matters.[26]

Investments in the region between 2010 and 2015 for just the raw materials cluster are calculated to be more than $150 billion. This is undoubtedly good news. Nevertheless, countries face the challenge of finding ways to add value, increase productivity, improve innovation, and diversify their production and exporting bases. In 2003–5, Latin America concentrated only 3.6% of the world's direct investment in technology linked to R&D, according to ECLAC. This number decreased in 2008–10 to barely 3.2% of the worldwide total.[27] In 2010, the data looked more encouraging, although far from the levels reached by Asia. The medium-high technology sectors reached 28% participation, or in other words 12 percentage points higher than in 2009. Brazil received more than half of the direct technology investment made in the region. Even so, although the public sector makes great effort where R&D is concerned, the private sector lags behind.

[25] See Javier Santiso, *Latin America's Political Economy of the Possible*, Cambridge, Mass., MIT Press, 2007.

[26] See Enrique Krauze, *Redeemers: Ideas and Power in Latin America*, New York, Harper, 2011.

[27] See the report on the CEPAL, available at www.eclac.cl/publicaciones/xml/9/ 43289/2011-322-LIE-2010-WEB_ULTIMO.pdf.

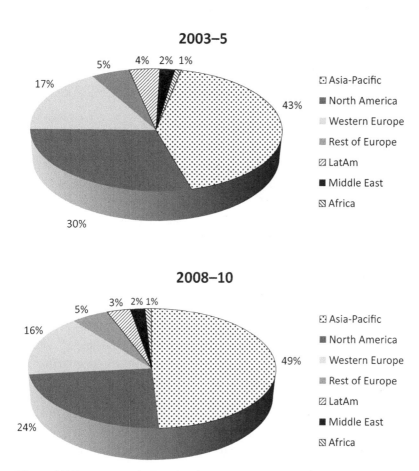

Figure 5.5 Percentage of FDI related to R&D, 2003–5 and 2008–10.
Source: ECLAC, 2011.

Brazilian companies invested an average of barely 0.6% of their income in information technology research and development according to the OECD, a figure far from the 1.8% invested by OECD companies (Figure 5.5).

The importance of innovation, technology and knowledge is common to all countries in the region. One way to explain the time lag compared to Asia is to point to the differences in productivity. While in Latin America labour productivity only grew at an annual average of 1.4%, in Korea it grew at an annual rate of 3.9%, while general

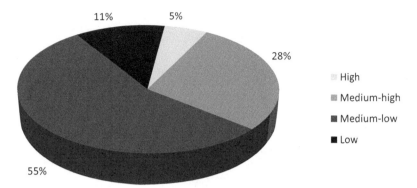

Figure 5.6 FDI in 2010, according to technological intensity.
Source: ECLAC, 2011.

productivity grew at a rate of 8.4% during the period 2009–11.[28]
Another assessment involves observing how Latin American cities
(where the bulk of the economic impulse is concentrated) show a
shortfall in economic achievement, wealth creation, business environment and, above all, R&D. Recent research by McKinsey[29] shows
that Latin American cities lag behind the benchmark (the average of
New York, Helsinki, Singapore and Toronto) used in all these areas
(Figure 5.6 here).

Productivity in Monterrey (the largest of the Latin American cities
analysed) is barely 52% of Helsinki's; Bogotá's productivity is among
the lowest of the eight cities analysed, at 27% of Helsinki's. In terms
of innovation, there are important differences: Buenos Aires is the city
with the highest annual average number of patents granted on the
continent; its six annual patents are far fewer than New York's 850.
Río, one of the best-educated Latin American cities, produces annually
some 240 technology research publications, far from Singapore's 2,800
(Figure 5.7).

---

[28] See McKinsey, *Building Globally Competitive Cities: The Key to Latin
American Growth*, Boston and Washington, DC, McKinsey Global Institute,
August 2011. Available at www.mckinsey.com/mgi/publications/Building_
globally_competitive_cities/PDFs/MGI_Latin_America.pdf; also see Christian
Daude, 'Innovation, Productivity and Economic Development in Latin
America and the Caribbean', OECD Development Centre, Working Paper 288,
February 2010. Available at www.oecd.org/dataoecd/4/36/44581147.pdf.
[29] See McKinsey, *Building Globally Competitive Cities.*

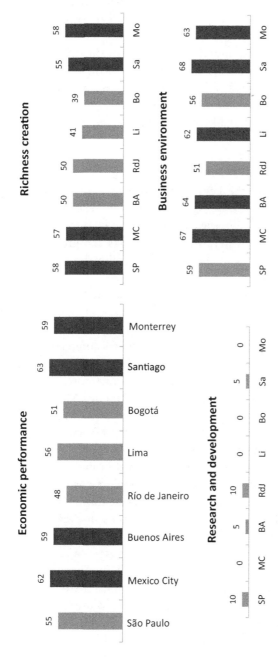

Figure 5.7 Situation of the most important Latin American cities in relation to the benchmark. *Source:* McKinsey Global Institute, 2011. Note: the 'benchmark' is the average of Helsinki, New York, Singapore and Toronto.

Improving technological clusters, the links between academia and the private sector, cooperation between researchers and businesses, as well as the quality of urban infrastructure, are some of the tasks necessary to improve and change this situation. Initiatives, such as those promoted by the Tec de Monterrey in the area of clusters, or Río in 2020 in the area of urban planning, are increasing. Access to finance, and in particular venture capital, is another of the pending subjects, where as we shall see, progress is being made.

Increased venture capital

In addition to FDI, the keys to climbing the value added chain are venture capital and private equity – both long-term capital bets. This was the lesson learned in the case of Israel, a country with no natural resources, not even water, which today has the greatest density of technology companies in the world and, with the USA, the highest number of companies quoted on NASDAQ.

Latin America lags behind in these areas, but many new initiatives with governmental and private support are opening an unprecedented area for more public–private partnerships. This will be the key for the decade 2010–20. We need plenty of innovative companies to take part in these initiatives and grow on a global scale from the region. We already know that Latin America can generate companies in cutting edge sectors such as telecommunications (América Móvil) or aeronautics (Embraer). It is possible to envisage the births of Latin Huaweis or Facebooks. As evidence of the enormous pool of talent in the region, one of the founders of Facebook, Eduardo Saverin, is Brazilian. Much of this local talent was raised and educated in the United States, and this group today represents an excellent pool of startup entrepreneurs.

As proof that something is happening in Latin America, companies like Google have started to buy startups in Brazil (for example the social networking site Orkut or technology company Akwan). The giants of South African and French media, Naspers and Vivendi respectively, became, along with Buscapé and GVT, companies born with the help of local and international venture capital. These venture capitalists are now looking towards Latin America. Many of them, however, like Chilean Scopix, are located in Chile but rely heavily on Silicon Valley for international expansion and capital. This is also the case of Letmego, headquartered in New York and co-founded by a Colombian, a Mexican and other Latin Americans; and of Smowtion, an

Argentine company located in California with offices in Mexico, Miami and Buenos Aires.

The governmental programme Start Up Chile, launched by President Piñera and operated with the support of the Chilean development agency CORFO, hopes to generate 1,000 startups in four years, and is largely based on attracting global talent to the country. Digital social networking sites like Sonico (with 40 million users), finance company sites like Wamba, or startups like Popego and TedCrunch, proliferate in Chile, as does the Mexican ClaseMovil.

In Brazil, BNDES plays a central role in attracting venture capital. FINEP, part of the Ministry of Science and Technology, launched the Inovar programme a decade ago. This supported the country's first generation of venture capital and development fund managers, today estimated to number nearly 200, according to Getulio Vargas. In the course of a decade, FINEP invested in around seventy startups, and in 2010 Brazil had around 125 science universities, 400 incubators and 1.7 million IT professionals. There are now a dozen VC funds specialised in startups that move underlying assets of nearly $2 billion, according to LAVCA. A VC fund such as Monashees Capital, with a dozen professionals, has a portfolio of a dozen startups, many of them with strong links to the Palo Alto and Tel Aviv hubs. Ideiasnet, another technology fund, has fifteen startups in its portfolio.

Some new funds are a very respectable size, promoted by veterans of the Brazilian market, like Stratus Venture Capital, which is raising a fund of $300 million for Brazil. CEOs of startups such as Samba Tech, Predicta/BTBuckets, Compra3 and Silicon Reef no longer need to go to Palo Alto to raise capital. Technology fairs that bring together startups and venture capital are starting to multiply. These fairs include the famous Punta del Este, which in mid January 2011 reunited in the Punta Tech Meet Up around 200 businesses, or the Campus Party Brazil which welcomed more than 300 projects for its 'Campuseros Emprenden' competition. In Mexico, Argentina and Peru, entrepreneurs and technology developers are organising clubs like Tequila Valley, Palermo Valley or Lima Valley. Telefónica launched Wayra incubators in eight countries during 2011–12 (more than 10,000 projects have been received and 150 startups accelerated in the region).

Voluntarism and good faith are clearly not everything. To reach more companies and enterprises, time and a favourable ecosystem are needed, including state of the art education, sufficient financing and, above all, entrepreneurs. Nevertheless, the good news is that from Mexico to Chile, by way of Colombia or Brazil, many countries in the region are now in the race. The private sector will also be key in strengthening the capacity to finance business innovation, in particular in high-tech sectors related to health, logistics, and even raw materials and agro-industry.

For now, investment in venture capital and private equity in Latin America still remains small, representing barely 2% of the world's total (comparable to Africa). In 2009, of the more than $3.5 trillion raised in the world by this type of vehicle, barely $4.4 billion was aimed at Latin America. While these types of funds (key in the rise of Palo Alto or Tel Aviv and for the cutting-edge startups and industries of the USA and Israel) represent 0.3% of the US GDP, in Latin America they only represent 0.03% of regional GDP, below the world and European averages of 0.17% and 0.19%, respectively. In the first half of 2010 more than $3.1 billion was raised, and as we have already seen, 2010 closed with a record of more than $8 billion.

Global investors are also watching the region. Global specialists in these industries, such as Apax, Carlyle, Silver Lake and TPG, are now interested in Latin America. In September 2010, the American giant Blackstone invested in the Brazilian investment company Patria Investimentos, taking a 40% stake for $200 million, and confirming the appetite of investors for Brazil. Carlyle, another American giant in the sector, created a $230 million fund to invest with Banco do Brasil.

At the start of 2011, in order to attract more venture capital (VC) and private equity (PE), the government reduced the tax rates for foreign capital flows intended for VC/PE. Technology multinationals, equipped with venture capital funds, also began looking to the region, and especially Brazil, with more intensity (although still giving priority to India or China). In 2001 the BlackBerry Partners Fund,[30] a venture capital fund promoted by Research In Motion Ltd, Thomson Reuters and Royal Bank of Canada, announced plans to raise a fund exclusively dedicated to BRICs, including Brazil, for a total of $150 million to support software companies and application suppliers for mobile phones. Telefónica founded and launched Amerigo, a VC network fund with teams in Colombia, Chile, Brazil and Spain – and $300 million of capital mobilised.

---

[30] See www.blackberrypartnersfund.com/.

In New York, entrepreneurs such as Michael Nicklas, a business angel who created the Social Smart Ventures fund, have specialised in internet investments focused solely on Brazil. In the EMPEA/Coller Capital Emerging Markets Private Equity 2010 survey,[31] Brazil was placed just behind China as the emerging market with the greatest potential for the VC/PE. Some successful IPOs like TIVIT, purchases such as Orkut by Google, and investments such as the Bostonian fund Great Hill Partners in Buscapé (earning a return on investment of nearly 900% in barely four years after selling for $340 million to Naspers), are beginning to put Brazil on the map of startups, venture capital and private equity funds.

Local pension funds are also beginning to invest in venture funds and the private equity industry. Mexican pension funds plan to invest more than $600 million in private equity. The asset portfolios under administration represent an average of 20.5% of the GDP of those countries in the region that have developed a private pension system. For now, the potential is still limited for venture capital investments. In mature markets (United States, Britain, Canada, Holland, the Scandinavian countries and Japan), private pension funds invest on average 3–5% of the total of their assets in private equity/venture capital (VC/PE), and contribute 25–30% of the total capital of VC/PE funds. Even more, the participation of VC/PE instruments in the total portfolio of pension funds could reach 8–10%, as in the United States and Sweden, while in Latin America it represents an average of 2%.[32]

The fourteen Mexican official pension funds (Afores) dedicate 8% of their $100 billion in managed assets to invest in unlisted companies. All of the states in the region are also launching programmes to promote innovation. Foreign multinationals are also striving, along with local operators, to create and promote centres for innovation and development with headquarters in the region. Among the most interesting initiatives are the government sponsored programmes. From

[31] See EMPEA and Coller Capital, *Emerging Markets Private Equity Survey 2011*, London, Coller Capital / EMPEA, 2011. Available at http://spanish. collercapital.com/uploaded/documents/News/2011/EMPEA_Coller_2011_ Survey_-_final.pdf.

[32] See Alberto R. Musalem and Fernando Baer, 'Latin American Pension Funds Investing in Private Equity and Venture Capital', Centro para la Estabilidad Financiera, Working Document 36, July 2010. Available at www.cefargentina. org/files_publicaciones/12-00wp-n%BA36-abstract-espaxol.pdf.

Brazil to Chile, by way of Colombia, Peru and Mexico, initiatives to create a dense fabric of private venture capital or seed capital funds are multiplying (the English expression 'venture capital' perhaps best captures the ideas of adventure, risk and audacity involved in the process).

This impulse is welcome in a region where innovation is still largely limited to the public realm (contrary to what is happening in South Korea), as is stressed in the report *Innovalatino,* published in 2011 jointly by INSEAD and OECD's Center for Development, with the support of the Fundación Telefónica.[33] And this is probably the appropriate starting point. Contrary to the commonly expressed idea, the venture fund industries in the United States and Israel were not born spontaneously or created exclusively by the action of the market's invisible hand. As Josh Lerner, professor at the University of Harvard Business School and expert on the subject, underlines in his latest book, the American government was crucial in creating Silicon Valley.[34]

Also in Israel, the role of the government was key in promoting the Yozma Venture Capital programme early in the 1990s and transforming Israel into an incubator of innovation enterprise. Today Tel Aviv is, ahead of Boston and just behind San Francisco, one of the cities in the world with the most venture capital activity. In 2010, the seed capital industry in Israel included more than sixty private funds that managed more than $10 billion. The ratio of venture capital to GDP in Israel is one of the highest in the world (almost 0.5% of GDP).

Josh Lerner also alerts us to the (numerous) failures of public regulation. This is something that the drivers of programmes to promote seed capital in Latin America are very aware of when designing new initiatives. Everyone, from Chileans to Colombians, wanted to learn from the successful (or unsuccessful) experiences of cutting-edge countries such as the United States, Singapore and Finland. One of the keys has been to encourage private initiatives and make the fabric of private seed capital funds denser.

Latin America is at a crossroads. The waves of investment in raw materials must not end in premature celebration. This is the decisive

---

[33] OECD, INSEAD and Fundación Telefónica, *Innovalatino: Fostering Innovation in Latin America,* Ariel/Fundación Telefónica, 2011, also see www.innovalatino.org/.

[34] See Josh Lerner, *Boulevard of Broken Dreams: Why Public Efforts to Boost Entrepreneurship and Venture Failed and What to Do about It,* Princeton University Press, 2009.

moment to wager on innovation and diversification, convert short-term capital into long-term capital, and aim to create Latin American Huaweis or Facebooks during the next decade. A short time ago, the president of the Inter-American Development Bank, an important player in the region, wrote in the *Financial Times* that the decade of 2010 could be the decade of Latin America. One of the keys will be the regional capability to innovate and develop, not only new products, but also new processes. What we are witnessing invites optimism: an urgency for innovation now permeates the region.

Governments, left or right wing, from Brazil to Chile, Colombia to Uruguay, are aware of the imperative to move up the value chain. In Chile, the right wing government of Sebastián Piñera launched one of the most ambitious programmes to boost entrepreneurship and star-tups. The programme, called Start-Up Chile,[35] put the country on the map of innovation and technology. Entrepreneurs who choose to move to Chile for at least six months receive a grant of $40,000. Additionally, the programme provides free office space and moving assistance. It also facilitates networking and business connections.

Start-Up Chile received more than 1,600 applications from seventy countries, with most coming from the USA. Nearly 500 entrepreneurs have participated so far in the programme and there are now 220 foreign startups in Chile that employ 180 locals and 143 abroad. The first batches of foreign startups have raised $8 million in venture capital financing from firms in Argentina, Brazil, France, the USA and Uruguay. Most important, Silicon Valley-style entrepreneurship has been spreading in and around the South American countries. An annual budget of about $15 million per year put the small commodity based country of Chile in the radar of venture capitalists and entrepreneurs.

This programme followed another one launched in 2000 with the ambition of making Chile an IT outsourcing hub, another effort to break its economic dependence on the mining industry. By offering massive subsidies, the Chilean government created an outsourcing industry that generated $800 million in revenue and employed 20,000 people in 2012. These Chilean programmes are not isolated: in 2012, the Brazilian BNDES launched a major initiative to boost venture capital and private equity funds in the country with more than $540 million mobilised, a programme inspired by the ones launched by Israel.

---

[35] See http://startupchile.org/.

BNDES currently has fifteen private equity and fourteen venture capital funds, which together have invested in 199 new enterprises since 2000. Colombia also launched major initiatives in 2011 with the creation of several sovereign funds, one devoted to boost innovation. In 2012 the government launched INNpulsa, a tool managed by Bancoldex, in order to boost entrepreneurship and innovation in the country.[36] This initiative followed a major effort by several Ministers, among them Diego Molano (Information Technologies and Communications) and Juan Carlos Echeverry (Finance) – replaced by Mauricio Cárdenas in 2012.

In a nutshell, and in order to summarise the key messages of this chapter, the rules of the game are not written. Latin America is showing signs of taking off also in terms of technology and innovation. The rise of (some) Multilatinas 2.0 testifies to this new trend. However, the region is lagging behind others that are catching up even more quickly, in particular Asia, with India and China as the frontrunners. The biggest challenge – and also opportunity – in the near future comes precisely from the East, namely from Asia and in particular from China. As we will see in the next chapter, the rise of China was one of the major events of the decade 2000–10 worldwide and this has also been a major reality for Latin America. This emergence is a wake up call for the region and its multinationals: it is both a market opportunity (that has massively benefited players like Vale and Petrobras, for example) but also a challenge for the more technological firms (like Embraer). China's shadow looms large now over Latin America and it will shape its future.

---

[36] See www.innpulsacolombia.com/.

6 | *China: a wake up call*

As we have seen in the previous chapter, Latin American multinationals are on the rise in technological sectors. This trend is a promising one but it also faces challenges. The biggest one is related to the risks (and opportunities) that are linked to the rise of China. In the decade 2000–10 we have been witnessing a major shift of the economic and trade relations of Latin America, once centred in the Atlantic (USA and Europe) and now centred in the Pacific (Asia). This shift is good news for the region: emerging Asian economies are set to contribute close to 58% to global growth in the current decade and China will be the highest contributor with almost 30% of global growth.

The rise of China is dramatic and, since 2010, it has caught up with Europe as Latin America's second largest partner. Commodities are about half of the total exports. As we will see, China has become the top trading partner for Brazil, Chile and Peru and the second largest one for Argentina and Colombia. However, the risk for the region is the commoditisation of the exports and de-industrialisation of the countries. Latin American exports towards China are heavily concentrated on commodities reaching more than 80% of the total (while Asian and Chinese exports in particular for Latin America are 80% manufactured products with more value added). The big question therefore is if the rise of China will stop the trend we have been describing in the previous chapter: the rise of more value added and technological multilatinas.

The numbers are indeed pointing to challenges. There is some evidence that China might be behind the renewed Latin American concentration on exports of commodities and increase the region's dependence on commodities.[1] In any case, China is challenging industrial

---

[1] See Matt Ferchen, Alicia García-Herrero and Mario Nigrinis, 'Evaluating Latin America's Commodity Dependence, on China', BBVA Research, Working Paper 12/08, May 2012.

players from the region with Latin currencies that are appreciating and Chinese competitors that are increasingly moving abroad. Brazil, for example, the largest industrial country of the continent, increasingly exports products to China with lower technological content and increasingly imports products with higher technological content. In 1994, Brazilian high and medium technological products exports reached 19% of the total, while in 2007 they went down to 12%. In the meantime Brazilian imports of high and medium technological products from China jumped from 59% of the total to 67%.[2] In a nutshell, China's rise is bringing major benefits to the region, as we will see, but also poses new risks and challenges. The decade 2010–20 will tell if the region manages to ride this wave and mitigate some of the costs involved in the rise of China.

A close analysis if the trade data does not confirm the trend of deindustrialization. In fact, according to some recent research by BBVA's economists,[3] Brazilian exports of high technological content and high quality have increased more than the average and more than low technological and low quality exports in recent years. Overall, the emergence of China has been supporting a displacement of Brazilian exports, not only towards natural based products but also to goods with higher quality and higher technological content. The story is therefore not yet complete.[4] The good news is that Latin American governments from Brazil to Colombia are more and more aware of the urgency to upgrade their manufacturing and industrial outputs, to climb the value chain and at the same time to transform the Chinese boom into an opportunity and a blessing, that is, to draw an analogy to

---

[2] See www.bbvaresearch.com/KETD/fbin/mult/120507_Sino-Latin_American_Economic_Relations_AGH_tcm348-317221.pdf?ts=1352012. See also K. C. Fung, Alicia García-Herrero and Mario Nigrinis Ospina, 'Latin American Commodity Export Concentration: Is There a China Effect?', BBVA Research Working Paper 12/07, May 2012.

[3] See Enestor dos Santos and Soledad Zignago, 'The Impact of the Emergence of China on Brazilian International Trade', in K. C. Fung and Alicia García-Herrero (eds.), *Sino–Latin American Economic Relations*, London, Routledge, 2012, pp. 224–53.

[4] For a discussion see Rhys Jenkins and Alexandre de Freitas Barbosa, 'Fear for Manufacturing? China and the Future of Industry in Brazil and Latin America', *China Quarterly*, 209, March 2012, pp. 59–81, and Kevin Gallagher, 'A Catalyst for Hope: China's Opportunity for Latin America', in Javier Santiso and Jeff Dayton-Johnson (eds.), *The Oxford Handbook of Latin American Political Economy*, Oxford University Press, 2012, pp. 233–61.

Hirschman, to make China a 'catalyst for hope' rather than a catalyst for despair.

The rise of China

During the decade 2000–10, China established itself as one of Latin America's great business partners. Business between the regions increased more than 50% in 2010 to reach a record of nearly $180 billion. As early as 2014, China will take the place of the European Union as the continent's second largest trading partner. From this point of view, the decade 2000–10 was one of increasing relations between the regions. In the current decade it is very probable that we will see a new relationship forged that is more financial and industrial. The data from 2010 confirm both trends.

From a trade point of view, the relationship between China and Latin America has been firmly established. Chile leads the trend as the Asian giant's largest trading partner. China absorbed 24.5% of all Chile's exports in 2012 (compared to 11.5% only five years earlier). China also became Brazil's largest trading partner in 2010, absorbing 17% of its total exports (compared to 6% by the mid-2000s). Another country that is looking to Asia and China is Peru, with more than 12% of its exports going to China. Venezuela and Argentina in turn send 10% and 9% of their exports to China. As the Economic Commission for Latin America and the Caribbean (ECLAC) pointed out in its latest report on Chinese–Latin American relations, the Asian giant could take the European Union's place as its second largest trading partner midway through the decade of 2010–20[5] (Figure 6.1 and Table 6.1).

In all these cases, the relationship is founded on the exports of raw materials and agricultural products such as copper, oil and soy, while China mainly exports manufactured products to the region. That is to say, in this current decade Latin America is having to work out how to change this imbalance and export more value added products to China, a country where consumer habits are changing and will

---

[5] See ECLAC, *La República Popular China y América Latina y el Caribe: hacia una nueva fase en el vínculo económico y comercial (The People's Republic of China and Latin American and the Caribbean: Ushering in a New Era in the Economic and Trade Relationship)*, Santiago de Chile, ECLAC, June 2011. Available at www.eclac.org/comercio/publicaciones/xml/4/43664/People_Republic_of_China_and_Latina_America_and_the_Caribbean_trade.pdf.

Table 6.1 *China: a strategic trade partner for Latin America, 1990–2010 (in $ million).*

	Exports			
	1990–5	1995–2000	2000–5	2005–10
Latin America-Caribbean	32.2	17.8	26.8	31
Asia-Pacific	26.5	9.3	20.3	13.8
USA	36.7	16.1	25.6	11.7
EU	26.3	15	28.8	16.4
Rest of the world	8.8	7.1	26.6	17.2
World	19.1	10.9	25	15.7
	Imports			
	1990–5	1995–2000	2000–5	2005–10
Latin America-Caribbean	14.5	12.7	37.6	27.7
Asia-Pacific	32.4	12.2	23.9	14.6
USA	19.7	6.8	16.8	15.9
EU	18.2	7.6	18.8	17.9
Rest of the world	11.2	13.4	26.8	15.8
World	19.9	11.3	24	16.1

Source: ECLAC, 2012.

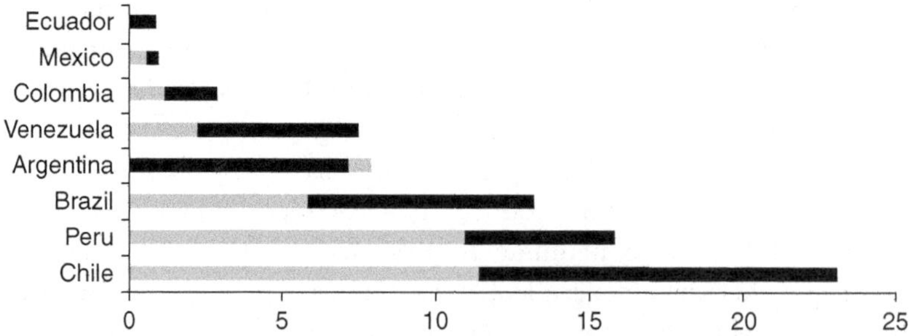

Figure 6.1 Exports to China as percentage of total exports in 2009.
Source: Based on JP Morgan, 2011. Grey for 2005; black for 2009.

continue to change in the future (creating business opportunities for astute exporters).

We are also seeing how the region is becoming more sensitive to Chinese growth. The work of IADB economists suggests that the transmission of global shocks (positive and negative) is now under Chinese influence for Latin America.[6] Although Chinese growth should remain strong until the middle of the current decade (and thus its appetite for raw materials), growth may slow in the second half of the current decade and so negatively affect Latin America.[7]

The region is also exposed to fluctuations in Chinese exchange rates. An appreciation of the renminbi could positively affect countries such as Mexico that export manufactured products to third countries (USA) and compete directly with Chinese products.[8] However, for the majority of countries in the region that export products to China for processing (raw materials), an appreciation would be negatively felt.[9] Fluctuations in the exchange rate of the renminbi and the dollar will be relevant for the future of the region (and other developing economies).[10]

Another trend worth noting is something that largely explains President Obama's focus on the region in 2011–12: the exports of Argentina, Brazil and Chile to China are greater than their exports to the United States. These countries (two of which received a visit

---

[6] See Ambrogio Cesa-Bianchi *et al.*, 'On the Transmission of Global Shocks to Latin America before and after China's Emergence in the World Economy', Inter-American Development Bank, Working Paper. Available at www.iadb.org/res/centralBanks/publications/cbm58_649.pdf.

[7] See Yongzhen Yu, 'Identifying the Linkages between Major Mining Commodity Prices and China's Economic Growth – Implications for Latin America', IMF Working Paper 11–86, April 2011. Available at www.imf.org/external/pubs/ft/wp/2011/wp1186.pdf.

[8] On China's negative impact on Mexico's economy (both export manufactured products and compete in the USA, the main export market of both economies), see Gordon Hanson, 'Why Isn't Mexico Rich?', *Journal of Economic Literature*, 48(4), 2010, pp. 987–1004. Mexico is one of the ten emerging economies that is most exposed to China's boom (more than 75% of its exports are manufactured), see Gordon Hanson and Raymond Robertson, 'China and the Manufacturing Exports of Other Developing Countries', in Robert Feenstra and Shang Jin Wei (eds.), *China's Growing Role in World Trade*, University of Chicago Press and NBER, 2010, pp. 137–59. Available at http://irps.ucsd.edu/assets/022/8776.pdf.

[9] See Barry Eichengreen and Hui Tong, 'The External Impact of China's Exchange Rate Policy: Evidence from Firm Level Data', IMF Working Paper 11–155, July 2011. Available at www.imf.org/external/pubs/ft/wp/2011/wp11155.pdf; and Hanson and Robertson, 'China and the Manufacturing Exports of Other Developing Countries', pp. 137–59.

[10] See Christopher Garroway, Burcu Hacibedel, Helmut Reisen and Edouard Turkisch, 'The Renminbi and Poor Country Growth', OECD Development Centre, Working Paper 292, September 2010. Available at www.oecd.org/dataoecd/22/55/45950256.pdf.

from President Obama) are already looking more towards Asia than
to the north. For Colombia, Ecuador, Venezuela, Mexico and Peru,
the United States remains their largest trading partner, but for some
nations, such as Peru, Asian business is already unstoppable. Mexico is
the country in the region that trades the least with China. In 2010 Mexican exports to the Chinese dragon only reached 1.4% of its total, far
from the 83.5% of Mexican exports absorbed by the United States. In
addition, barely 2% of Ecuador's total exports go to China. Colombia
is another country that is experiencing a major shift towards Asia. In
only five years, between 2005 and 2010, exports to China went from
1% to 5% of its total, a notable increase that is explained by the rise
in raw material exports.

China's FDI towards Latin America: the big news of the 2010s decade

The big news since 2010 has been the increase in Chinese foreign direct
investment to the region. In 2010 we witnessed an unprecedented
boom in Chinese investment throughout Latin America. This was little
more than $30 billion until 2009, but in the following year alone
nearly twenty large Chinese acquisitions and share transactions were
announced in Latin America (totalling $33 billion).

We made these estimates from various corporate announcements,
including investments made through offshore centres such as the
Netherlands, Switzerland and Luxembourg, through which Chinese
investment is often channelled towards Latin America. FDI figures
tend to be difficult to calculate and differ between various bodies
(for example UNCTAD and ECLAC). ECLAC estimates that Chinese transnationals invested more than $15 billion in the region in
2010, becoming the third largest investor in Latin America and the
Caribbean with a 9% share, after the United States (17%) and the
Netherlands (13%).[11] The amount suggested by ECLAC for the single
year 2010 is more than double the amount invested by China in the
two previous decades from 1999 to 2009! And it has been speeding up
since.

[11] See ECLAC, *Foreign Direct Investment in Latin America and the Caribbean*
(*La inversión extranjera directa en América Latina y el Caribe 2010*), Santiago
de Chile, ECLAC, May 2011; and the presentation of the report available at
www.eclac.org/noticias/paginas/8/33638/2011-283-IED-Presentacion-es.pdf.

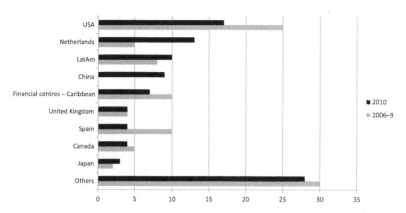

Figure 6.2 FDI in Latin America: China is an important direct investor in Latin America, 2010.
Source: ECLAC, 2011.

In fact the numbers may be even larger. If we consider that part of what is invested through the Netherlands is also direct investment from China, then the Asian giant has become the second largest investor in Latin America, ahead of the European powers, including Spain. Chinese investments announced since 2011 total $22.7 billion (Figure 6.2 and Table 6.2).

China is now one of the main investors on the Latin American continent. The nineties and the following decade saw a European investor boom in the region, particularly Spanish investors. This is not over, as the multimillion dollar investments in 2010 and 2011, particularly in Brazil, by companies such as Telefónica, Iberdrola and Santander show. The big news in 2010 was, however, China's centre stage entrance as an investor in Latin America. The region was waiting for the Chinese Godot for nearly a decade. In 2010 Godot took the stage. A flurry of deals have taken place since 2010 in the region involving Chinese companies (Table 6.3).

Among the largest Chinese deals agreed in 2010 were: a $3.3 billion contract between state-run Chinese Wisco and local LLX for an iron and steel operation in the heart of Río de Janeiro; an agreement with Brazil's Petrobras ($10 billion); a share purchase in the Argentine oil company Bridas ($3.1 billion for 50% of the company); a $3 billion rights purchase to the Peregrino Brazilian oil field (Sinochem buying from Norwegian Statoil); and the Toromocho copper mine ($2.2 billion investment by Chinalco).

Table 6.2 *China: FDI in selected Latin American and Caribbean economies (in $ million).*

	Confirmed investment		Planned investment
Country	1990–2009	2010	After 2011
Argentina	143	5,550	3,530
Brazil	255	9,563	9,870
Colombia	1,677	3	–
Costa Rica	13	0.05	700
Ecuador	1,619	41	–
Guyana	1,000	–	–
Mexico	127	5	–
Peru	2,262	84	8,640
Venezuela	240	–	–
TOTAL	7,336	15,241	22,740

Source: ECLAC, 2011.

Table 6.3 *Key Chinese investments in Latin America in 2010.*

Country	Month	Chinese company	Amount (in $ million)	Sector
Chile	March	State Grid	1,050	Copper
Brazil	March	East China Minerals	1,200	Iron
Argentina	March	CNOOC	3,100	Oil
Venezuela	April	CNPC	900	Oil
Mexico	April	Foton	250	Automotive
Peru	May	China Sci-Tech	255	Copper
Peru	May	Chinalco	2,200	Mining
Brazil	May	State Grid	1,720	Energy
Brazil	May	Sinochem	3,070	Oil
Brazil	August	Chery	700	Automotive
Brazil	September	Sany Heavy Industry	100	Metallurgy
Brazil	October	Sinopec	7,100	Oil
Argentina	November	CNOOC	3,000	Oil
Argentina	December	Sinopec	2,450	Oil
Brazil	December	State Grid	1,000	Electricity
Brazil	December	China Investment Corp	300	Banking
Brazil	Unconfirmed	Wuhan Steel & Iron	5,000	Steel

Source: Author's estimates, 2012; based on official data and press, Bloomberg, Financial Times, and local Latin American and Chinese sources.

Many sectors are now active in foreign investment: from electrical services to agro-industrial, by way of automotive parts and telecommunications. In December 2010, three sovereign funds, ADIC of the United Arab Emirates, GIC of Singapore and CIC of China bought shares in BTG Pactual bank for $200 to $300 million each, more proof of the Chinese (and Arab and Asian) appetite for Brazil. In Peru, a Chinese consortium invested more than $2 billion to increase the capacity of the port of Tacna and another $8 billion to connect this port by road and rail to Bolivian mining zones.[12]

Chinese oil companies invested $15 billion in the region during 2010. One of the most recent operations was agreed by China Petroleum Corporation for the purchase of a subsidiary of Occidental Petroleum in Argentina for $2.5 billion. A few months earlier, the Chinese oil company CNOOC had bought part of Pan American Energy, also in Argentina, for more than $3 billion. This boom will not stop here. In Cuba, the China National Petroleum Corporation (CNPC) began in 2011 to expand the Cuban Cienfuegos refinery with an investment of $6 billion, one of the largest in the history of Cuba (China's Eximbank financed 85% of the refinery's modernisation). Other oil companies, such as Malaysian Petronas, Indian Oil, Natural Gas Corporation and PetroVietnam, in addition to Petrobras and PDVSA, have also contracted oil blocks in Cuban waters.

In the Peruvian mining sector, firms such as Chinalco and Minmetals/Jiangxi Chinalco have invested more than $1.4 billion and Chinese companies plan to invest another $4.5 billion while trade relations continue to respond to the free trade agreement that took effect in 2010. In turn, Ecuador signed bilateral agreements for more than $5 billion with China in 2010 for hydroelectric, oil and infrastructure investments.

We are also witnessing more activity from Chinese sovereign funds in the region. Stocks owned by Chinese sovereign fund CIC in the Brazilian stock market barely represent 4% of the total invested outside the country (CIC is an important investor in the Vale mine, for example). But bilateral visits are multiplying and China is preparing the way for future investments in Mexico, Brazil and the Andean countries. We

[12] For an overview on Chinese FDI in Peruvian mineral sectors, see Rubén González-Vicente, 'Mapping Chinese Mining Investment in Latin America: Politics or Market?', *China Quarterly*, 209, March 2012, pp. 35–58.

are also witnessing a strong increase in bilateral Chinese credit lines to countries in the region, in particular Argentina, Brazil, Venezuela and, to a lesser degree, Ecuador – the total amount reaching more than $50 billion over the three years 2010–12. These amounts contrast, for example, with the $11 billion that the Inter-American Development Bank invests in the continent every year.

Brazil receives a great part of this investment and accounted for more than $17 billion in Chinese investments between 2009 and 2011 according to figures compiled by APEX-Brasil, something never before seen. This is close to half of the amount represented by the 40% stake in the Brazilian subsidiary of Spanish oil company Repsol YPF ($7.1 billion). The flow of Chinese capital for productive activities totalled a third of the $38.5 billion received from direct investment, according to the Brazilian Banco Central. These estimates are always difficult to make because China (like other foreign investors) often uses fiscal vehicles in Luxembourg or other countries such as the Netherlands and Switzerland. Among the larger operations are investments by Sinochem ($3 billion), State Grid ($1.7 billion), ECE ($1.2 billion) and Wisco ($400 million) – all linked to energy sectors and raw materials.

In the first decade of the twenty-first century, China established itself as one of Latin America's great trading partners. In this second decade of the new century, China will also establish itself as one of the great direct investors. Both of these Chinese initiatives (trade and investment) show that Latin America is no longer a 'backyard' for the USA. The hope now is that Latin America will move strategically to find Chinese investors in high value added businesses, and not just investors in raw material assets. Potential investors in high value added areas could include: Huawei or ZTE in the telecommunications sectors; BYD, Chery or Geely in the automotive sectors; and Haier among others in manufacturing. If these investors choose to invest in Latin America then 2010–20 will truly become a Latin decade.

The region's exports to China have grown substantially but are dominated by raw materials. Exports in 2000 from the majority of Latin American countries to China barely reached 5% of exports, but in 2010 Chile sent a third of its exports to China, Peru sent 15% of its total, and Brazil sent 13%. At the same time, imports from China increased significantly between 2000 and 2010. In the case of Argentina, imports multiplied by 10, in Mexico by 14, in Brazil by 20, and in the cases of Peru and Colombia by more than 15, according to recent calculations made by researchers at the Brookings Institution.[13]

An unequal relationship between the countries of the region and China became even more pronounced, with some exporting low value added products and China exporting more intensively value added products and technology. This unequal relationship also has a potentially problematic turning point for Latin America: as China gets closer to the $15,000 per capita level, it will start reducing its demand for raw materials, something the Brookings Institution estimates will happen around 2015. This will present an even more intense challenge, given that China will be industrially 'graduating'[14] and moving towards products that are more technology intensive and value added (making Latin America's road towards these same goals of higher added value and better technology more difficult)[15] (Table 6.4).

The imbalance in trade relations between China and Brazil is systemic, for example. While Brazilian exports to China are mostly raw materials and low value added products, China mainly exports manufactured products with high added value to Brazil. This unbalanced relationship became more pronounced between the decades of the 1990s and the 2000s, as Figure 6.3 shows.[16] As a result, there is (growing) interest and pressure on the part of Brazil to change this

[13] See Mauricio Cárdenas and Adriana Kluger, 'The Reversal of the Structural Transformation in Latin America after China's Emergence', Washington, DC, Latin American Initiative, August 2011. Available at www.brookings.edu/~/media/Files/rc/papers/2011/0802_structural_transformation_cardenas/0802_structural_transformation_cardenas.pdf.

[14] See the work of World Bank chief economist Justin Lin, 'From Flying Geese to Leading Dragons: New Opportunities and Strategies for Structural Transformation in Developing Countries', World Bank Policy Research Working Paper 5702, June 2011; and the presentation: http://sitesources.worldbank.org/DEC/Resources/Uzbekistan-final.pdf.

[15] See the impact on Latin America and Africa analysed by Margaret McMillan and Dani Rodrik, 'Globalization, Structural Change and Productivity Growth', Harvard University, Kennedy School, Working Paper, February 2011. Available at www.hks.harvard.edu/fs/drodrik/research.html.

[16] See Enestor dos Santos and Soledad Zignano, 'The Impact of the Emergence of China on Brazilian International Trade', Madrid, BBVA Research Working Paper 22, September 2010. Available at www.bbvaresearch.com/KETD/fbin/mult/WP_1022_tcm348-231940.pdf?ts=1082011; and more generally on Latin America Eliana Cardoso and Márcio Holland, 'South America for the Chinese? A Trade Based Analysis', OECD Development Centre, Working Paper 289, April 2010. Available at www.oecd.org/dataoecd/41/39/45041460.pdf.

Table 6.4 *Chinese–Latin American trade (in $ billion).*

	Chinese exports to			Chinese imports from			Chinese trade balance		
	1990	2000	2010	1990	2000	2010	1990	2000	2010
Argentina	0.0	0.6	6.1	0.3	0.9	6.8	−0.3	−0.3	−0.7
Brazil	0.1	1.2	24.5	0.5	1.6	38.0	−0.4	−0.4	−13.6
Chile	0.1	0.8	8.0	0.0	1.3	17.8	0.0	−0.6	−9.7
Colombia	0.0	0.2	3.8	0.0	0.0	2.1	0.0	0.1	1.7
Mexico	0.1	1.3	17.9	0.1	0.5	6.8	0.0	0.8	11.1
Peru	0.0	0.1	3.6	0.1	0.6	6.1	−0.1	−0.4	−2.6
Uruguay	0.0	0.2	1.5	0.1	0.1	1.2	−0.1	0.1	0.3
Venezuela	0.0	0.3	3.6	0.0	0.1	6.6	0.0	0.2	−2.9

Source: Brookings Institution, 2011.

imbalance and limit the (relative) decline of Brazilian industry when faced with China's rise.[17] BNDES, the investing and industrial arm of the Brazilian state, has echoed this concern[18] (Figure 6.3).

Chinese investments in the region are mainly in the raw material sectors, while Latin American investments in China are barely significant.[19] In other words, the relationship between the regions is dominated by this dependence on raw materials. Research by BBVA confirms this imbalance in trade relations and FDI between the two countries.[20] This pattern is repeated throughout the region. While

[17] On the (growing) rivalry between Brazil and China, see Carlos Pereira and Agusto de Castro Neves, 'Brazil and China: South South Cooperation or North South Competition', Brookings Foreign Policy Paper Series 26, March 2011. Available at www.brookings.edu/papers/2011/03_brazil_china_pereira.aspx.

[18] See Fernando Puga and Marcelo Nascimento, 'O efeito China sobre as importações brasileiras', Río de Janeiro, BNDES, Visao do Desenvolvimento, 89, December 2010. Available at www.bndes.gov.br/SiteBNDES/export/sites/default/bndes_pt/Galerias/Arquivos/conhecimento/visao/visao_89.pdf.

[19] See the IADB report that summarises the imbalanced evolution of the two regions during the decade 2000–10, BID, Inter-American Development Bank (IADB), *Ten Years after the Take-off: Taking Stock of China – Latin America and the Caribbean Economic Relations,* Washington, DC, IADB, 2010. Available at http://idbdocs.iadb.org/wsdocs/getdocument.aspx?docnum=35410652.

[20] See Enestor dos Santos and Soledad Zignano, 'The Impact of the Emergence of China on Brazilian International Trade', Madrid, BBVA Research Working Paper 22, 2010. Also see Kevin Gallagher, 'China and the Future of Latin American Industrialization', Boston University Issue Brief 8, October 2010. Available at www.bu.edu/pardee/publications/issues-in-brief-no-18/.

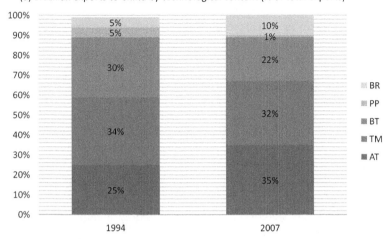

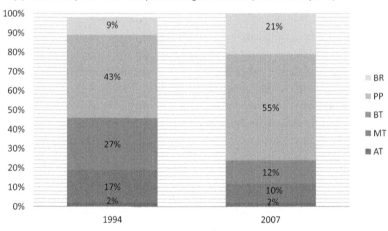

Figure 6.3 China and Brazil: an unbalanced trade relationship.
(a) Brazilian exports to China by technological content (percentage of total exports).
(b) Chinese exports to Brazil by technological content (percentage of total exports).
Source: BBVA Research 2012. *Note:* BR (based on natural resources); PP (primary products); BT (low technology); MT (medium technology); AT (high technology).

Chinese exports to Latin America are concentrated in manufactured products with a certain level of technology (90% of Chinese exports to the region), Latin American technology exports barely represent 12% of the total exported by the region to China.[21]

Walking the Talk with China: rebalancing technology and innovation

This will be one of Latin America's greatest challenges in the current decade 2010–20: to position itself as a competitive region that offers innovation and added value. China could become an ally in this endeavour providing the Latin American governments present a different relationship, and foster investments in technology areas. Contrary to the widespread stereotype, China is not only a manufacturer of cheap products. It is rapidly repositioning itself in highly technological and value added sectors; and companies such as Huawei and ZTE have become two of the world's top suppliers to the telecommunications industry.

Latin America could also encourage the deployment of factories and centres for these emerging multinationals. In some cases (still exceptions) steps are being taken in this direction, in particular in Brazil, although until now the majority of Chinese FDI in this country has been concentrated in low value added sectors. A report by Brazil's Ministry of Development, Industry and Trade shows that 84.5% of the $37.1 billion that Chinese companies invested in the country between January 2003 and January 2011 was concentrated in the metallurgy and energy sectors.

Thus, in addition to investments in raw material sectors, some technology sectors are receiving investment. The Chinese appliance group Haier also agreed a deal that creates mixed companies in Venezuela, and a research and development centre focused on clean technology products. Both countries also agreed to create an airline to operate in Venezuela with $300 million of initial investment. Also, in April 2011, Brazil and China signed several technology cooperation agreements,

---

[21] See Alicia García Herrero, 'China – Latam: Going beyond Conventional Wisdom', Hong Kong, BBVA Research, presentation made at the China–Iberoamerican Dialogue, Madrid, SEGIB, September 2010. Available at www.bbvaresearch.com/KETD/fbin/mult/101007_AliciaChina-LATAM_tcm348-234062.pdf?ts=27122010.

one of which will lead to the establishment in Brazil of a $400 million Huawei factory for manufacturing components for the telecommunications industry. In turn, the other big Chinese technology company that supplies the telecommunications industry, ZTE, also announced after a meeting of its managing director with the president Dilma Rousseff that the Chinese firm would start producing tablet computers in Brazil (investing some $250 million in the project until 2014 and hiring 2,500 employees). ZTE will also build a research and logistics centre, the first of its kind for the company in Latin America.

A few months later, in July 2011, Brazil and China announced an agreement in which China would invest more than $4.5 billion in the Brazilian nanotechnology sector. In the short term, Brazil and China will jointly invest some $6.4 million in the construction of a nanotechnology and space science research centre in the city of Campinas (São Paulo), in an initiative that results from an association between Brazil's Ministry of Science and Technology and the Chinese Academy of Sciences (CAS). The objective of the Brazilian government is to use and increase the research infrastructure of the National Nanotechnology Laboratory and profit from Chinese experience as it is one of the leading countries in the research of new materials and nanotechnology.

In the automotive sector, the Geely and Chery groups are looking to establish themselves in the region. Chery Automobile entered the market in Brazil in 2010, becoming the first Chinese car group to show an interest in the country and invest $400 million in a plant in the state of São Paulo. Chery has another factory in Uruguay, and in 2011 it announced the construction of a third factory in Venezuela with an investment of $200 million. Geely sells its cars in Peru, Uruguay, Cuba and Venezuela. In Uruguay, Geely also entered into a partnership with a local manufacturer that produces cars for Mercosur, for a total investment of $40 million. Also in 2011, the Chinese heavy construction machinery company Xuzhou Construction Machinery Group (XCMG) announced that it would invest $206 million in a factory in Minas Gerais. Sany Group, a Chinese manufacturer of heavy engineering equipment and machinery, is eager to take advantage of the push for the Games and the World Cup and is planning to construct a new $200 million factory and R&D centre, turning Brazil into one of its main markets outside China.

The Chinese push extends to other sectors, such as railways and in particular high-speed trains, in which the French leader Alstom will now be challenged by Chinese companies for projects uniting Río de Janeiro–São Paulo and Buenos Aires–Cordoba in Argentina. In 2011, more Chinese constructors announced plans for Brazil: JAC Motors announced the construction of its first installation in São Paulo, a $600 million plant to produce 100,000 units annually. Also in 2011, Lifan signed a $100 million agreement with Effa (with Uruguayan and Chinese capital) to build a plant to produce 10,000 vehicles per year. The Chinese brand also announced the construction of a $70 million R&D centre in São Paulo. This centre will be the first built by the company outside China.

In Argentina, China Railways International and the local group, Roggio, won a bid to construct the metro in Cordoba, the country's second largest city. Most of the $10 billion awarded in early 2011 will be spent in several stages, with $2.5 billion spent during the first four years to repair two stretches of rail lines, of which 85% will be financed by the Chinese Development Bank. Another $1.8 billion will be used to construct four metro lines in Cordoba.

Another of the more ambitious Chinese projects in the region is in Colombia, where the construction of a rail line was announced in 2011 as an alternative to the Panama Canal and connecting the Atlantic to the Pacific via Colombia. If the $7.6 billion project goes through, it will be one of China's most ambitious in the region (to be financed by the Chinese Development Bank and operated by China Railway Group). In 2012, President Santos from Colombia, and his team of ministers, including the leading economist Mauricio Cárdenas turned mining minister, travelled to China and signed no fewer than nine pacts there. Interestingly, these included a financing facility from China Development Bank for a pipeline through Venezuela and Colombia to the Pacific Coast, but also value added deals.

The revival of industrial policy in Latin America (renewed and led by Brazil) points also to potential changes in the relationship with China, as we have seen.[22] But it could go even further. Why not imagine

---

[22] On the revival of industrial policy in Latin America, and Brazil in particular, see Luciano Coutinho, Joao Ferraz, André Nassif and Rafael Oliva, 'Industrial Policy and Economic Transformation', in Javier Santiso and Jeff Dayton-Johnson (eds.), *The Oxford Handbook of Latin American Political Economy*, Oxford University Press, 2012, pp. 100–33.

that Bolivia, which possesses large lithium reserves, a main ingredient in batteries for electric cars and mobile phones, might also install a research and development centre for an industrial battery plant in the country, taking advantage of this Chinese interest and momentum? The world lithium market is significant and totals almost a billion dollars. But the world market for lithium-based batteries is estimated at $25 billion in the current decade, and the market for cars that run on lithium-based batteries at more than $200 billion. (In 2010 Bolivia barely exported eighty-six product categories to China, 87% of which were raw materials, while it bought 3,734 different product categories from China, according to the Bolivian Institute for Foreign Trade.)

China spends more than 2% of its GDP on R&D, and patents more than 100,000 licences per year (75% of them Chinese and the remainder from multinationals operating in the country) while spending on R&D in Latin America barely reached 0.6% of GDP and 35,000 patents were registered in the entire continent (almost 90% of them by foreign multinationals). Cooperation with China could well mean research and development laboratories in Latin America.

China has become an economic and political power and its growing presence on the Latin American continent is further proof of this rise. International organisations have noted this wave, making an ever larger space in their decision-making bodies for China – as is the case of the International Monetary Fund, or, by awarding key positions, as in the case of the World Bank's chief economist. In Latin America, the IADB (Inter-American Development Bank) already has China as a member, along with Korea and Japan. The CAF (Andean Development Bank) is increasing its regional agreements and cooperation with China. There is no subject on today's global and regional political and economic agenda in which China is not essential. The rise of China represents one of the great changes in this massive shift of wealth and power towards emerging markets.

The year 2011 confirmed the massive bets of China in Latin America. The region received, according to UN ECLAC, a record of $153.4 billion (a jump of 33% compared to the previous year). While Europe was the biggest investor in Latin America, accounting for almost 40% of total FDI (ahead of the USA, 18%, and Japan, 8%), China has been the fastest growing investor in the region. In 2011

Chinese FDI in Latin America reached a new high: $23 billion (surpassing the previous year, $15 billion).

Symbolic of the increasing linkages between the two regions, China and IADB agreed in 2012 to a billion dollar investment fund.[23] According to some estimates, between 2005 and 2011 China provided loan commitments upwards of $75 billion to Latin American countries. China's loan commitments of $37 billion in 2010 were more than those of the World Bank, Inter-American Development Bank and United States Export-Import Bank combined for that year.[24]

Latin America should take advantage of this relationship to rebalance relations with China in a less asymmetric mode. The region needs to leverage on its resources in order to boost more Chinese FDI of value added. If China wants the coal of Colombia, why not build truck factories in the country in order to transport the mineral from the heartland to the coast? If China wants the lithium of Bolivia or Chile, why not have the battery manufacturer BYD or automobile players like Geely installing factories in the Andean countries? In 2012, China Construction Bank showed interest in the Brazilian assets of WestLeb, the troubled German bank. Beyond the commodity clusters, the Chinese are now looking to jump into more value added sectors, and Latin America should take advantage of this. In the same range of ideas, the region should promote more openness from China to its manufactured products and build trade-offs in order to open the doors of the Chinese markets.[25]

The rise of China in Latin America has changed the region. It has also provoked a rebalancing of powers within the Americas. The USA is not the sole player in Latin America anymore. Likewise, Europe, and Spain

---

[23] See www.iadb.org/en/news/news-releases/2011-03-28/china-eximbank-latin-america-investment-fund,9323.html.

[24] See Kevin P. Gallagher, Amos Irwin and Katherine Koleski, 'The New Banks in Town: Chinese Finance in Latin America', *Inter-American Dialogue Report*, March 2012. Available at www.thedialogue.org/PublicationFiles/TheNewBanksinTown-FullTextnewversion.pdf.

[25] See Rolando Avendaño and Javier Santiso, 'Economic Fundamentals of the Relationship', in Adrian Hearn and José Luis León-Manriquez (eds.), *China Engages Latin America: Tracing the Trajectory*, London, Lynne Rienner Publishers, 2011, pp. 67–101; and Rolando Avendaño and Javier Santiso, 'Asian Opportunities and Diversification Strategies: An Outlook for Latin American Trade', in K. C. Fung and Alicia García Herrero (eds.), *Sino-Latin American Economic Relations*, London, Routledge, 2012, pp. 36–69.

in particular, has to reset its approach to the region according to this new reality. The expropriation of Repsol by Argentina in 2012 cannot be understood if we do not incorporate into the equation the fact that Spain and Europe carry much less weight nowadays than in the past (and will continue to do so in the future). Latin America looks East more and more. For the West this is also a wake-up call.

7 | Spain and Latin America

We have seen in previous chapters how the multilatinas are leading the way to a new Latin American destiny. Various countries in the region, other than Brazil and Mexico, have started investing abroad, initiating a process of expansion that now includes Europeans as well. Europe is also on the investor radar of these multilatinas, a novelty that prompts us to reconsider the relationships that Spain has traditionally maintained with the continent. As underlined also in Chapter 6, Europe (and the USA) – the West – is no longer the sole player and investor in Latin America: China has been taking an increasing role.

The relationships with Spain in particular need to be revisited in the light of the new realities, both the rise of Latin America and the rise of China, that is, the rebalancing of the world towards emerging markets. For decades, relations between Spain and Latin America have been special. Latin America helped to put Spain politically on the world map, enjoying a liaison with the European Union when Spain joined the EU. In an economic and business sense, Latin America has been crucial in transforming Spanish companies and banks into multinationals, which in fact dominated foreign investment activity in Latin America throughout the decade 2000–10.[1] Business relations between Spain and Latin America have been established since the 1990s by waves of Spanish investors.

However, over the years, the horizons for Spanish companies expanded and they began investing in the United States, Europe and Asia, while not forgetting Latin America. The region has not stopped being attractive for large Spanish companies, as the deals made by Telefónica, Santander and Iberdrola in 2010 show. After a notable number of operations in the 1990s resulting from the processes of liberalisation and privatisation, a new generation of Spanish investors –

---

[1] See the extensive work done by Pablo Toral, *Multinational Enterprises in Latin America since the 1990s*, London and New York, Macmillan, 2011.

manufacturers and suppliers of unregulated services – are now taking centre stage in Spanish operations in Latin America.[2]

Trends are appearing that may represent another great Latin American opportunity for Spain. The (increasing) investor interest for Europe, in particular on the part of other emerging multinationals, could be used to encourage these firms to locate in Spain. The example of China, which we develop here in detail, is symbolic of the potential that could be set in motion. Chinese multinationals are expanding strongly, especially in Latin America and Europe. Spain, because of its presence in Latin America, already appears on the radar – as the association of Chinese multinationals with Repsol, Telefónica and BBVA shows.

Spain could thus become a Latin American hub for the corporate headquarters of foreign multinationals. There are other opportunities as well: Spain could position itself to welcome Latin American technology startups in search of European expansion, and beyond that, contact the diaspora of Latin American executives in positions of influence in multinational technology companies and encourage them to relocate their European headquarters to Spain.

A final option that is probably the most important (and the subject of a subsequent chapter) is that Spain could enhance its role as a bridge to Europe for the multilatinas. In this way, Spain could capitalise on the business relationship established in the past (from the Latin American expansion of Spanish multinationals) and become a European hub for multilatinas in search of international expansion.

Spain and Latin America: a special relationship

Latin America is a trump card that many Spanish companies have used to become multinationals. Business relationships since the 1980s between Spain and Latin America have been close. The first 'multilatinas' were Spanish, a process that Mexicans and Brazilians now emulate from the other side of the Atlantic. This close relationship is even more relevant now with Europe and Spain in crisis; the profit and

---

[2] See the work of Esteban García Canal and Mauro Guillén, 'The Expansion of Spanish Businesses into Latin America: An Analysis', *Journal of Globalization, Competitiveness, Governability, Georgetown University*, 2(2), 2008, pp. 18–45. Available at www.unioviedo.es/egarcia/GCG.articulo_91_1216827229514.pdf.

loss accounts of many multinationals in the 'Ibex 35' (Spanish stock exchange index) have been largely saved by their presence in Latin America.

Spanish companies internationalised quickly in recent decades, with a large Latin American presence.[3] Spain is one of the countries that has made the most progress in the Fortune 500 index, which classifies the largest multinationals; while there were eight Spanish multinationals in 2005 (all linked to Latin America), there were twelve in 2009, double the number of Sweden and equal to the Netherlands. In 2012, the overseas revenue of the 'Ibex 35' companies topped more than 60% for the first time, with Latin America the origin of most of the income (Telefónica, Santander, BBVA, Repsol, Iberdrola and Mapfre, among others). Another way to measure this internationalisation is to examine the attraction of Spanish publicly traded companies for foreign investors. These investors now control more than 40% of their capital, a historic record. Among these investors are several sovereign funds from emerging countries – attracted by this exposure to the Latin American continent.

In October 2010, Qatar Holding, the sovereign fund of Qatar, purchased 5% of Santander Brazil for nearly €2 billion. A few months later, in March 2011, the same fund bet heavily on a publicly traded Spanish company by investing €2 billion in Iberdrola – buying more than 6% of the Spanish multinational. In both cases, the sovereign fund aimed to win exposure to the emerging markets of Latin America, and in particular Brazil, where both Spanish companies have a solid presence. Latin America represents more than 40% of the total revenue of these groups and the region accounts for more income than the peninsula. In other words, while the Arab investment has focused on Spain, the investors have bought into groups whose strategy is based on emerging markets, in particular Latin America.

These deals affirm that many Spanish companies acted wisely by investing in Latin America. These holdings have made Spanish firms

---

[3] For more information on this phenomenon, see the essays of Ramón Casilda, *Multinacionales españolas en un mundo global y multipolar* (*Spanish Multinationals in a Global and Multipolar World*), Madrid, ESIC, 2011; Mauro Guillén and Esteban García Canal, *The New Multinationals: Spanish Firms in a Global Context*, Cambridge University Press, 2010; Mauro Guillén, *The Rise of Spanish Multinationals: European Business in the Global Economy*, Cambridge University Press, 2005.

attractive to Middle Eastern sovereign funds, as in the cases of Santander and Iberdrola; or for Chinese investors, as in the case of Repsol. Latin America has become a trump card. More than ever, the history of many Spanish firms is written with a Latino accent, and now Arab and Chinese as well. More than ever, these companies have become 'euro-emerging multinationals' – multinationals located in OECD countries but with strong ties to emerging countries.

It is difficult to envisage the international projection of Spanish companies without the stepping stone of the Latin American continent. This special relationship is even more relevant today with the global economic crisis, which was triggered in the OECD countries and is now punishing Spain. The world balance is reversed, and the emerging countries are overtaking the developed ones. Business opportunities increasingly exist in the emerging economies and the risks are becoming more relevant. In mid 2011 for example, although the sovereign risk to insure finance for Venezuela or Argentina was greater than that of Greece, the premiums for Brazil, Peru or Chile were less than for Spain, Ireland, Hungary or Iceland.

Moreover, one of the paradoxes of the current global crisis is that Latin America (like Asia) has become the lifejacket of many European – and especially Spanish – companies. Without the Americas (and the international markets) it would be difficult to see how the majority of Ibex 35 firms could ride out the storm, given that the excellent results achieved by many of these firms are largely thanks to contributions from Latin America.[4] The bulk of the profits from Telefónica, BBVA and Santander are now from the Americas. In the case of Telefónica, Latin America is responsible for 62% of the €29 billion earned in 2011. The DNA of the two principal Spanish banks is also very Latino. For Santander, Latin America accounted for 45% of profits in 2011, with Brazil the main source. In the case of its rival BBVA, Mexico represented 30% of returns in 2011, compared to 30% for the Spanish market, 18% for South America, 15% for Eurasia and 5% for the USA. The BBVA does nearly 60% of its business abroad, mainly in

[4] For a detailed analysis of the internationalisation process and adjustments of Spanish multinationals in recent years see ESADE, *La multinacional española ante un nuevo escenario internacional (The Spanish Multinational Faced with a New International Scenario). Second annual report of the Observatorio de la Empresa Multinacional Española (OEME) (Spanish Multinational Business Observatory)*, Barcelona and Madrid, ESADE Business School and ICEX, 2010.

Latin America. Generally speaking, the importance of foreign transactions for Ibex 35 companies has increased with the crisis in Spain and Europe. Some, like Ebro Foods, Acerinox and Gamesa made more than 90% of their 2011 sales abroad. In the case of Santander, this was more than 80%, and for Telefónica foreign sales reached 72%, an amount similar to that of OHL which has a strong presence in Mexico and Brazil.

Paradoxically, investors were previously worried about the 'excessive' exposure of Spanish companies to Latin America, and now these worries have been reversed. Investors worry about Latin American exposure to the risk of European, and particularly Spanish, contagion. Although the numbers seem partially to justify these fears, they still seem somewhat excessive. Between 2008 and 2009, the crisis in Spain was felt on the Latin American continent. Exports to the peninsula plummeted from $6 billion to under $1.2 billion. The impact was limited, however. Spain receives barely 1.6% of its imports from Latin America. This is less than trade with China (7.5% of the total exported in 2009 by the Latin American continent). Europe represents little more than 14% of the total Latin American exports, mainly raw materials. In the financial realm, the role of Spain is more important. The assets of Spanish banks on the continent total more than $380 billion, according to BIS and JP Morgan, in other words more than 50% of the banking credits and loans of European banks and double those of the United States.

Concerns were also raised specifically about an eventual silent death of Iberian foreign direct investment (FDI) towards the continent. It is true that the record volumes were reached in years past (in 2002, the peak year for investment, Spain represented 22% of the total FDI received by Latin America). In the mid-2000s, at the crest of the Spanish investment overseas boom, FDI to Latin America totalled 50% of investments made abroad by Spanish companies. In 2009, Spanish FDI stock in Latin America dropped to 13% of the total; and FDI to Latin America represented only 10% of the total invested abroad by Spanish companies.

This does not mean that interest in the continent has waned. The relative lessening of the importance of Spanish investment is due to the increase in new Asian investors, as well as the investor boom by Latin Americans in their own continent. The appetite of Spanish companies remains intact, as the operations of technology companies and banks on the Latin American continent show. Banco Santander took complete control of its Mexican subsidiary, while Telefónica did the same with Vivo in Brazil. Together, they have invested nearly $10 billion in Mexico and Brazil in the years 2010–12, during the most severe years of the Spanish crisis. Oil company Repsol announced in 2010 that it would continue to work on the continent, with some $5 billion in hydrocarbon exploration projects in Brazil for example, a country where it would also like to emulate the strategy of Santander and take its local subsidiary public. For a group like OHL, more than 85% of its portfolio is in international activity, with Latin America leading the way. Many Spanish groups like BBVA, Santander or OHL started to list their subsidiaries in Mexico or Brazil.

For many companies with more limited Latin American and international investments than those mentioned above, the current crisis in Spain may accelerate their plans for expansion outside the peninsula. This is the case for Indra, which multiplied its contracts in the region during 2010, particularly in Brazil, Peru and Chile. In 2010, Acciona signed the largest loan granted in Latin America for renewable energies ($375 million); Abengoa announced an investment of $180 million to develop the largest co-generation plant in Mexico; while in 2011 Indra announced an acquisition for nearly $150 million in Brazil. Major infrastructure projects being carried out throughout the continent are reasons to look for business in a region that was growing faster than Europe in 2012, according to the latest estimates of the BBVA's research department.

Spain as a Latin American hub for corporate headquarters

Spain could look to capitalise on its presence in Latin America by attracting the Latin American corporate headquarters of multinationals, in particular from emerging countries that want to strengthen their international expansion into Europe and Latin America.

We will use the case of China as an example, doubly interesting for its expansion into Latin America and the growing business relationships with those Spanish multinationals that are strongly established in Latin America. The logic developed here could extend to India, Korea, Singapore or Taiwan. Nevertheless, the global rise of China is exceptional and Spain's connection with Latin America offers the best opportunity of this type for Spain.

For Spain, this arrival of China on the Latin American stage represents challenges and opportunities. The visit to Spain of Li Keqiang in early 2011 stressed the growing importance of China for all the world's economies, including Europe, and Spain in particular. A paradox of history is that the emerging economies such as China's have now become the lifeline for many of the developed economies. Since the global crisis in 2008, all sovereign debt sales go through Beijing. In the case of Spain, the visit reminds us that China already owns nearly 20% of the bonds issued by the Spanish treasury (equivalent to €43 billion).

This visit also invites us to think about the opportunity for Spain to establish a strategic relationship with China, positioning the country as a hub for China to enter Europe and Latin America. This is an idea that I have developed in an ESADE Position Paper published by ESADE's Centre for Global Economy and Geopolitics,[5] and based on a meeting of Club España 2020 (a platform that encourages dialogue between key Spanish executives on the peninsula and those outside the country in many European and American multinationals).

Chinese companies have agreed important deals with Spanish companies during the course of 2010. These represent an opportunity to encourage some of these firms to locate their European corporate headquarters (including Latin American) in Spain. In October 2010, for example, the oil company Sinopec bought into Repsol Brazil, acquiring 40% of the company. A month before, BYD (Build Your Dreams), one of the world leaders in the sector of electric batteries (which will be key for the future electric car industry), signed an agreement with the Basque group Bergé for distribution in Spain. Also in October 2010, the presidents of ENDESA and BYD signed a cooperation agreement. Currently, another important Chinese automobile group, Chery, is looking to expand into Europe and Latin America. In 2010 Chery decided to construct an industrial plant in Brazil and have a project for Europe, possibly in Spain (Catalonia). For their part, the Chinese ICBC has decided to open offices in Spain to compete in retail banking. This is one of the largest Chinese banks, with almost 400,000 employees and market capitalisation that approaches $170 billion. It has 18,000 branches worldwide and a presence in 110 countries. The

---

[5] See www.esade.edu/research-webs/eng/esadegeo/publications/position.

Spanish branch will report for now to the Chinese bank's affiliate in Luxembourg.

All these operations open the door to opportunity for Chinese partners to locate their European (and/or Latin American) headquarters in Spain. To this end, a concerted public–private action between the government and companies could be launched. For now, Chinese multinationals do not have any of their international corporate headquarters in Spain, neither for Europe nor for Latin America. Sinopec, for example, has various affiliates with headquarters in Europe, mainly in London. For now it does not have an integrated headquarters for Europe and/or Latin America. The operation with Repsol YPF presents a unique opportunity for these companies to locate their European headquarters in Madrid, in the same way that Mexican Pemex, another emerging multinational and shareholder in the Spanish company, did in the past (in 2011, Pemex doubled its equity ownership in Repsol to around 10%). Also, because of Repsol's ties with Latin America, Madrid could also be the best choice for the Latin American operational headquarters.

In the case of BYD, the European affiliate is in Rotterdam, but there is probably no reason why it could not be transferred to Spain. In addition to facilitating expansion to Europe from this base, BYD could also use it to expand its operations into Latin America, in such a way that Spanish executives can use their knowledge of the region. The decision to relocate the European headquarters is currently open. For now, Germany is considered a possible location since BYD also made an agreement with Daimler in Stuttgart in 2010. In 2010, BYD selected Los Angeles for its North American headquarters. The Spanish Bergé Group also has many connections with Latin America. Why not locate BYD's European and Latin American headquarters in Spain, making Bilbao and/or Madrid their operational centres?

In addition to BYD, Bergé Automoción is also the Spanish distributor for other Chinese automobiles, Chery and Geely, both in full international expansion. Chery entered the market in Brazil in 2010, becoming the first Chinese automobile group to invest in this country. The company is also studying an investment in Western Europe, possibly in Catalonia. Barcelona welcomed, in June 2011, the first Chinese delegates to the Barcelona Summit, a summit promoted by ESADE and Barcelona's Chamber of Commerce to promote Chinese investment. (In 2012 an ESADE China Europe has been created.) It is easy to imagine that, in addition to an industrial plant, Chery could also install its European headquarters and even its Latin American headquarters in Barcelona.

To these examples we can add others: the Chinese Investment Corporation, a Chinese sovereign fund, is currently looking for a location for its European headquarters; telecommunications suppliers Huawei and ZTE have their European headquarters in London and Paris but have one of their largest global clients (Telefónica) in Spain; Hutchinson has invested $400 million in the port of Barcelona; Citic, the strategic Chinese partner of BBVA, may open offices in Madrid to distribute Chinese funds in Europe and even use this platform for Latin America.

Spain has many trump cards in its hand to reposition itself internationally. The wager on emerging markets is undoubtedly one of these cards. Many Spanish companies have focused on these markets masterfully. This expertise could become a strategic asset and enable Spain to become a central axis for the expansion of emerging multinationals, including the Chinese.

Spain as a European hub for Latin startups

We have seen that the technology dimension is central to the concerns of many Latin American countries. In Chapter 5 we also saw how Multilatinas 2.0 are sprouting up throughout the region. We can glimpse this next wave as an opportunity for Spain.

We can imagine that the European commercial platforms of Latin American startups could be located in Spain. Several of the more dynamic Latin American entrepreneurs live in Spain, like Martin Varsavsky, a creator of several startups. Venezuelan Ana María Llopis also created several companies, among them the startup ideas4all. Mauricio Prieto, a Mexican entrepreneur, is the co-founder of Odigeo, one of the largest European startups with nearly €4 billion of revenues in 2012. Ecuadorian Eduardo Arcos launched Hipertextual, while Hispano-Argentine Gustavo García achieved one of the greatest Internet successes in the country with the sale of BuyVip to Amazon for €70 million. Also, some of the most active venture capitalists in the country are Latin Americans based in Spain, such as Mexican José Marín, founder of IG Expansión, and Alberto Gómez, founder of Adara Venture Partners, a Venezuelan who graduated from MIT and Harvard. Also living in Madrid is Uruguayan Gonzalo Rodríguez, who started several startups, is a business angel, and runs BtoB Factory.

Few Latin American startups, however, have established bases for European expansion in Spain. Of the twenty largest listed (rather arbitrarily) in Table 7.1, none except Dridco has a presence in Spain or manages European expansion from Spain. The case of Dridco is interesting. This Internet startup arrived in Spain in July 2011 with an investment of €2 million. Its international ambition is strong. It projects a total investment in all the countries where it operates of €23 million for this year. In Spain the company invested €2 million in 2011, and €6 million until the end of 2013, to compete in the Spanish market with ZonaJobs.com (search engine and job search portal), ZonaProp.com (online platform for real estate purchase, sale and rental), and DeMotores.com (vehicle sales). Dridco has 320 employees working in offices in Argentina, Chile, Colombia, Mexico and Venezuela. Its sites are also available in Costa Rica, Ecuador, Panama and Peru. In Spain, the company opened its offices in Madrid in July 2011 and had a team of around fifty by the end of December 2011.

From Barcelona, ESADE Business School is looking to attract startups from Latin America and other regions. To show what a business school can do, in 2009 it developed a new campus, Creapolis, as an innovation park housing more than fifty multi-sector companies. Among these is the Brazilian technology company Goods That Talk. Latin American consulting firm Global Business is also based in the park.

Telefónica has launched the Wayra initiative, a project that was deployed in eight Latin American countries and Spain in 2011 with the goal of creating a network of incubators. In one year of life, Wayra became one of the largest incubators on earth, with nearly 10,000 startup Latin American (or Spanish) projects submitted. Campus Party, the largest event that unites digital 'campuseros', has become more Latin American in recent years and multiplied its operations in Latin America. In turn, La Red Innova now gathers the best Spanish and Latin American startups in Madrid, generating an unprecedented location for entrepreneurs and investors from both continents to work together. Under Wayra, which means 'wind' in the Andean Quechua language, entrepreneurs get an average of about $50,000, space and six months of mentoring. Telefónica receives a 10% stake in each business and a preference right to buy a successful product.

Very few of the main Latin American technology companies have a presence in Europe, and of those that do, barely any locate their corporate headquarters in Spain. Although Mexican Softtek has chosen

Table 7.1 *Top twenty Latin startups.*

Startup	Origin	Founder	Year	Website	Global presence	European presence
BuscaPé	Brazil	Romero Rodrigues	1999	buscape.com	16	Yes
PagosOnline	Colombia	Martin Schrimpff	2003	pagosonline.com	6	No
Vostu	Brazil	Joshua Kushner and Mario Schlosser	2007	vostu.com	2	No
Mentez	Brazil	Juan Franco and Jaime Roldán	2006	mentez.com	4	No
Eventioz	Argentina	Pablo Aquistapace		eventioz.com	15	Yes
Restorando	Argentina	Frank Martin and Franco Silvetti	2010	restorando.com	2	No
Smowtion	Argentina	Andrés Alterini, Mariano Elizari and Santiago Pinto	2008	smowtion.com	4	Yes
Junar	Argentina	Javier Pájaro and Diego May	2011	junar.com	3	No
Movile	Brazil	Fabricio Bloisi	2003	movile.com	6	No
DeskMetrics	Brazil	Bernardo Porto	2010	deskmetrics.com	N/A	No
Welcu	Chile	Nico Orellana and Sebastián Gamboa	2007	welcu.com	2	No
Peixe Urbano	Brazil	Alexander Ferraz and Julio Vasconcellos	2010	peixeurbano.com	N/A	No
fnbox	Argentina/USA	Rodrigo Teijeiro	2002	fnbox.com	3	No
Locaweb	Brazil	Gilberto Mautner and Michel Gora	1999	locaweb.com	3	No
Scopix	Chile/USA	Luis Vera and Ariel Schilkrut	2006	scopixsolutions.com	N/A	No
Tiaxa	Chile	Felipe Valdés and Sergio Gutiérrez	2000	tiaxa.com	9	No
Dridco	Argentina	Luis Saguier, Guido Grinbaum, Mariano Nejamkis, Daniel Serra and Gabriel Dantur	2008	dridco.com	11	Yes
Weemba	Argentina	Constancio Larguia, Pablo Larguia and Carlos Maslatón	2008	weemba.com	3	Yes
Clasemovil	Mexico	Alejandro Moctezuma	2009	clasemovil.com	N/A	No
Socialmetrix	Argentina	Martin Enriquez and Juan Manuel Damia	2009	socialmetrix.com	5	No

Source: ESADEgeo, 2012, based on reports and websites.

Spain for its main European office, it is an exception, along with the Mexican Neoris (technology affiliate of Cemex), whose president for Europe, Africa and the Middle East is based in Madrid.

Brazilian TOTVS uses Lisbon as a base for European expansion, while technology company Brightstar, founded by Bolivian Marcelo Claure and headquartered in Miami, uses London as its European headquarters. Globant operates in Europe from London, Stefanini from Brussels, and Bematech, one of the first hardware companies in Brazil to go public (in 2007), uses Berlin as its European base. The group Positivo, which has 3,000 employees, has a European presence in Portugal and London, but not in Spain. Redecard is an affiliate of the Itaú Unibanco bank (which possesses 50%) and provides financial services only in Brazil. B2W Varejo is an Internet portal resulting from the merger of Americanas.com and Submarino. Vivo was acquired by Telefónica in 2010. B2W, affiliate of retailer Lojas Americanas, has 1,500 employees and revenue of more than $2.3 billion and its internationalisation in Argentina and Mexico now points to India, China, Chile, Uruguay and the United States.

Latin America's case is not isolated. There are no large American technology companies or startups with European corporate headquarters in Spain. The majority have chosen London, Dublin, Paris or Luxembourg for their European headquarters. Nevertheless, in the framework of a more general strategy that would include the United States, Taiwan, Korea, Japan and Israel, we might imagine an effort to attract Latin American (and other) technology corporate headquarters to Spain.

The new Latin American argonauts

Spanish and Latin American entrepreneurs located in key posts in US telecommunications companies could be allies in this effort. They are in key decision-making positions and could be facilitators for implanting corporate technology headquarters in Spain. Alex Ceballos, for example, a Dominican responsible for the corporate global strategy of Amazon, directs operations from Seattle; Christian Hernández, a Central American director for international business development for Facebook, is based in London, as is another Latino, Ezequiel Vidra, director of strategic alliances in the EMEA (Europe, Middle East and Africa) region for Google.

The role of the business diaspora has been key in the development of many countries, including the United States. In the 1990s, 25% of technology startup entrepreneurs in Silicon Valley were Asian or of Asian descent. Latin Americans and Hispanics (born in the USA) represent 8% of all entrepreneurs. If we add all the emigrants and natives outside the country, more than 40% of startups from Silicon Valley were launched by members of these entrepreneurial diasporas.[6] California's power of attraction (and retention) is striking. More than 100,000 international students are concentrated in California (with an impact of $3 billion of the nearly $19 billion generated by the United States).[7]

A recent study by the National Venture Capital Association (NAVCA) of the United States shows the importance of foreign entrepreneurs for creating business empires and multinationals in the USA.[8] Since the mid-1990s, foreign entrepreneurs have been responsible for 25% of companies created and supported by venture capital funds. The market capitalisation of companies launched by foreign entrepreneurs now tops $500 billion and the number of employees surpasses 200,000 in the United States and 400,000 in the world. Multinationals the size of Intel, Sun Microsystems, eBay, Yahoo and Google were founded and co-founded by foreigners. Andy Grove, of Hungarian origin, was one of the co-founders of Intel; Indian Vinod Khosla co-founded Sun Microsystems with a German; another Indian, Pradeep Sindhu, created Juniper Networks, the main competitor today of Cisco; Jerry Yang, co-founder of Yahoo!, arrived in the United

---

[6] See Robert Fairlie and Aaron Chatterji, 'High Technology Entrepreneurs in Silicon Valley: Opportunities and Opportunity Costs', University of California, Santa Clara, Department of Economics, October 2010. Available at http://people.ucsc.edu/~rfairlie/papers/; also see Robert Fairlie, *Race and Entrepreneurial Success: Black, Asian, and White-owned Businesses in the United States*, Cambridge, Mass., MIT Press, 2008.

[7] For estimations see John Douglass, Richard Edelstein and Cecile Hoareau, 'A Global Talent Magnet: How a San Francisco/Bay Area Global Higher Education Hub Could Advance California's Comparative Advantage in Attracting International Talent and Further Build US Economic Competitiveness', University of California, Berkeley, Center for Studies in Higher Education, Research and Occasional Paper Series, May 2011. Available at http://cshe.berkeley.edu/publications/docs/ROPS.CalBayAreaHEHub.6.13.2011.pdf.

[8] See NAVCA, *American Made: The Impact of Immigrant Entrepreneurs and Professionals on U.S. Competitiveness*, Arlington, Virginia, NAVCA, 2011. Available at www.nvca.org/index.php?option=com_content&view=article&id=254&Itemid=103.

States as an adolescent; the founders of eBay, France's Pierre Omydiar, and of Google, Russia's Sergey Brin, arrived as children in the United States.

The list goes on. In all cutting-edge sectors (semiconductors, biotechnology, Internet and software) foreign entrepreneurs abound, in particular from India, France, Britain, Iran, and now also China. The Indian diaspora has been the most productive of those analysed by the previously mentioned study (a total of thirty-two firms, or 22%), ahead of Israel (seventeen, or 12%) and Taiwan (sixteen), all ahead of Canada, France, Britain, Germany, Australia, China and Iran. The capacity to attract entrepreneurial talent goes beyond the companies founded by foreigners. Today many of the managing directors of US multinationals are foreign, the deans of the Chicago, Cornell and Harvard Schools of Business are from India, and the president of the largest law firm in the United States, Baker & McKenzie, is Brazilian. Much of this talent comes into the country by way of universities. MIT, Stanford and Harvard are talent pools of foreign entrepreneurs who are looking later to settle in the United States.

For emerging economies the connection with Silicon Valley has also been key for the development of economic clusters. Ties to the Indian, Israeli and Taiwanese diasporas of Silicon Valley have been the main driving force behind technological industries and services taking off in their countries of origin. Mumbai, Tel Aviv and Taipei today have some of the highest concentrations of technology companies on the planet.[9] In all cases, there was an active policy to mobilise this talent, either directly or indirectly.

Today, the accelerated launch of the emerging economies in parallel with the crisis of the 'advanced' countries is causing a return flow towards the emerging countries; this pendular movement is another aspect of the shift in the wealth of nations. In 2009, 108,000 Chinese students doing advanced studies outside the country (mainly in the USA) returned to China, 56% more than the previous year, and in

---

[9] See Anna Lee Saxenian, *The New Argonauts: Regional Advantage in a Global Economy*, Cambridge, Mass.: Harvard University Press, 2006; on China and India see Khanna Trun, *Billions of Entrepreneurs: How China and India Are Reshaping Their Futures and Yours*, Cambridge, Mass.: Harvard Business School Press, 2008; and on the Indian diaspora in technology industries, see Ramana Nanda and Tarun Khanna, 'Diasporas and Domestic Entrepreneurs: Evidence from the Indian Software Industry', Harvard Business School Working Paper 3, 2008. Available at www.hbs.edu/research/pdf/08-003.pdf.

2010 the numbers were even higher, with 135,000 returning. In a study by the Kauffman Foundation, using LinkedIn and a poll, 60% of Indians and 90% of the Chinese polled who returned to their country did so because the economic opportunities were more advantageous.[10] In all, 72% of the Indians and 81% of the Chinese considered that the opportunities to start a business were better in their countries of origin than in the United States. The impact of these 'returnees' on the creation of technology companies and the IT sector in general in their home countries is significant: 56% of those who returned to India worked in technology companies, a figure higher than China's 33%.

Does Latin America possess similar potential to encourage innovation? The large number of Hispanic and Latin American businessmen and executives at the helm of multinationals in the USA and Europe is striking, whether as the directors of multinationals or as creators and developers of startups in various technology sectors. These new argonauts could be mobilised by their respective countries, even creating advisory committees at the highest levels of government. (In Israel, for example, there is an innovation committee directly linked to the prime minister.)

In large technology multinationals, there are many Latin American directors who could form the first circle of councils and advisors. The management committee of Nokia in Finland included Alberto Torres, board member and executive vice president for the key area of technology solutions. In the Franco-American multinational Alcatel Lucent is Argentine Victor Agnellini, one of the senior vice presidents of the company. In Madrid is his compatriot Guillermo Ansaldo, a member of Telefónica's steering committee, and formerly the head of the Spanish market (he will direct, after organisational remodelling, an area called 'global resources'). The Brazilian-born Eduardo Navarro is in charge of the global strategy of Telefónica, also in the top management. Paraguayans Mario Zanotti and Regis Romero preside over operations in Latin America and Africa, respectively, in the telecom multinational Millicom International Cellular, headquartered in Luxembourg.

In the United States, Latin American and Hispanic executives also stand out in leading technology companies. These include Orlando

---

[10] See Kauffman Foundation, *The Grass Is Indeed Greener in India and China for Returnee Entrepreneurs*, Kansas City, Kauffman Foundation, April 2011. Available at www.kauffman.org/uploadedfiles/grass-is-greener-for-returnee-entrepreneurs.pdf.

Ayala, Colombian president of emerging markets for Microsoft, a group that includes compatriot Hernán Rincón and Venezuelan Horacio Gutiérrez, who is at the helm of the legal area and licensing protection; and Mexican Enrique Rodríguez in charge of the television, video and music business. Chilean Marcela Pérez de Alonso is part of the HP technology management team as the director of human resources and member of the company's steering committee. Until 2008, Mexican Héctor Ruiz was the president of AMD, Intel's largest competitor. Notable at Visa is Puerto Rican Antonio Lucio, head of worldwide marketing for the company and member of the executive committee. Many Latinos are also presiding over Latin American divisions, such as Mexican Jaime Vallés for Cisco, a company with another compatriot, Enrique Rodríguez, as senior vice president/general manager in the video technology group.

Hispanics born or raised in the United States are also an executive talent pool. In 2010, Symantec, a large US technology company, was in the hands of Enrique Salem, a US-trained Hispanic engineer who became president of the group. The executive leader of giant AT&T is Cuban American Ralph de la Vega, member of the multinational's steering committee in Dallas. Another high-level executive in this company is Hispanic Thaddeus Arroyo, chief investment officer. In Cisco, Carlos Domínguez is senior vice president in the office of the chairman and CEO and plays a key role in the multinational. In this same firm another Hispanic is in a notable position: Angel Méndez, senior vice president in charge of customer value chain management and member of the multinational's emerging countries council.

This management diaspora is not limited to multinational executives. We can also find many Latinos among technology startup creators or seed capital investors. Argentine Martin Varsavsky, founder of technology companies such as Jazztel and FON, lives in Madrid. Also in Madrid, the ex-president of Costa Rica, José Figueres, is promoting innovation and startups on the continent via La Red Innova, along with Argentinean entrepreneur Pablo Larguia.[11] Mexican José Marín founded a venture capital firm, IG Growth, that intends to support technology startups. The Venezuelan Alberto Gómez has been one of the founding partners of another leading Venture capital fund based in Madrid, Adara, while Ana María Llopis and Alberto Benbunan, also

---

[11] See www.redinnova.com/.

from Venezuela, created ideas4all and Mobile Dreams Factory respectively, startup ventures based in Madrid, and are also active business angels. One of the leading Spanish-speaking bloggers, Eduardo Arcos, from Ecuador, is also based in Madrid. Steven Posner, a Colombian entrepreneur based also in Madrid, founded Vodka Capital, one of its ventures, and is also an active business angel. Other Latin American entrepreneurs are betting on Spain: in 2012 Luis Machado from Venezuela and Hans Christ from Guatemala created Xopso, a retail online store.[12] Of the largest European startups, Odigeo, an online travel agency, that happens to be also the largest one from Spain, with a turnover of nearly 4 billion euros in 2012, was co-founded by two Mexicans, namely Mauricio Prieto and Javier Pérez Tenessa.

In Boston, one of the most active centres for startups in the United States, along with Palo Alto, there are various technology companies, many created by former students of MIT, such as Puerto Rican Javier Segura (CEO of Tap 'n' Tap), and Chilean Sandro Catanzaro (co-founder of DataXu). In Austin, Roy Sosa and his brother are at the head of the technology company incubator MPower Ventures. In New York is Francisco Álvarez Demalde, an Argentine who is founding partner of Riverwood Capital, a venture capital fund specialising in technology companies, headquartered in Menlo Park, California. Some of this firm's investments include outsourcing companies such as Globant, with headquarters in Buenos Aires and a presence throughout the Latin American continent; and Allus, headquartered in Colombia. Initiatives such as Traweln, which brings together entrepreneurs and investors in technology areas to work with companies in Latin America, were also born in Silicon Valley. In Palo Alto is Bling Nation, a pay-by-mobile startup created by Wences Casares, also founder of Meck, a venture capital firm based in Chile and a clear example of the connection between Silicon Valley and Latin America. Also in California is NewScale, a technology company founded by Chilean Rodrigo Flores.

Bolivian Marcelo Claure, CEO of Brightstar, has created the largest Hispanic empire in the United States, based in Miami with revenue of nearly $10 billion in 2012. In 2010, this businessman invested a billion dollars in the creation of the first lithium investment fund

---

[12] See http://technewseurope.com/2012/04/19/xopso-es-the-new-spanish-daily-deal-startup/.

(an essential mineral in technology components, abundant in Argentina, Chile and particularly Bolivia) and which is traded on the New York Stock Exchange as Global X Lithium.

Also in Miami is the Internet company Weemba, founded by Constancio Larguía, the man who created the Patagon site during the Internet boom, along with Wenceslao Casares. It was recently sold for $550 million to Banco Santander. In this same city are the main headquarters of Neoris, a global business consulting and IT company, founded and developed by Latin Americans (the current director is Claudio Muruzábal). This is a sector in which the Assa group, based in Buenos Aires and managed by another Argentine, Roberto Wagmaister, also stands out.

These argonauts do not only come from Europe and the USA. Uruguayan Pablo Brenner co-founded in Israel a company that would eventually be traded on the NASDAQ. He is currently partner of a Uruguayan venture capital fund, Prospéritas Capital Partners, which specialises in technology companies, and is chairman of Taho (supplier for Acceso Inalámbrico in Brazil). There is also the Bolivian and now German citizen Guillermo Wille, who is director in Bangalore, India, of the GE John F. Welch Technological Centre, one of the major innovation and development centres for multinational General Electric.[13]

Latinos are also participating in global venture capital companies such as Intel Capital, an affiliate of the giant Intel dedicated to seed capital. Brazilian Ricardo Arantes is one of its directors, based in São Paulo, and managing investments mainly in Brazil (in Brazilian companies like Digitron, Neovia, Yavox, Atomatos and Certidesign) but also others in the region such as Chilean Sonda. Another director is Marcos Battisti, also Brazilian, who manages Western Europe and Israel from London. There are also companies that connect Silicon Valley and Latin America (like LatinValley). Many of the VC companies in Brazil, for example, were created by Brazilians many of whom were trained at MIT, who had returned from the United States to their home country, like the founders of Ideasnet.

With networks of connections that are being created in Palo Alto, Boston, New York and Madrid, and in the Latin American region itself (Palermo Valley in Buenos Aires, Lima Valley, Tequila Valley in Mexico City and Tech Valley in Brazil), companies that are linked to

---

[13] See http://ge.geglobalresearch.com/locations/bangalore-india/.

the Internet, new technologies, outsourcing, social networking, etc. are being structured throughout the region. La Red Innova is looking to connect Europe and Latin America in the area of technology startups. Recently, some national governments and institutions in the region have wanted to systematise these networks. At the request of several governments, the World Bank's KD4 Program provided advisory support to develop pilot initiatives in Chile, Mexico and Argentina. In Chile, the Fundación Chile, along with other institutions and the Chilean government, launched Chile Global, an initiative inspired by GlobalScots, which is looking to connect the Chilean executive diaspora and investments in technology sectors. In Mexico, CONA-CYT (National Commission on Science and Technology) is leading the development of Mexico's talent network abroad.

In their work on the importance of networks and the spread of venture capital, Isin Guler and Mauro Guillén propose that professional contact networks are important in explaining the spread of venture capital outside the United States. They show that in the decade of the 1990s the international expansion of investors in startups was focused mainly in Britain and Canada, two countries with strong connections to the USA. It then stretched to Israel, where the Israeli diaspora played an important role, as did the Indian and Chinese diasporas, two of the other emerging countries included in the top ten destinations for American venture capital.[14]

These diasporas could play a role in making Spain a hub for corporate headquarters for Europe, the Middle East and Africa. They could also consolidate Spain as a Latin American technology base; and the region's startups and technology companies could locate their European expansion bases in Madrid, Barcelona, or other cities on the peninsula. Nevertheless, beyond the possibilities explored here with startups, the trump card that Spain can play is to encourage the location on the peninsula of corporate headquarters for multilatinas looking to explore new investment opportunities in Europe, Africa and the Middle East. This is the issue that we will explore in the following chapter. As we have insisted already in previous chapters, the rise of

[14] See Isin Guler and Mauro Guillén, 'Home Country Network and Foreign Expansion: Evidence from the Venture Capital Industry', *Academy of Management Journal*, 53(2), 2010, pp. 390–410; Isin Guler and Mauro Guillén, 'Institutions and the Internationalization of US Venture Capital Firms', *Academy of International Business*, 41, 2010, pp. 185–205.

Latin America invites the resetting of relations with the continent and this is specially true for Spain.

Spain could take advantage of some emerging trends: startups of Latin American and technological companies of the continent will look to new markets (Europe is one and Spain could be an entry point); Chinese multinationals have been building special ties with some Spanish ones (Sinopec with Repsol, Huawei or China Unicom with Telefónica, etc.) and this could open the opportunity for locating European and Latin American headquarters of Chinese firms in Spain. Last but not least, and probably the most important and promising avenue, is that multilatinas themselves are expanding in Europe, the Middle East and Africa and this represents also an opportunity for Spain.

8 | *Spain as a Latin hub*

Latin multinationals have been focusing their attention on foreign markets, first on the Latin American continent and later beyond. The United States, Europe and Spain now appear to be the objectives.

Grupo Bimbo, the largest bread manufacturer in Latin America (with 102,000 employees and sales in 2010 of $9.5 billion), acquired American conglomerate Sara Lee Corporation, the leading American bread manufacturer, for nearly a billion dollars in 2010. Since 2002, this Mexican multinational has increased its acquisitions, buying a total of six companies in the United States, China, Brazil and Mexico. Previously, Bimbo was the world leader with 3% of global sales, 11% in the United States and 14% in Mexico. With the acquisition of Sara Lee, its market share jumped to 17% of American sales and 4% of global sales. In mid 2011 it also made a bid for Bimbo in Spain, showing once again its thirst for international expansion. In 2012, another Mexican multinational, América Móvil, offered $3.4 billion to raise its stake to 28% in KPN, the former Dutch telephone monopoly.

These examples illustrate what we have seen in previous chapters: the emergence of Latin America as a global investor. Brazil is leading this boom. In 2011, the thirty principal Brazilian multilatinas held nearly $90 billion in assets abroad and employed almost 200 million people in other countries. The total stock of Brazilian multinationals in foreign direct investments was around $160 billion at the end of 2010, making Brazil the seventh largest investor abroad among emerging economies.

However, this boom now involves much more than the multinationals of the region's two main economies, Mexico and Brazil. Multinationals from Argentina and now also Chile, Peru and Colombia have become involved in this Latin expansion. Peruvian soap and detergent producer Romero is now in seven neighbouring countries. Colombian Grupo Nacional de Chocolates has more than 28,000 employees in different countries. Chilean wine producer Concha y Toro recently bought an American brand. Chilean Sigdo Koppers (SK) announced the purchase of Belgian industrial group Magotteaux in August 2011 in a transaction estimated at $680 million. Argentine Tenaris, an iron and steel manufacturer with 24,000 employees in a dozen countries, has been even more radical, locating its worldwide headquarters in Europe, specifically in Luxembourg.

More proof of this multilatina vitality is the purchase in mid 2011 by Colombian Suramericana of the Dutch ING Latin American pension funds; Suramericana won out over Metlife, Prudential, Chilean Saieh and Grupo Bolívar. Suramericana has become one of the main Colombian multilatinas, thanks to a transaction that is one of the largest made by a Colombian company – the purchase of BAC Credomatic for $1.9 billion (which includes one of Colombia's principal banks, the Banco de Bogotá, and the pension fund Porvenir).

This new reality invites reflection on restructuring relations between Spain and Latin America while reconsidering the business connections between them. The decades of unilateral relations, in which Spain was an investor in the region, have ended, leaving room for more balanced relations and potential in Europe to capitalise on Latin America's investment boom abroad.

The multilatinas: a great opportunity for Spain

This trend could represent a unique opportunity for Spain to be on the receiving end, rather than the providing end, of Latin American capital and welcome Latin American corporate headquarters in Europe.

In terms of investment, Spain is tentatively on the Latin American radar. Nevertheless, the potential for the continent's business investors to take a major role is great. In 2010, capital flows out of Latin America and the Caribbean increased nearly 70%, reaching $76 billion (compared with $112 billion of direct investments received in the region). Of this, $43 billion was foreign direct investment, an increase of 56% over the previous year (this exceeds Spanish FDI, which was €26 billion).

Latin America is now a major issuer of capital, totalling 17% of direct investments made by emerging markets in 2010 compared to a meagre 6% in 2000. Brazil continues to be an important issuer; but in 2010, Mexico, Colombia and Chile had record foreign direct investments according to ECLAC data.[1] The bulk of transactions

[1] See www.eclac.cl/publicaciones/xml/9/43289/2011-322-LIE-2010-WEB_ULTIMO.pdf.

Table 8.1 *Principal trans-border acquisitions made by multilatinas, 2010 (in $ million).*

Acquired company	Country	Sector	Acquiring company	Country	Value
BSG Resources Guinea Ltd	Britain	Mining	Vale SA	Brazil	2,500
BAC Credomatic GECF Inc.	Panama	Financial services	Grupo Aval Acciones y Valores	Colombia	1,920
Gerdau Ameristeel Corp	Canada	Manufacturing	Gerdau	Brazil	1,607
Cimpor Cimentos de Portugal	Portugal	Manufacturing	Camargo Corrêa Portugal SGPS	Brazil	1,894
Keystone Foods LLC	United States	Agro-industrial	Marfrig Alimentos SA	Brazil	1,260
Univision Communications Inc.	United States	Audiovisual services	Televisa México	United States	1,200
Cimpor Cimentos de Portugal	Portugal	Manufacturing	Votorantim	Brazil	1,192
DECA II	Guatemala	Energy/services	Empresa Pública de Medellín	Colombia	605
Farmacias Ahumada SA	Chile	Trade	Grupo Casa Saba SAB	Mexico	604
Bar-S Foods Co.	United States	Agro-industrial	Sigma Alimentos SA	Mexico	575
PetroRig III Pte Ltd-PetroRig	Norway	Services	Grupo R SA de CV	Mexico	540
Cintra Concesionaria de	Chile	Services	Interconexión Eléctrica SA (ISA)	Colombia	499
Infraestructura de Transporte					
Cia Minera Milpo SAA	Peru	Mining	Votorantim Metais Ltd.	Brazil	419
Sunoco Chemicals Inc.	United States	Manufacturing	Braskem SA	Brazil	350
Pasadena Refining System Inc.	United States	Manufacturing	Petrobras	Brazil	350
Ecuador	Ecuador	Soft drinks	Embotelladoras Arca SAB	Mexico	345
Devon Energy Corp.-Cascade	United States	Oil/gas	Petrobras	Brazil	180
IBI México	Mexico	Financial services	Banco Bradesco SA	Brazil	164
Dana Hldg-	United States	Manufacturing	Metalsa SA	Mexico	150
417 Fifth Avenue, New York, NY	United States	Real estate services	Inmobiliaria Carso SA	Mexico	140

Source: ECLAC, 2011.

(nearly 50%) now take place within the region, or in other words, direct investments by Latin American countries are still concentrated in the region.

However, we are also seeing operations in other regions. Eight of the eleven main FDI transactions made in 2010 were in North America and Europe. Or, in other words, although the first stage of the internationalisation of the multilatinas was concentrated in Latin America, we are witnessing the emergence of a second stage that spans other geographies, including OECD countries such as the United States and Canada, or Europe, with Portugal, Britain, Norway and Spain receiving the bulk of attention. Direct investments only account for part of the story, and trade flows are also important. Europe, and Spain in particular, continue to be important partners, perhaps not so much for Mexico but for the Southern Cone (Table 8.1).

Spain as a European hub for multilatina corporate headquarters

Latin American investment in Spain is scarce at the moment. Nevertheless, several multilatinas have located their European corporate headquarters in Spain. In other words, receiving Latin American FDI is not the only way to strengthen business relations with the region. Another approach for Spain would be to position itself as a location for European corporate headquarters of multilatinas.

This is already the case, in particular for some Mexican multilatinas. Cemex and Pemex have located their corporate headquarters in Madrid. Grupo Modelo (owner of Corona beer) is in Guadalajara, from where operations are run for Europe, Africa and the Middle East. Brazilian companies Alpargatas (owner of the Hawaianas brand) and Gerdau also have their European headquarters in Spain (in Madrid and Bilbao respectively). Argentine Arcor is located in Barcelona, as is Chilean shipping company Sudamericana de Vapores, while Chilean LAN is headquartered in Madrid. The Corporación Andina de Fomento (CAF), an international financial organisation created by the Latin American states, has opened its European office in Madrid.

Spain is therefore already a (budding) Latin hub that could grow further. Brazilian banks (Bradesco, Itaú Unibanco, Banco do Brasil, BTG Pactual) are internationalising. Spain could be the location for a European parent company. The same goes for Mexican Banorte, Colombian Bancolombia and Venezuelan Mercantil. The Chilean or Brazilian sovereign funds may consider opening European offices in Spain, as could those funds recently created by Colombia and Panama. Spain could be the gateway to Europe for many of the multilatinas that are not in Europe, or whose corporate headquarters are outside Spain.

How many companies are we talking about? What does the current map of multilatina European headquarters look like? We have analysed these points in detail, based on new research and a new database.

A map of multilatina European headquarters

Most multilatinas operate from European cities outside Spain. They have chosen these cities despite the cultural similarity that the peninsula offers; and despite the scarcity of air connections and limited number of business and economic links found outside Spain. We have a long way to go to bring them to Spain.

The Brazilian development bank BNDES selected London for its European office, as did Petrobras. Chilean Antofagasta, an affiliate of mining group Luksic, also has its global corporate headquarters in London. Others such as Argentine group Tenaris relocated their global corporate headquarters to Luxembourg, while Brazilian construction company Odebrecht decided to operate in Europe, the Middle East and Africa from Lisbon.

To document the potential of a systematic relocation strategy for multilatina European corporate headquarters, we carried out a systematic analysis of the largest and most international multilatinas, identifying the location of each of their European headquarters. The principal result of this research, original and unprecedented, is that we found that most multilatinas have their European corporate headquarters outside Spain, although many are in Spain, confirming the potential of Spain for this group.

In total we analysed 147 multilatinas and the largest firms appeared on various databases and rankings (in particular América Economía and the Vale Centre of the University of Columbia in New York). For each multilatina, we have identified its international and European offices. Table 8.2 below presents a total sample, and identifies the European city and country where the corporate headquarters are located. The majority of the companies are Brazilian (sixty), followed

Table 8.2 *Multilatinas with European headquarters, 2011.*

#	Origin	Multilatina	European headquarters	Country	European activity	Sector
1	Brazil	Votorantim Cimentos	Hamburg	Germany	Yes	Cement
2	Brazil	Sabó Ind. y Com. De Autopeças	Heilbronn	Germany	Yes	Auto parts
3	Brazil	Weg	Nivelles	Belgium	Yes	Machinery
4	Brazil	Metalfrio	Aalestrup	Denmark	Yes	Household appliances
5	Brazil	Marcopolo	Suez	Egypt	Yes	Auto parts
6	Brazil	Gerdau	Bilbao	Spain	Yes	Steel
7	Brazil	Embraer	Paris	France	Yes	Aerospace
8	Brazil	Natura	Paris	France	Yes	Cosmetics
9	Brazil	Petrobras	London	Britain	Yes	Petroleum
10	Brazil	TAM			Yes	Airlines
11	Brazil	Duas Rodas	N/A		No	Food products
12	Brazil	Lupatech	N/A		No	Engineering
13	Brazil	Grupo JBS (Friboi)	London	Britain	Yes	Food products
14	Brazil	Itaú – Unibanco	Lisbon	Portugal	Yes	Banking
15	Brazil	Construtora Norberto Odebrecht	Lisbon	Portugal	Yes	Engineering
16	Brazil	Camargo Côrrea Cimentos	Lisbon	Portugal	Yes	Cement
17	Brazil	Grupo Camargo Côrrea	Lisbon	Portugal	Yes	Construction/engineering
18	Brazil	Tigre (Tubos De Conexión)	N/A		Yes	Construction materials
19	Brazil	Artecola	N/A		No	Chemicals

(*cont.*)

Table 8.2 (cont.)

#	Origin	Multilatina	European headquarters	Country	European activity	Sector
20	Brazil	Andrade Gutierrez	Porto Salvo	Portugal	Yes	Construction/engineering
21	Brazil	Cia. Siderurgica Nacional	Paio Pires	Portugal	Yes	Steel
22	Brazil	Vale	London	Britain	Yes	Mining
23	Brazil	Marfrig	Northampton	Britain	Yes	Food products
24	Brazil	Sadia	Worcester	Britain	Yes	Food products
25	Brazil	Aracruz Celulose	Nyon	Switzerland	Yes	Cellulose
26	Brazil	Bematech	Berlin	Germany	Yes	Technology
27	Brazil	Randon	Gelsenkirchen	Germany	Yes	Professional automobiles
28	Brazil	Stefanini	Brussels	Belgium	Yes	Technology
29	Brazil	Ultrapar	Brussels	Belgium	Yes	Holdings
30	Brazil	Spoleto	Madrid	Spain	Yes	Food – franchises
31	Brazil	Marisol	Madrid	Spain	Yes	Textiles
32	Brazil	TOTVS	Braga	Portugal	Yes	Technology
33	Brazil	América Latina Logística	N/A		No	Construction/engineering
34	Brazil	Alusa			No	Engineering and Telecommunications
35	Brazil	DHB	N/A			Auto parts
36	Brazil	Escolas Fisk	N/A		No	Education – languages
37	Brazil	Ci&T	London	Britain	Yes	Technology
38	Brazil	Politec	N/A		No	Technology

			City	Country		Industry
39	Brazil	Localiza	N/A		No	Vehicle rental
40	Brazil	Cia Providencia				Textiles
41	Brazil	Brasil Foods	Budapest; Milton Keynes	Hungary & Britain	Yes	Food products
42	Brazil	Suzano Papel e Celulose	Signy	Switzerland	Yes	Cellulose and paper
43	Brazil	Cemig	N/A		No	Electricity
44	Brazil	Eletrobrás	N/A		No	Electricity
45	Brazil	Magnesita	Hilden	Germany	Yes	Mining
46	Brazil	Minerva				Food products
47	Brazil	Telemar (Oi)	Lisbon	Portugal	Yes	Telephony
48	Brazil	Coteminas	N/A		No	Textiles
49	Brazil	Itautec	Madrid	Spain	Yes	Technology
50	Brazil	Tupy		Germany	Yes	Auto parts
51	Brazil	Duratex	Sint-Martens-Latem	Belgium	Yes	Wood
52	Brazil	Iochpe	N/A	Belgium	Yes	Auto parts
53	Brazil	Klabin			Yes	Paper
54	Brazil	Alpargatas	Madrid	Spain	Yes	Footwear
55	Brazil	Banco do Brasil	Vienna	Austria	Yes	Banking
56	Brazil	BNDES	London	Britain	Yes	Banking
57	Brazil	Bradesco	Luxembourg	Luxembourg	Yes	Banking
58	Brazil	ABInBev	Leuven	Belgium	Yes	Soft drinks
59	Brazil	Braskem	Rotterdam	Netherlands	Yes	Petrochemicals
60	Brazil	Usiminas	Copenhagen	Denmark	Yes	Mining
61	Colombia	Grupo Argos	N/A		No	Cement

(cont.)

Table 8.2 (cont.)

#	Origin	Multilatina	European headquarters	Country	European activity	Sector
62	Colombia	Nutresa (previously Nacional de Chocolates)	N/A		No	Food products
63	Colombia	Carvajal	Madrid	Spain	Yes	Editorial
64	Colombia	Colombina			No	Food products
65	Colombia	ISA	N/A		No	Electrical distribution
66	Colombia	Terpel	N/A		No	Petroleum distribution
67	Colombia	Ecopetrol	N/A		No	Petroleum
68	Colombia	Empresas Públicas de Medellín	N/A		No	Electrical distribution
69	Colombia	Grupo Mundial	N/A		No	Construction
70	Mexico	Cinépolis	N/A		No	Entertainment
71	Mexico	Grupo Casa Saba (Fasa)	N/A		No	Retail trade
72	Mexico	América Móvil	N/A		No	Telecommunications
73	Mexico	Cemex	Madrid	Spain	Yes	Cement
74	Mexico	FEMSA	Madrid	Spain	Yes	Soft drinks
75	Mexico	Telmex	N/A		No	Telecommunications
76	Mexico	Grupo Alfa	Madrid	Spain	Yes	Auto parts/petrochemicals
77	Mexico	Grupo Bimbo	Madrid	Spain	No	Food products
78	Mexico	Grupo Modelo	Guadalajara	Spain	Yes	Soft drinks
79	Mexico	Grupo Televisa		Spain	Yes	Media
80	Mexico	Gruma	London	Britain	Yes	Food products

81	Mexico	Grupo Elektra			No	Retail trade
82	Mexico	Mexichem			No	Petrochemicals
83	Mexico	Vitro	León	Spain	Yes	Glass
84	Mexico	P.I. Mabe	Toledo	Spain	Yes	Diapers
85	Mexico	Pemex	Madrid	Spain	Yes	Petroleum
86	Mexico	Grupo México			No	Mining
87	Mexico	Industrias Ch			No	Steel
88	Mexico	Cementos de Chihuahua			No	Cement
89	Mexico	Xignux				Holdings
90	Mexico	Corporación Durango				Paper
91	Mexico	Interceramic				Non-metallic minerals
92	Mexico	San Luis Corp.	Stuttgart	Germany	No	Auto parts
93	Mexico	Accel			Yes	Food products
94	Mexico	Grupo Carso			No	Holdings
95	Mexico	Grupo Kuo			No	Holdings
96	Mexico	AHMSA			No	Steel
97	Mexico	Aeroméxico	Madrid	Spain	Yes	Airlines
98	Mexico	Top Radio	Madrid	Spain	Yes	Entertainment
99	Mexico	Laboratorios Silanes	Madrid	Spain	Yes	Research
100	Mexico	Softtek	Coruña	Spain	Yes	Technology
101	Mexico	Omnilife	Madrid	Spain	Yes	Health, well-being
102	Argentina	Impsa (Pescarmona)	N/A		Yes	Food products
103	Argentina	Tenaris	Dalmine	Italy	Yes	Steel
104	Argentina	Arcor	Barcelona	Spain	Yes	Food products
105	Argentina	Laboratorios Bagó	Moscow	Russia	Yes	Research

(*cont.*)

Table 8.2 (cont.)

#	Origin	Multilatina	European headquarters	Country	European activity	Sector
106	Argentina	Techint	Bergamo	Italy	Yes	Holdings
107	Argentina	Molinos Río de la Plata	Fara San Martino	Italy	Yes	Food products
108	Argentina	Grupo Los Grobo	N/A		No	Agro-industrial
109	Argentina	Cresud	N/A		No	Agro-industrial
110	Argentina	Roemmers	N/A		No	Research
111	Argentina	Tecna	Madrid	Spain	Yes	Engineering
112	Argentina	Iecsa (Grupoods)	N/A		No	Construction
113	Argentina	Citrícola San Miguel			Yes	Agro-industrial
114	Argentina	BGH	N/A		No	Technology
115	Argentina	CLISA	N/A		No	Holdings
116	Argentina	Petroq. Río Tercero	N/A		No	Mining/petroleum
117	Argentina	Grupo Assa	N/A		Yes	Agro-industrial
118	Argentina	Grupo Plastar	N/A		No	Petrochemicals
119	Argentina	Sancor Coop.	N/A		No	Food products
120	Argentina	Havanna	Barcelona	Spain	Yes	Food products
121	Argentina	Bio Sidus	N/A		No	Technology
122	Chile	Enap	N/A		No	Petroleum and gas
123	Chile	Cencosud	N/A		No	Retail sales
124	Chile	Falabella	N/A		No	Retail sales
125	Chile	Sudamericana de Vapores	Barcelona	Spain	Yes	Shipping
126	Chile	LAN (now LATAM)	Madrid	Spain	Yes	Airlines

127	Chile	Arauco	Leiden	Holland	Yes	Forestry/cellulose
128	Chile	Antofagasta PLC	London	Britain	Yes	Mining
129	Chile	D&S	N/A		No	Retail sales
130	Chile	CMPC	London	Britain	Yes	Forestry
131	Chile	CGE	N/A		No	Electricity and gas
132	Chile	Molymet	Guildford	Britain	Yes	Mining
133	Chile	SQM	Antwerp	Belgium	Yes	Industrial
134	Chile	Ripley	N/A		No	Retail sales
135	Chile	Farmacias Ahumada	N/A		No	Retail sales
136	Chile	Embotelladora Andina	N/A		No	Food and beverages
137	Chile	CCU	N/A		No	Food and beverages
138	Chile	Madeco	N/A		No	Forestry
139	Chile	Masisa	N/A		No	Industrial
140	Chile	Salfacorp	N/A		No	Industrial
141	Chile	Interoceánica (CCNI)	Madrid	Spain	Yes	Shipping
142	Chile	Viña Concha y Toro	Wheatley	Britain	Yes	Beverages
143	Chile	Sonda	N/A		No	Technology
144	Chile	SQM	Antwerp	Belgium	Yes	Mining
145	Peru	Ajegroup	Madrid	Spain	Yes	Food products
146	Peru	Yanbal	Madrid	Spain	Yes	Cosmetics
147	Peru	Gloria	N/A		No	Holdings

Source: ESADEgeo, 2012; based on websites, corporate reports, América Economía, and Vale Center Columbia University.

by Mexican (thirty-two), and then Chilean (twenty-three), Argentinean (twenty-nine), Colombian (nine) and finally Peruvian (three) (Table 8.2).

Of the 147 multilatinas selected (the continent's largest as identified by cross-referencing the databases of América Economía and Vale Centre of the University of Columbia) not all have European headquarters.

We have identified a total of seventy-seven with corporate headquarters in Europe, or almost half of the largest multilatinas (52% of the total). Some are purely commercial headquarters, while others manage operations not only in Europe, but also in the Middle East.

In some cases (Antofagasta, ABInBev, Tenaris) the headquarters are not only regional but global, or in other words some have their parent companies in Europe. None, however, is located in Spain. Britain is the most popular location, followed by Belgium, and then Luxembourg.

An analysis by country of multilatinas with a European presence shows us a clear winner, Brazil, and three runners-up: Mexico, Chile and Argentina. In addition to being the most numerous, Brazilian multinationals are the most likely to have a European headquarters. Whether as an effect of the size of the companies or because of an international focus, 72% of the Brazilian multinationals analysed have a presence in Europe; of these, forty-two companies have their EMEA (Europe, Middle East and Africa) headquarters in Europe. This percentage decreases in the case of the runners-up (at around 40%) and increases again with a scale effect in Peru (which only has three companies with EMEA headquarters) (Figure 8.1).

If we exclude Mexico (to avoid slanting the sample towards Spain, since we are only able to list headquarters based in Spain for this country), the most popular location for corporate headquarters is Britain (thirteen), ahead of Spain (twelve), Portugal and Belgium (eight each), and Germany (seven). Many of the multilatina headquarters are in small towns and cities – such as Signy in Switzerland, Hilden in Germany, Guildford and Wheatley in Britain, Dalmine and Fara San Martino in Italy. In other words, the location of the headquarters does not always correspond to international connections or regional or national centrality. This is also corroborated in the case of Spain with Gerdau (Bilbao), Softtek (Coruña), Toledo (Mabe) and Modelo (Guadalajara) (Figure 8.2).

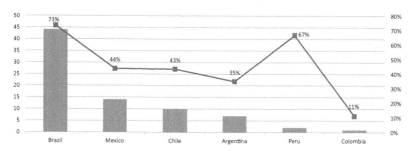

Figure 8.1 Multilatinas with a presence in Europe and EMEA headquarters. *Source:* ESADEgeo, 2012. Multilatinas by country of origin with EMEA headquarters in Europe (left axis) and percentage of multilatinas with presence in Europe, by country (right axis).

The classification of headquarters by country confirms the relative attractiveness of Spain, since one-third of multilatinas have their European corporate headquarters in the country (even when Mexico is not included in the sample the number is significant). Nevertheless, research also shows the potential: fifty-two European corporate headquarters of these multilatinas are not in Spain.

If we look at the potential of each country in detail, the case of the Brazilian multilatinas is particularly striking: Embraer and Natura are in Paris; Votorantim, Bematech and Sabó in various German cities; Metalfrío and Usiminas in Denmark; Petrobras, JBS Friboi, Vale, Marfrig, Brasil Foods and Bematech in Britain; Stefanini, InBev, Ultrapar and Randon in Belgium; Aracruz and Suzano in Switzerland; Braskem in the Netherlands, etc. Only Itaútec, Alpargatas, Marisol, Gerdau and Spoleto are in Spain. In other words only five of the forty-three European headquarters (as mentioned above, only forty-three of the sixty Brazilian multilatinas in the sample have operational European headquarters).

Portugal, with eight, has the highest number of European corporate headquarters belonging to Brazilian multilatinas. This may seem logical given the cultural and linguistic similarity; however, this number equals that of Britain, a country that has more European corporate headquarters belonging to Brazilian multilatinas than Spain. The number in Spain is comparable to Germany, which also has five corporate headquarters, and fewer than Belgium. In Portugal's case, historic,

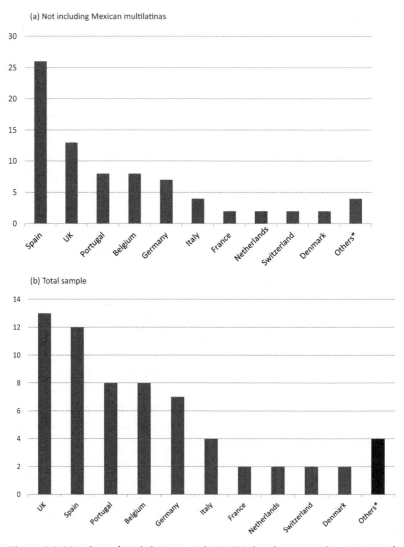

Figure 8.2 Number of multilatinas with EMEA headquarters, by country of origin. (a) Not including Mexican multilatinas. (b) Total sample.
Source: ESADEgeo, 2012, based on websites, corporate reports, América Economía and Vale Center Columbia University, 2012.

cultural and business connections explain the reason for the location of the headquarters; however in Germany's case, it has more to do with the industrial connection since Brazil is one of German industry's largest overseas centres for production. In Belgium's case, the explanation has more to do with the presence of European institutions, particularly in the Belgian capital, even though many multilatinas located in this country are not in Brussels, but in other cities such as Nivelles for WEG, Sint-Martens-Latem (near Ghent) for Duratex, and Louvain for ABInBev.

An analysis of revenue also reveals that the offices located in Spain have smaller parent companies than those located in Britain. Gerdau (whose European corporate headquarters is in Spain) had sales in 2010 of nearly $19 billion, far behind Petrobras and Vale (both headquartered in Britain) with $128 and $50 billion respectively in sales for 2010. In qualitative terms (the power of the parent companies supporting them), Britain is probably the European country with the highest concentration of large Brazilian multilatinas. Agro-industrial giants Brasil Foods, JBS Friboi and Marfrig operate from Britain.

If we focus on Chilean multilatinas, the results indicate more of the same. Although some have their corporate headquarters in Spain, the majority are outside the country. Of a total of twenty-three Chilean multilatinas included in the sample, only ten have a European headquarters we can identify. Of these, only three are in Spain, one in Barcelona (shipping company Sudamericana de Vapores) and the other two in Madrid (shipping company Interoceánica and LAN Chile airlines). The rest of the Chilean multilatinas have their European headquarters in Britain (four), Belgium (three) and Holland (one). Chilean multilatina Antofagasta deserves mention for locating its worldwide headquarters in London.

Argentina has twenty multilatinas in the sample, seven of them with European corporate headquarters. Arcor and Havanna selected Barcelona, but all the others are located in European cities other than Spain. Argentina's case is interesting because a few groups such as Techint have opted to move their worldwide corporate headquarters to Europe. Specifically, Tenaris and Ternium now have their worldwide headquarters in Luxembourg. We could envisage these HQs being relocated to Spain, meaning that not only the European corporate headquarters would move, but also the worldwide headquarters, with more employees and resources.

Potential for consolidation

Three observations stand out from this analysis: the first is that Spain has had some success in attracting multilatina European corporate headquarters, in particular in the case of Mexico. The second observation is that there is great potential to attract others to (re)locate their European and even worldwide corporate headquarters to Spain. This is the case of the Brazilians in particular, who have the most multilatinas, but who have almost no European corporate headquarters in Spain. Chile and Argentina also deserve more attention, in particular for having three worldwide headquarters in Europe (Antofagasta, Tenaris and Ternium). The third observation is that the largest multilatinas on the continent chose to locate their headquarters in countries like Britain, which do not share cultural connections in the same way as Portugal and Spain.

The most important conclusion is probably relative to Brazil – a nation with many global companies. According to the Vale Center at the University of Columbia, the thirty major public Brazilian companies have nearly $90 billion in assets abroad and nearly 180,000 employees outside Brazil. The bulk of those assets outside the country nevertheless continue to be concentrated in just a few companies: Vale, Petrobras and Gerdau control nearly 75% of the assets of Brazilian companies abroad. In terms of sales and employees, agro-industrial JBS Friboi has $17 billion in sales abroad and employs 80,000 people outside Brazil (45% of the people employed abroad work for the thirty largest Brazilian multilatinas).

In other words, the level of Brazilian internationalisation, although it has been important, still has room to grow. It is very probable that the future will see even more international activity from these multilatinas. In short, only nine of these thirty major Brazilian multilatinas have assets abroad worth more than a billion dollars. Many began in Europe with important acquisitions, as in the case of Gerdau in Spain (in 2005 it bought 40% of Sidenor for €450 million and in 2008 another 20% for €206 million) and Magnesita in Germany (where it bought LWB Refractories for nearly a billion dollars). Now 20% plan to grow abroad in the future through acquisitions. To this group we can add those that plan to internationalise by establishing their own production bases (33%), or those that are planning to export with support from offices abroad (29%).[2]

There are various Brazilian multilatinas that have developed an important Spanish presence and so Spain may represent a sensible location for these firms to locate their European corporate headquarters. Several are on the peninsula through the acquisition of Spanish companies, or through participation in Portuguese groups. One of the most active is the multi-sector group Camargo Correa, which invoices some $10 billion with activities ranging from fashion to construction, including cement, concessions, electricity, shipyards, crude oil and steel production. The company arrived in Spain in 2006 with affiliate Santista's purchase of Tavex, a textile company that trades on the stock market and has production plants in Spain, Morocco and Latin America. In 2010 Camargo Correa also acquired 33% of Portuguese cement producer Cimpor, which produces in Brazil, Egypt, China, India, Turkey, Peru and South Africa, and is already one of the largest cement producers in Spain.

Brazilian steel producers are very interested in Spain. The Gerdau group, based in Porto Alegre, and the largest producer of long steel in Latin America as well as the second largest iron and steel manufacturer in the USA, bought Corporación Sidenor in 2006. The company, with fourteen plants in America, Europe, and Asia and 25 million tons of production, later acquired SGSB Acero, which acquired CIE Automotive. CSN, another large Brazilian steel producer, acquired Extremaduran Gallardo in 2011 for nearly a billion euros. The purchase enabled CSN (eighth largest group by market capitalisation among the large mining and steel producers) to consolidate itself in Spain for expansion into Europe.

Another of the large Brazilian multi-sector groups, Odebrecht, also has an eye on Spain. Its construction division, one of the largest in the world with projects in thirty-five countries, has had important projects in Germany and Britain. Odebrecht already has a Spanish affiliate and has partnered with Spanish construction and engineering companies in Latin America. It won contracts such as the Centro Intermodal in Miami with OHL, a refinery in Mexico with Técnicas Reunidas,

---

[2] See www.vcc.columbia.edu/files/vale/documents/EMGP-Brazil-Report-2010-Final.pdfmal.

and the Panamanian Metro with FCC. Another group with European ambition is Braskem, one of the world's largest plastic producers, which continued its international expansion in the USA with another important acquisition for $350 million.

In other sectors, Spain could play a key role. We have already highlighted the importance of Spain's business relations with Latin America, which constitute a solid base on which to capitalise. As if this were not enough, there are additional initiatives, such as that of the Madrid stock market, created in the early 2000s as a platform for the multilatinas to trade in euros. In 2011, Latibex included thirty-four stocks traded from six countries (Argentina, Brazil, Chile, Colombia, Mexico and Peru). It is the third largest Latin American stock market by market capitalisation, with €540 billion. These listed firms could form the basis of a 'priority test group' for locating European headquarters in Spain.

Many of the multilatinas are located in cities that lack the air connections that Madrid and Barcelona offer. In addition, there are different national contexts that could favour Spain. Weg, for example, one of the main auto part companies, has its European headquarters in Belgium, a nation with a smaller car industry than Spain. Also with an EMEA headquarters in Belgium (Antwerp) is Chilean Soquimich. TOTVS has its corporate headquarters in Braga, Portugal, a country where the bank Itaú, construction companies Odebrecht and Andrade Gutiérrez, the conglomerate Camargo Correa and iron and steel manufacturer CSN are also located. All these companies have their operational headquarters in cities that are not capitals and lack the connections that Madrid, for example, could offer. This is also the case with Brazilian Metalfrío, which is based in Aalestrup, Denmark, a nation with few direct connections to Brazil. The number of air connections with Brazil is relevant. Iberia has direct flights to various Brazilian destinations, including São Paulo and Río where most of the corporate headquarters of the thirty main Brazilian multilatinas are located (twenty-two headquarters in total).

Multilatinas that have embarked on European adventures represent another type of case. Lupatech, for example, is a Brazilian multinational with 3,600 employees, composed of businesses that mainly focus on equipment and services for the oil and gas sector. This company has an industrial presence in Brazil, Argentina and Colombia. In July

2011, Lupatech acquired 7% of Vicinay Marine SA (for $16.3 million), a company headquartered in Bilbao and belonging to Grupo Vicinay, which has a variety of business lines focused on the oil and gas industry.

Few multilatinas have located in Spain because of direct investments.[3] Between 1990 and 2000, the main destination for Mexican investment, for example, was the USA with 50%. Spain was second with 13%, but then the Mexican focus began increasingly to shift towards Latin America, which between 2001 and 2008 displaced Spain and Brazil to become the second largest destination for Mexican FDI.

Mexican investments in Spain during 2001–8 took ninth place overall, ahead of other Latin American countries and ahead of European countries such as Switzerland and Sweden, as well as Japan and India. The imbalance of investment is obvious when we compare those made by companies from both countries. During the decade 2000–10, direct investment by Spanish companies in Mexico topped €26 billion, compared with the €4 billion invested by Mexican companies in Spain during this same period. Even so, Mexico is the sixth largest investor in Spain in terms of stock, and more importantly, the largest Latin American investor.

The opening of representative offices or corporate headquarters is another method for becoming established in a country. Spain does not come out badly in this respect, as the location of various Mexican multilatina headquarters in the country shows; nevertheless, this process could be enhanced in light of the previous analysis. The sale in 2012 of Bimbo in Spain by the Sara Lee group and the interest shown by Mexican Bimbo confirm that opportunities exist. This sale took place in 2012. Also in 2011, the country's wealthiest man, Carlos Slim, bought into La Caixa for a symbolic amount (almost €7 million). An affiliate (Condumex) of the controlling conglomerate (Carso), specialising in cables for the automotive industry, has been in Spain for twenty years since its first acquisition in the country. Also, giant Televisa holds 40% of Spanish broadcaster La Sexta, an entity in which it has invested more than €125 million over several years.

---

[3] See the study available at http://gcg.universia.net/pdfs_revistas/articulo_124_1248713270240.pdf.

Brazil's case is even more telling. This country, a member of the G20 and head of the BRICs, invests little in Spain by way of FDI. Spain was in twenty-seventh place for total investments during the period 2000–8. As we have seen, there are very few Brazilian multilatina corporate headquarters in Spain – with London, Lisbon and German cities taking the prizes.

Madrid and Barcelona

Nevertheless, Spain and its main cities, Madrid and Barcelona, have become valued locations over the years, even for distant countries like Japan.

In the ranking of the twenty most attractive cities in the world, as ranked by MORI Memorial Foundation in 2009 (the main ranking of this type in Japan), Madrid was placed eleventh, just behind Hong Kong.[4] In 2010, and despite the crisis, Madrid continued in the top twenty worldwide, specifically in fifteenth place.[5] In other rankings of this type, Madrid remains among the world's top twenty. In AT Kearney's ranking it was seventeenth in 2010, losing ground since the previous year, when it was ranked fourteenth.[6] Agencies that promote local investment (Madrid Emprende in Spain's capital and ACC1Ó in Barcelona), as well as the national agency (Invest in Spain), have performed an important job and could become even more important in the framework of a strategy for corporate headquarters.

We must not deceive ourselves here. Competition in Europe is strong and the initial impulse must come from the highest state and local levels. Unfortunately, Spain does not stand out as a central hub for corporate headquarters. Neither Madrid nor Barcelona is in the world's top twenty cities for corporate headquarters, either by sector or by revenue. Tokyo, New York, London and Paris head the ranking, and Chinese cities such as Beijing, Shanghai and Hong Kong are beginning to appear as well.

---

[4] See www.mori-m-foundation.or.jp/english/research/project/6/pdf/GPCI2009_English.pdf.
[5] See www.mori-m-foundation.or.jp/english/research/project/8/index.shtml#report.
[6] See www.atkearney.at/content/misc/wrapper.php/id/50369/name/pdf_urban_elite-gci_2010_12894889240b41.pdf.

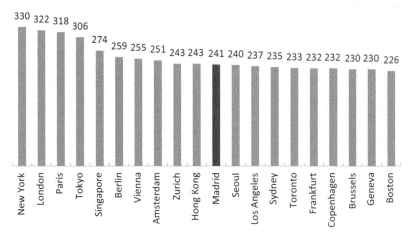

Figure 8.3 Global Power City Index Ranking, 2009.
Source: Mori Memorial Foundation, 2011.

The potential is great, however. Spain is one of the countries with the fewest restrictions on FDI. In the index prepared by the OECD it is in the world's top ten, even ahead of Germany and all the emerging economies including China, India and Brazil.[7] Moreover, Spain has improved considerably in the ranking since 2006 when the index was first published (Figure 8.3 and Table 8.3).

Spain occupies a commendable twelfth place from a total of forty in the Reputation Index, and is valued in particular for its way of life. Nevertheless, in matters of perceived technology, Spain lags behind in twentieth place; the same is true for perceived market and company recognition (seventeenth place), and perceived quality of goods and services (eighteenth place).[8] This index shows the limits of Spain's image and position. Within this world map relative to image, Spain is in line with Greece, Portugal and Latin American countries, all associated with leisure and enjoying life, unlike its immediate European neighbours such as France and Germany, which are associated with economic reputation, technology and product quality (Figure 8.4).

[7] See OECD, *OECD's FDI Restrictiveness Index. 2010 Update*, Paris, OECD, 2010. Available at www.oecd.org/dataoecd/32/19/45563285.pdf.
[8] See Javier Noya and Fernando Prado, *Estudio reputación de España en el mundo*, Madrid, Instituto de Análisis de Intangibles, 2010. Available at www.institutointangibles.com/.

Table 8.3 *Analysis of cities as corporate bases.*

(a) Sectors that generate the most revenue and cities where they are concentrated.

RK 2011	Sector	City	Country	No. of HQs	Revenue (in $ trillion)
1	Industrial	Tokyo	Japan	46	855.39
2	Financial	New York	USA	33	616.45
3	Information technology	Tokyo	Japan	14	425.19
4	Consumer discretionary sectors	Tokyo	Japan	17	424.67
5	Energy	The Hague	Netherlands	2	301.17
6	Materials	Tokyo	Japan	18	279.34
7	Basic services	Paris	France	3	259.32
8	Sanitation	New York	USA	11	248.63
9	Staple goods	Paris	France	6	224.76
10	Telecommunications	Tokyo	Japan	3	173.95

(b) Top 'hub cities' by sector.

RK 2011	City	Country	Sector	No. of HQ	Sales (in $ trillion)
1	Tokyo	Japan	Industrial	46	855.39
2	New York	USA	Financial	33	616.45
3	London	Britain	Financial	19	609.22
4	Paris	France	Financial	14	539.43
5	Tokyo	Japan	Information technology	14	425.19
6	Tokyo	Japan	Discretionary consumption	17	424.67
7	Fayetteville	USA	Discretionary consumption	1	408.21
8	Paris	France	Industrial	18	365.22
9	Tokyo	Japan	Financial	34	338.55
10	San José	USA	Information technology	21	306.65
11	The Hague	Netherlands	Energy	2	301.17
12	Nagoya	Japan	Discretionary consumption	5	292.19
13	Seoul	Korea	Industrial	19	290.35
14	Dallas	USA	Energy	3	286.33
15	Tokyo	Japan	Materials	18	279.34
16	Moscow	Russia	Energy	5	276.90
17	Houston	USA	Energy	16	276.14
18	Beijing	China	Financial	12	259.58
19	Paris	France	Basic services	3	259.32
20	New York	USA	Sanitation	11	248.63

(c) Top twenty hub cities, by sales volume

RK 2011	City	Country	No. of sectors	No. of HQs	Total sales (in $ trillion)
1	Tokyo	Japan	10	163	3,115.02
2	Paris	France	10	61	1,956.69
3	New York	USA	10	84	1,541.5
4	London	Britain	9	59	1,416.25
5	Seoul	Korea	9	42	758.01
6	Beijing	China	7	34	707.66
7	Dallas	USA	9	18	558.77
8	San Francisco	USA	8	17	540.33
9	Chicago	USA	9	32	497.13
10	Nagoya	Japan	6	19	464.01
11	Osaka	Japan	8	34	439.96
12	Fayetteville	USA	2	2	435.03
13	Munich	Germany	6	10	434.95
14	Moscow	Russia	6	17	383.3
15	Houston	USA	7	28	380.05
16	Minneapolis	USA	7	14	375.85
17	The Hague	Holland	3	4	363.12
18	Hong Kong	China	9	49	347.49
19	Shanghai	China	7	16	340.49
20	San José	USA	4	25	324.82

Source: GaWC, 2010.

Madrid is in thirteenth place of twenty cities with the most corporate presence worldwide. Barcelona possesses important attributes and a strong image for creativity and innovation. It is telling that some multilatinas like Argentinean Arcor and Chilean Sudamericana de Vapores have located in Barcelona. In terms of attractiveness for investors, Barcelona also stands out, as the latest Ernst & Young poll places Barcelona and Madrid among the top ten most attractive cities in Europe to establish business operations. Nevertheless (and this is an important pending subject),[9] neither of the two is perceived as a

---

[9] The most recent work of economists and urbanists dwells on innovation and creative urban centres, capable of attracting talent and promoting business. See Edward Glaeser, *Triumph of the City: How Our Greatest Invention Makes Us Richer, Smarter, Greener, Healthier, and Happier,* New York, Penguin Press, 2011.

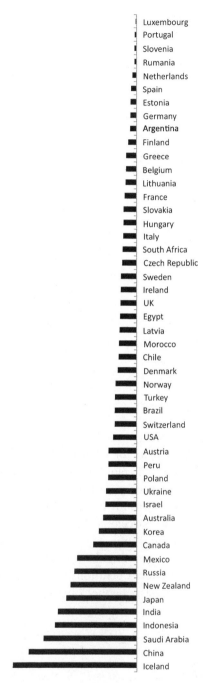

Figure 8.4 2010 OECD index of restrictions on foreign direct investment. *Source:* OECD, 2011.

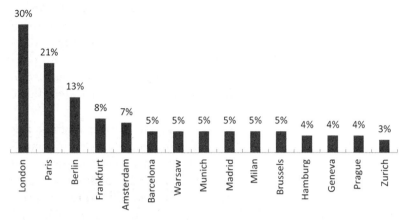

Figure 8.5 Cities preferred by investors, 2010.
Source: Ernst & Young, 2011.

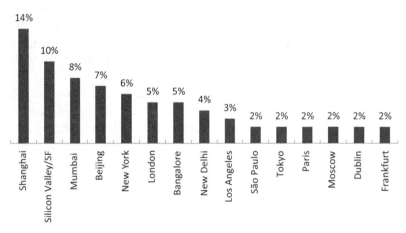

Figure 8.6 Where will the next Google or Facebook be born? The world's most innovative cities in the future.
Source: Ernst & Young, 2011.

place of innovation (the simplest question related to this perception asks where the next Facebook or Google will be born). This ranking puts emerging cities like Shanghai in the lead, which in 2011 pulled ahead of Silicon Valley/San Francisco, or Mumbai and Beijing, both of which were ahead of New York and London. São Paulo also displaces Tokyo and Paris (Figures 8.5 and 8.6).

Spain stands out for the quality of its infrastructure, is the top EU country for motorways, and also leads for the number of high-speed rail kilometres. It also has forty-six international seaports and forty-nine airports with 250 airlines operating in the country. All this positions Spain as an ideal bridge between Europe and Latin America, in addition to being a potential hub for Europe, Africa and the Middle East.

When deciding where to locate, companies consider multiple factors, but the transport and logistical infrastructure, telecommunications infrastructure, and regulatory and normative transparency and stability take the prizes, with 63%, 62% and 62% of business people surveyed considering these variables to be crucial.[10] To remain competitive, investors also consider an attractive tax system (34%) and low labour costs (28%) to be essential.[11] When investing in cities, the quality of urban infrastructure (38%) and technical innovation parks (31%) are also considered relevant (Table 8.4).

In the decade from 1999–2009, Spain became the world's second largest investor in Latin America with 9% of the total, behind the United States (with 37%), but ahead of Canada (7%) and any other European country including France, Britain and Germany (each with only 5%).

This business connection with Latin America is a great asset for the future. Some multinationals like Danish Vestas, American Blackrock, French Axa and British BT and Bupa, have established their Latin

---

[10] See the report by Ernst & Young, *Restart: Ernst & Young's European Attractiveness Survey*, Ernst & Young, 2011. Available at www.ey.com/Publication/vwLUAssets/Eurospe_attractiveness_2011_web_resolution/$FILE/Eurospe_attractiveness_2011_web_resolution.pdf.

[11] On the impact of tax rates, in particular on DFI, see M. P. Devereux, B. Lockwood and M. Redoano, 'Do Countries Compete over Corporate Tax Rates?', *Journal of Public Economics*, 92, 2008, pp. 1210–35. Corporate policies for fiscal optimisation have prompted many multinationals to accumulate cash pools, international liquidity, outside the parent company's country, in international regional headquarters, something also to take into account when we consider the question of corporate headquarters regions. Many of these cash pools are being located in regions such as Europe and Asia, outside the national territory of the parent company. It is estimated, on average, that US corporations have $15 billion in cash pools located outside the country. See Zoltan Pozsar, 'Institutional Cash Pools and the Triffin Dilemma of the U.S. Banking System', IMF Working Paper, 190, August 2011. Available at www.imf.org/external/pubs/ft/wp/2011/wp11190.pdf.

Table 8.4 *The twenty cities with the greatest corporate presence in the world (GaWC Index, 2011).*

RK 2011	City	Corporate Headquarters	RK 2011	City	Corporate Headquarters
1	London	368	11	Brussels	187
2	New York	357	12	Sydney	186
3	Hong Kong	253	13	Madrid	182
4	Tokyo	244	14	Toronto	182
5	Paris	235	15	Amsterdam	180
6	Singapore	229	16	São Paulo	168
7	Chicago	213	17	San Francisco	164
8	Los Angeles	201	18	Zurich	157
9	Frankfurt	193	19	Washington	154
10	Milan	191	20	Mexico City	148

Source: GaWC, 2011.

American headquarters in Spain. Perhaps the greatest potential for capitalisation in the future is attracting the European headquarters of the multilatinas.

More locations could also be promoted. Why not imagine French multinational Schneider Electric, which acquired software network affiliate Telvent from Abengoa in mid 2011 (for €1.4 billion), installing its Latin American headquarters in Spain? In 2010, before the purchase of Telvent, the emerging markets already represented 37% of company sales. With the acquisition of the Spanish group, this amount will increase. In mid 2011, Schneider Electric located their worldwide office for Safe Energy Systems for Industry and Infrastructures in Barcelona. Also in 2011, Spaniard Julio Rodríguez, executive vice president for the EMEAS division of Schneider Electric, which includes Europe, the Middle East, Africa and South America, started working from Barcelona. He is the company's most senior executive, a member of the worldwide executive committee, and president of Schneider Electric Spain. From the central headquarters in Barcelona, Schneider Electric now manages business in Europe, the Middle East, Africa and South America.

Also, why not imagine French Suez Environnement, which finalised its purchase of Aguas de Barcelona (Agbar) in 2010, doing the same? Its managing director, Jean Louis Chaussade, is also very familiar with the region and with Spain, where he lives. This purchase will increase the French group's exposure in Latin America. In 2010, the region represented 4% of its total revenue, an amount comparable to Asia but lagging behind Africa and the Middle East (7%). Agbar has a broad presence in Latin America, in particular in Mexico, Colombia, Peru and Chile.

Spain, with Madrid and Barcelona leading the way, could position itself as a Latin hub, or in other words provide central locations for multilatina corporate European headquarters. Spain could provide locations for Latin American and European headquarters for emerging multinationals, in particular those that have developed strategic connections with Spanish groups that are well established in the region, as we have seen in the case of China. Finally, Spain could also be the place to locate the Latin American headquarters of European groups that, because of their history in Spain and Latin America, could be given some priority. The possibilities explored here do not exhaust the options, but do show the importance of promoting and reconsidering the business relationship with Latin America.

Last but not least, Latin firms, such as CEMCA from Mexico or Ajegroup from Peru, could also decide to locate their global operations for expansion overseas in Spain, not only towards Europe but also towards Africa, the Middle East or even Asia (as Ajegroup is already doing).

9 | Conclusions

We have seen how 2010–20 is proving to be the decade of the multi-latinas. Latin American companies are contributing to the acceleration of an internationalisation process that will see them become increasingly global multinationals. Many continue to restrict their ambitions in terms of internationalisation to Latin America, but an increasing number are now venturing into the United States, Europe, Africa and even Asia. This process is a blessing in disguise for Spain, which has traditionally been a firm supporter of the region. The growth of the multilatinas means that Spain has an opportunity to position itself as a unique point of entry into Europe and as a home to the European corporate headquarters of many of these companies.

However, the international expansion of Latin American companies will bring other opportunities. We have also seen how the region's multinationals and technological startups could be another group of companies for Spain to watch within the framework of a European positioning strategy. The close links that Spain has forged with Latin America since the 1990s may lead multinationals from emerging countries such as China to choose the peninsula for establishing the corporate bases from which to do business with Europe and Latin America. Many Chinese companies have created close links with Spanish multinationals that have strong presences in Latin America. Finally, Latin American argonauts, i.e. Latin American executives in technological (or other) multinationals, could also become allies in a strategy to position Spain as a Latin hub for corporate headquarters.

Innovation in international cooperation

However, the potential for future relations between Latin America and Spain is much broader and international cooperation is an arena of particular interest, in which Spain stands out as the continent's main ally among OECD countries. Somewhat unusually among OECD countries – the international cooperation efforts of which tend to focus on Africa – most of Spain's international cooperation is directed towards Latin America. Nevertheless, there is scope for Spain to go still further with innovation and fresh impetus.

Innovation abounds in the business world, and not just in startups or the R&D departments of global multinationals. We are also witnessing significant changes and disruptive innovation at a state level. Indeed, international cooperation is an area in which there are exciting changes following the emergence of investment vehicles designed to stimulate the creation and development of companies in the emerging and border markets of Asia, Africa and Latin America.

The so-called European development finance institutions (EDFI) are development financing institutions that have been growing for decades and which are gaining increasing relevance as players in and promoters of new capital flows towards developing countries.[1] These vehicles are designed to promote and invest in financially viable companies and projects with a development impact. They therefore operate at a different level from the more traditional assistance or subsistence-orientated development aid models by encouraging business creation and innovation, as well as employment and added value. There are currently around fifteen institutions of this type which, according to the Dalberg consultancy firm, boast a combined investment portfolio of just over €18.5 billion. Each year, a new investment portfolio adds another €4 billion to this figure. However, these amounts are still rather modest when compared to the official aid development budget, and account for just 6% of bilateral aid. There is therefore much scope for growth.

Spain could attempt to position itself through an innovative approach, committing funds and increasing institutional density in this area. Spain's COFIDES is one of the aforementioned development agencies. However, its portfolio is rather modest: at the end of 2009 it was less than €500 million and new investments that year totalled

---

[1] For a more detailed vision of the new players and capital flows in the area of development, see Andrew Mold, Annalisa Prizzon, Emmanuel Frot and Javier Santiso, 'Aid Flows in Times of Crisis', a paper prepared and presented at the Conference on Development Cooperation in Times of Crisis and on Achieving MDGs, IFEMA Convention Centre, Madrid, 9–10 June 2010. Available at www.eu2010.es/export/sites/presidencia/comun/descargas/agenda/agenda_junio/pdf_grupo/ES/Mold_xFlujos_de_ayudax.pdf.

just over €150 million, which is a long way from the sums handled, for example, by the British CDC Group, with a portfolio exceeding €3.3 billion at the end of 2009 – and new projects for nearly €600 million. Of course, COFIDES was created only some twenty years ago, while CDC (the oldest) has been around for more than seventy years. However, Spain could be more ambitious in this regard, which means increasing efficiency and aid budgets, as well as moving towards private equity vehicles. It means, in short, creating and strengthening the institutional ecosystem. How can this be done?

The history of the CDC, a reference in the area, is a source of inspiration. In 2004, CDC became a fund of funds, i.e. it turned its attention to encouraging private equity investors to create funds dedicated to investment in developing countries (examples include Actis and Áureos, which operate from London with subsidiaries in developing countries). This institution has thus sought to provoke an institutional trickle down, acting as an incubator both in source countries and, more importantly, in host countries. This formula has the added virtue of encouraging the private sector to dedicate resources or fund managers to the funds that are created, thus multiplying the sums contributed to developing countries. The most notable example of this kind of cooperation is probably that of Norfund, the public Norwegian agency, which created an investment vehicle in conjunction with the country's water industry – one of the leading water industries in the world. Britain, together with Swedish, Dutch and a number of private banks, also created an infrastructure fund for Africa at the beginning of the 2000s. With the creation of FONPRODE in 2011, Spain has taken a significant step in this direction, creating a non-reimbursable aid instrument that enables it to operate as a venture capital fund of funds, as many of the aforementioned agencies have been doing.

For a country like Spain, which has a significant core of large companies operating on a large scale in emerging countries and in Latin America in particular, this formula could also multiply public contributions, which may be combined with private contributions for the creation of private equity funds or fund managers. Spanish-based venture capital management funds such as Axon Capital have developed projects that look towards Latin America, seeking to promote funds to boost investment in Spanish technological companies and startups, or technological companies seeking to develop from various countries in the region. Spain has a number of companies in the financial, construction, engineering, energy, telecommunications and new technology sectors that could participate in regional and/or sector-specific funds or fund managers, particularly directing resources to Latin America, a region with which Spain has a number of converging public and private interests. More importantly, it is a region from which both EDFIs and international cooperation – with notable exceptions such as that of Spain – are withdrawing.

Official development assistance is being directed en masse towards Africa, and rightly so: it is the poorest and neediest continent. However, aid is being withdrawn from middle-income countries, thereby punishing Latin America in particular, a region that continues to suffer significant levels of need, poverty and inequality, as well as limited funding for activities that generate employment, growth, and economic and social development. A glance at the EDFIs shows the reality of this trend. The portfolios of these institutions are not directed towards Latin America. According to the information presented in the Dalberg report referred to above, published in 2010, in the case of Britain's CDC, Latin America accounted for just 7% of its total portfolio in 2009 with this figure set to fall to 5%. The same trend can be observed at the Belgian agency, BIO, which plans to reduce its Latin American portfolio from 17% to 12%, and Finnfund, the Finnish agency, which plans to reduce the weight of its Latin American portfolio from 15% to 5%. For others such as the Danish IFU, Latin America was already practically absent from its portfolio, and will soon disappear almost entirely with its weight reduced from 4% to 1%. Other funds, such as Norway's Norfund which used to have a strong presence and considerable activity in Latin America, are also moving in the same direction; Norfund is reducing its Latin American portfolio from 36% to 18%.

The region has not fallen off the radar entirely, however. For some funds, such as the German DEG, a subsidiary of the giant KfW, Latin America still accounts for around 20% of the total portfolio (this fund's consolidated portfolio is one of the largest, amounting to €4.7 billion at the end of 2009). Some are even increasing investments in the region to a certain extent; this is the case of the French Proparco (with Latin America representing 9% of its total portfolio in 2009, compared to the region's 4% in the total consolidated portfolio); and the Swiss SIFEM (in which Latin America accounted for 16% of investment in 2009, compared to 13% in the total consolidated portfolio). FMO, the investment arm of Dutch cooperation, with a total portfolio, in

2010, of over €4.6 billion, still has some of these funds invested in private equity. Its Latin American portfolio represents around 23% (€200 million) of more than €1.1 billion for private equity investment. However, since 2009, some countries in the region, namely Brazil, Chile and Mexico, have ceased to be potential recipients – and future investment will be concentrated in Colombia, Peru and Central America.

Latin America is falling off the development radar for most countries and the pressure from OECD governments is increasingly on Africa and Asia. This is another place where Spain could set itself apart and innovate: not only by increasing the volume of investment dedicated to private equity, e.g. via a fund of funds, thereby contributing to increasing the density of the institutional ecosystem, but also by committing massively to a region that is experiencing widespread funding withdrawal. Spain's strategy in this sense would be to concentrate or focus its resources, rather than spread them out. International cooperation players and EDFI transactions already abound in Africa and Asia, yet they are becoming fewer in Latin America. This strategy for focusing assistance would also be more consistent with the efficiency objectives promoted by the OECD and members of the DAC donors' club. Overspreading or fragmenting aid often results in increased waste, loss and disruption in host countries.[2]

Furthermore, Spanish international cooperation may find some strong allies in this area for structuring field-specific (e.g. water, health, nutrition) or sector-specific (e.g. infrastructure, energy, telecommunications and new technologies) funds and fund managers. It could also attempt to innovate through public–private alliances such as those established by Norfund with Norway's water industry. This would also go some way towards alleviating the €600 million cut (10% of the total) in the official development assistance budget, which was decided in 2010 (and intensified in 2011 and 2012). There is nothing

---

[2] In this connection, see the papers presented at the OECD: Emmanuel Frot and Javier Santiso, 'Development Aid and Portfolio Funds: Trends, Volatility and Fragmentation', OECD Development Centre, Working Paper 275, 2008; Emmanuel Frot and Javier Santiso, 'Herding in Aid Allocation', OECD Development Centre, Working Paper 279, 2009; Emmanuel Frot and Javier Santiso, 'Crushed Aid: Fragmentation in Sectoral Aid', OECD Development Centre, Working Paper 284, 2010. Available at www.oecd-ilibrary.org/development/crushed-aid_218465127786.

to prevent Spain from aiming high here and leading the world with innovation in this area.

Spain has a large number of multinationals with deep roots in the region – via foundations and directly through their own activities. These multinationals have developed a variety of forms of cooperation and they contribute to the economic and social development of the countries in which they are present. Yet there is still scope for more public–private cooperation in the form of joint participation in the creation of development capital or seed capital funds, or funds for microenterprises and micro-entrepreneurs.

Telefónica, for example, is promoting the creation in eight Latin American countries of startup accelerators (called Wayra) to encourage entrepreneurship and help prevent business founders from leaving the country to create added value companies in the United States or Europe.[3] In an initial phase, Telefónica will contribute around $50,000 for each selected project, as well as physical resources such as offices and infrastructures for entrepreneurs. In June 2011, Telefónica Internacional created Wayra to manage this ambitious plan. One year later 13,000 projects had been received and 200 startups accelerated throughout the continent. At the same time, with the impulse of Telefónica also, a network of five VC funds, called Amerigo, and run by independent teams, had been created in four countries (Brazil, Colombia, Chile and Spain), with total capital mobilised of around $350 billion.

BBVA has launched a foundation for microfinancing on the continent with a budget of €200 million.[4] In 2011, it promoted the creation of Fondo Esperanza SpA with $20 million to provide the poor in Chile with access to the financial system, thus enabling businesses to be set up. The bank has also begun working with multilateral bodies. In 2010, the IFC, the private sector arm of the World Bank Group, invested $10 million in preferential shares of the Bancamía Microfinance Bank, an institution supported by BBVA's Microfinance Foundation. These microcredit funds have become particularly important in some of the countries in the region: in Bolivia, for example, they account for more than 11% of the country's GDP and almost one-third of the total credit

---

[3] See www.wayra.org.   [4] See www.mfbbva.org/castellano.html.

granted to the private sector. The importance of their role has become even more evident with the 2008–2012 global crisis.[5]

Brazil, an emerging donor

These new axes for international cooperation could also be strengthened by taking advantage of Latin America's newfound relevance.

Many countries in the region are now developed and their progress has resulted in good practices that could well be transferred to other countries. For example, Chile has become a country of reference for governance and it has also proved to be a very capable manager of its natural resources. In the past, Norway traditionally occupied a special position, as *the* international cooperator to watch in terms of governance, institutions and natural resource management; however, Chile could equally be hailed as an example today.[6] Indeed, Chile could become a benchmark of triangular cooperation for Spain, in terms of good tax practices for example, and Uruguay and Colombia could also inspire triangular cooperation of a similar nature. Spain would do well to reconsider its international cooperation relationship with these countries, and particularly with the continent's leading economy: Brazil.

A clear sign that times are changing is that emerging countries are also becoming global donors. The family of development players has now grown substantially, reaching significant numbers, depending on how these flows are calculated. According to recent reports by the UN and DAC (the OECD's Development Assistance Committee), non-traditional donors such as Saudi Arabia, China and India now

---

[5] See Gabriel di Bella, 'The Impact of the Global Financial Crisis on Microfinance and Policy Implications', IMF Working Paper 11–175, July 2011. Available at www.imf.org/external/pubs/ft/wp/2011/wp11175.pdf.

[6] In this connection, and for a comparison between Chile and Norway, see Gøril Havro and Javier Santiso, 'To Benefit from Plenty: Lessons from Chile and Norway', OECD Development Centre Policy Brief 37, OECD Development Centre, September 2008, available at www.oecd.org/dataoecd/23/12/41281577.pdf; and Gøril Havro and Javier Santiso, 'Benefiting the Resource Rich: Can International Development Policy Help Tame the Resource Crisis?', IDS Working Paper 35, February 2011. Available at www.ids.ac.uk/go/bookshop; and on the Social Science Research Network database http://papers.ssrn.com/sol3/papers.cfm?abstract_id=1761007.

contribute between 8% and 10% of official development assistance (ODA) worldwide. This group of the most advanced emerging countries is now being joined by the so-called 'CIVETS', another core group of emerging economies consisting of Colombia, Indonesia, Vietnam, Egypt, Turkey and South Africa, which have been described in a report by the Madrid-based Elcano Royal Institute as a 'third wave of development players'.[7]

In the first decade of this century, OECD countries and their technocrats at the organisation's Paris headquarters were astonished to see China's sudden entry into Africa, not just as an investor, but also as a donor. And the next ten years may well see the emergence of more developing countries as players in international aid, further surprising what we still call the 'developed world'. In Latin America, for example, one country that stands out in terms of economic significance and the rise of its multilatinas is Brazil.

This is yet another paradox of the shift in the world as we know it: countries such as China, India, South Africa and Arab nations are beginning to distribute aid when many of them are still struggling with poverty and inequality within their own borders. These countries are adding South–South cooperation and international investment in the form of financial vehicles known as sovereign wealth funds to the traditional development assistance mechanisms. It is therefore very probable that we are underestimating the current state of affairs, as we are using obsolete standards of measurement.

Brazil has developed an international cooperation agency (ABC) that still has a modest budget ($30 million per year). Dilma Rousseff, elected President in October 2010, said that, if elected, she would reform and strengthen the agency. Yet this agency is not the full extent of international cooperation in Brazil. A number of studies by the British think tank Overseas Development Institute (ODI) and Canada's International Development Research Centre (IDRC), two traditional donors, anticipate that total Brazilian aid could be fifteen times more than the ABC budget. Both institutions may well have underestimated the reality.

---

[7] See www.fride.org/publicacion/818/la-tercera-ola-de-actores-del-desarrollo; see also the Carolina Foundation report: www.fundacioncarolina.es/es-ES/nombrespropios/Documents/NPBAyllón0912.pdf.

Indeed, if we add Brazil's contribution to the UNDF ($25 million per year), its contribution to the worldwide anti-hunger programme ($300 million), aid in the form of technical cooperation ($440 million), funds committed to Haiti and Gaza (more than $350 million), and the commercial credits that the Brazilian Development Bank (BNDES) has granted to developing countries between 2008 and 2012 ($3.3 billion), then the total amount easily exceeds $4 billion. This places Brazil on a par with OECD countries such as Canada or Sweden in terms of development assistance. But the trend in these contributions is also noteworthy. The rate at which contributions are being made is increasing, particularly via BNDES: of the $3.3 billion contributed since 2008, half was provided in the first quarter of 2010.

However, Brazil exports technology and innovation as well as development funds. It is one of the world's leading producers of bioethanol, something that other energy-dependent developing countries are seeking to replicate with Brazilian aid and technology. Brazil is also an exporter of social innovation: the *Bolsa Família*, or family allowance programme, is now replicated by or has inspired governments and municipalities on every continent; even New York has drawn inspiration from this type of programme and it is also motivating initiatives in Africa.

Brazilian international cooperation has undergone a radical change in Africa. According to the UN, Brazil currently has some 300 cooperation projects operating in thirty-seven African states (at the beginning of the 2000s it had just twenty-one projects in seven states). One of the star projects is the Oswaldo Cruz Foundation (Fiocruz) which promotes the production of a vaccine against AIDS to tackle a disease that in 2010 affected more than 11% of the population of Mozambique. For its part, EMBRAPA runs projects for technical cooperation, training agricultural engineers and teaching food safety in Mali, Benin, Burkina Faso and other countries of the region.

In addition to this state-level activity, Brazilian companies are also in the process of international expansion. The construction company Odebrecht is setting up a sewage and water supply system in Angola and has become one of the largest employers on the entire African continent. Vale and Petrobras are supplementing their investments throughout Africa with a series of social programmes to help consolidate the viability of their investments and ensure acceptance by local communities. And their activity is not limited to Africa; they also operate similar strategies in the poorer Latin American countries.

A comprehensive report published in 2010 by the Madrid-based Ibero-American General Secretariat (SEGIB) contained a fairly explicit map of South–South cooperation, particularly in and from Latin America.[8] Brazil is obviously not the only country that is new to the world of international cooperation.[9] However, it is likely to be one of the most active in the second half of the 2010s, thereby joining China in surprising the traditional donors' club.

Triangular cooperation

The triangular cooperation arrangements between Spain and Latin American countries could also be echoed by triangular arrangements between Spain and Asian countries for the purposes of cooperating with Latin America. This is probably one of the most interesting axes yet to be explored.

Asian countries, particularly China, have become increasingly interested in the region and it is easy to imagine how joint cooperation vehicles could work. China set up the China Africa Development Fund (CAD Fund) in Africa in 2007,[10] with an allocation of a billion dollars from the China Development Bank and a further two billion dollars in 2010. This fund operates as a private equity fund, buying stakes in companies in order to develop the local productive fabric. The aim is to use this instrument to raise and invest a total of some $5 billion in Africa during the decade 2010–20.[11] Proof of the growing activity and relevance of China in the field of international cooperation is the production of its government's first white paper on assistance for development in 2011, which pointed out that such

---

[8] See SEGIB, *Informe de Cooperación Sur–Sur en Iberoamérica 2010* (Ibero-American South–South Cooperation Report), Madrid, SEGIB, 2010. Available at http://segib.org/actividades/files/2010/12/inf-coop-sur-sur-2010.pdf.

[9] For South–South cooperation, see www.cooperacionsursur.org/ in particular; also, the report jointly promoted by the Colombian Government and the OECD: www.oecd.org/dataoecd/14/39/46080702.pdf.

[10] See www.cdb.com.cn/english/.

[11] For relations between China and Africa, see Deborah Brautigam, *The Dragon's Gift: The Real Story of China in Africa*, Oxford University Press, 2009.

assistance had grown at an annual rate of 30% between 2004 and 2009.[12]

China is taking similar steps in Latin America. By the end of 2011, the Export-Import Bank of China (China Eximbank) presented a yuan-denominated sovereign wealth fund with a budget of a billion dollars to invest in Latin America, essentially for building infrastructure and in cooperation with the Inter-American Development Bank. It is envisaged that the fund will invest mainly in infrastructure, energy and natural resource projects, although particular attention will be paid to small and medium-sized companies involved in the distribution chains of these industries. The China Development Bank (CDB) also operates to a certain extent as a sovereign wealth fund, participating in transactions of great significance, particularly in the energy industry.[13] In Latin America, its main transactions have been with Brazil, Ecuador and Venezuela; and between 2005 and 2010, the CDB dedicated a total of over $40 billion of international cooperation financing to the continent's energy sector alone (Table 9.1).

The FONPRODE development fund was created by Spain – and represents a milestone in the (recent) history of Spain's foreign aid as it permits the creation of mechanisms that are common in other countries but not in Spain: namely, financial instruments and credits for public and private sectors. These can be allocated to common co-investment vehicles in the technology, renewable energy or infrastructure sectors, for which there is considerable demand in Latin America and in which Spanish and Chinese firms have a joint supply capacity. In total, the office that manages Fonprode[14] had a budget of €950 million in 2011, of which 68% constituted potential funds for development cooperation with no impact on the public deficit.[15] The budget allocation was €300 million in non-reimbursable aid and up to €645 million for financial cooperation activities with no impact on the deficit. In the annual plan for international cooperation, PACI 2011, Fonprode's

---

[12] See www.eu-china.net/web/cms/upload/pdf/nachrichten/2011-04-21Chinas-ForeignAid-WhitePaper.pdf.

[13] See Erica Downs, 'Inside China, Inc: China Development Bank's Cross-Border Energy Deals', John L. Thornton China Center at Brookings Monograph Series 3, Beijing and Washington, DC, March 2011. Available at www.brookings.edu/papers/2011/0321_china_energy_downs.aspx.

[14] This includes the state company, P4R, www.p4r.es/, as well as the AECID.

[15] See www.tecniberia.es/documentos/FONPRODE_AECID_15jun11mesa.pdf.

Table 9.1 *International activity of the China Development Bank in the energy sector, 2005–10.*

Year	Country	Borrower	Amount (in $ trillion)	Duration (years)
2005	Russia	Rosneft	6*	6
2008	Venezuela	BNDES	4	3
2009	Russia	Rosneft	15	20
2009	Russia	Transneft	10	20
2009	Brazil	Petrobras	10	10
2009	Venezuela	BNDES	4	3
2009	Turkmenistan	Turkmengaz	4	n/a
2010	Venezuela	BNDES	20.6	10
2010	Ecuador	Ministry of Finance	1	4

Source: Brookings Institution, 2011.
Note: *Includes funds of the ExIm Bank of China.

total funding amounted to just over €545 million, a considerable effort when viewed against total Spanish official development assistance (just over €4.2 billion, or 0.4% of GNI).[16]

Spain and China, for example, could contribute 100 million euros/dollars each and raise a further 100 million from Spanish and Chinese businesses. In total, we would be looking at a public–private fund of some 400 million euros/dollars. Chinese companies with significant interests in Latin America, such as Huawei and ZTE, as well as banks and oil companies, could all contribute. This would also go a long way towards changing China's image as a predator of raw materials in Latin America, something which Chinese authorities are increasingly keen to change, as demonstrated by the recent technology-related business agreements signed with countries in the region. Spanish companies with agreements and a significant presence in China could also participate.

Yet it is also possible to see how other players, particularly private players, could contribute. One example is BBVA, whose strategic partner, Citic (in which it has a 15% stake), is located in China. At the beginning of 2011, BBVA signed a major collaboration agreement with

[16] See www.aecid.es/galerias/noticias/descargas/2011/2011_03/
PACI2011Definitivo.pdf.

the China Development Bank to establish the bases for cooperation in various business areas in Latin American countries. This is the first alliance between a Spanish company and a Chinese bank. Cooperation between the two will focus on promoting project finance, commercial services, derivatives and corporate banking in various countries throughout Latin America. BBVA is currently the largest Spanish corporate investor in Asia and is active in the continent's main markets, with three branches in the region (Hong Kong, Singapore and Tokyo) and six representative offices (Beijing, Shanghai, Taipei, Mumbai, Sydney and Seoul).

Another example (in addition to those mentioned in previous chapters) was the inauguration in Chile in 2011 of the first Latin American laboratory with latest-generation LTE equipment, a joint initiative by the University of Chile and the Chinese company ZTE. The laboratory received an investment worth $11 million, financed almost entirely by ZTE, and the equipment was installed in the university's electrical engineering department. Four Latin American countries – Argentina, Brazil, Chile and Cuba – already have mixed committees for science and technology cooperation with China; these committees are responsible for establishing framework agreements, supervising the implementation of specific agreements, and reviewing cooperation.

China signed science and technology cooperation agreements with Brazil, Chile, Colombia and Ecuador in 2011, thereby accelerating progress in this area. In Bolivia, the Chinese company CAMC Engineering signed a technology transfer agreement with the government of Evo Morales for the industrialisation of Bolivian energy, as well as the construction of liquefied natural gas plants and hydroelectric plants (with financing from the Industrial and Commercial Bank of China). At the end of 2010, in a further show of its desire for technological cooperation, the Bolivian government and China's Great Wall Industry Corporation signed an agreement for the building and launch of Bolivia's first communications satellite in 2013. Thanks to this agreement, Bolivia will have a third-generation Chinese aerospace satellite with which to provide telecommunications services to the whole country, as well as support for educational and medical initiatives. The bulk of its financing is provided by the Chinese Development Bank ($251 million), with the rest being provided by Bolivia ($44 million).

This increase in technological cooperation is also related in part to the desire of countries in the region to create a more balanced relationship with China. The most emblematic case is, without a doubt, that of Brazil, which is currently endeavouring to incentivise technological transfer and Chinese added value in Brazil. A clear example of this is the investment agreement for technology transfer and local production signed by China Northern Railway (CNR) in 2011. In this agreement, CNR undertook (as part of an agreement to manufacture thirty-four trains for the Río de Janeiro government) to manufacture trains in Brazil from 2012 with an investment of almost $130 million for a plant in the city of Tres Ríos. One of the requirements of the tender for the purchase of the new trains was that they be manufactured in Río; the agreement also provides for the creation of 2,500 local jobs.

China is becoming an important player in international cooperation (if we consider this concept to mean more than belonging to the OECD donors' club). The *Financial Times* recently estimated that China lent more money to developing nations in 2009 and 2010 than the World Bank, highlighting Beijing's desire to increase its global influence. During the years 2010–12, China has lent at least $110 billion to governments and companies in developing countries, which exceeds the $100.3 billion contributed by the World Bank. These statistics were collated from public announcements made by banks, borrowers and the Chinese government. China has various public entities acting as international financial cooperation bodies: entities such as the China Development Bank, the Export-Import Bank of China and the Bank of China have granted large credits to Brazil, Venezuela and Russia in exchange for guaranteed oil reserves. Railroad projects in Argentina were also financed.

The importance of Chinese cooperation in Latin America is now a fact and, with the distribution of direct Chinese investment in Latin America, bilateral cooperation is also being consolidated. Proof of this is the new agreement signed between Venezuela and China in 2011 for $4 billion of financing for homes and a second agreement for the creation of a mixed oil, mining and construction company. The state company Petróleos de Venezuela agreed to provide financing, together with the Industrial and Commercial Bank of China (ICBC), for the construction of homes, an area for which the Venezuelan oil company is also responsible. This agreement supplements another agreed by the Venezuelan government in 2010 for a Chinese loan of $20 billion.

Korea is another potential candidate for triangular cooperation with Spain and Latin America. Spain and South Korea have a great opportunity to work together in Latin America within frameworks such as the Inter-American Development Bank (IDB), and combining Spain's experience in the area with the technological expertise of Korea (in 2004, Korea joined the IDB). Whether within or outside the framework of the IDB, Spain and Korea could work together as partners and members of this international body for the creation of joint projects – as both boast worldwide technological champions in the telecommunications and information technology sectors (e.g. Samsung and Telefónica), and have multinationals that are committed to Latin America (e.g. Santander and Posco). Recent studies by the new head of USAID (of Indian origin and a former employee of the Belinda and Bill Gates Foundation)[17] show that both direct and indirect (multilateral banks) cooperation centred on business support, technology transfer and new products are becoming more relevant and noticeable.

An example of the growing Latin American and Korean interest in cooperation is the recent initiative by the Korean multinational LG. In 2011, LG Electronics and the Chilean Sociedad de Fomento Fabril (SOFOFA) announced the creation of LG Chile's Incubadora Smart Funds to support technological entrepreneurial projects with $1.6 million contributed by South Korea. The initiative offers opportunities for local software developers and entrepreneurs to develop applications for the Smart platform (television and cell phones). With this initiative, LG will continue to support local talent. Furthermore, local applications that are developed in the incubator will be available for all of LG's Smart devices worldwide. Korea has also signed free trade agreements with Chile, Peru and Colombia, and is currently negotiating another agreement with Mexico and Mercosur. For its part, the Spanish bank BBVA opened an office in Korea in 2011: the first office opened by a Spanish bank in South Korea.

The Andean Development Corporation (CAF) also seeks to build bridges between Latin America and China. In 2011, it signed a framework cooperation agreement with the Institute of Latin American Studies of the Chinese Social Sciences Academy, China's largest institute

---

[17] See the study by William Perry, 'Growing Business or Development Priority? Multilateral Development Banks' Direct Support to Private Firms', Center for Global Development, CGD Brief, April 2011. Available at www.cgdev.org/content/publications/detail/1424992/.

for research on Latin America. In 2011, it also signed a technical cooperation agreement with the Asian Development Bank to encourage the
holding of bi-regional forums and seminars; exchange of best practices
in the areas of infrastructure, social development, environment and
financial policy; and research and studies and professional exchange
programmes. Spain is a member of the CAF, but, more importantly,
the CAF has its European office in Madrid (in 2012, the IDB moved
its European headquarters from Paris to Madrid also).

Another Madrid-based institution, the SEGIB, could constitute a
further channel. Portugal and Brazil's work with China within the
framework of the Portuguese-speaking forum can be considered as
providing a good general outline. At the end of 2010, China and
seven Portuguese-speaking countries signed a 2010–13 action plan for
economic and commercial cooperation in Macao, establishing a new
objective of extending the volume of trade over the coming years. This
agreement with China, which was made within the framework of the
third Ministerial Conference of the Forum for Economic and Trade
Cooperation between China and Portuguese-speaking countries, was
signed by Angola, Brazil, Cape Verde, Guinea-Bissau, Mozambique,
Portugal and East Timor.

Another country that is taking steps towards the region and could
be of interest in terms of possible triangular cooperation is India. As
we have seen in previous chapters, Indian investment in the region also
covers technology sectors. This technological interest is clear in the first
steps that India is taking towards international cooperation in Latin
America. In 2012 the Indian government opened a $10 million credit
line for Guatemala and increased the number of annual grants awarded
under the Indian Technical and Economic Cooperation programme
(ITEC). Above all, India, like China and Korea, could be another
potential candidate for the promotion of a fund of funds scheme similar
to that described above.

A public–private scheme involving Spain and other BRIC countries
could lead to the creation of a fund for Latin America. An Ibero-
American Development Fund – as the fund of funds could be called –
would benefit from the experience of these countries in official cooperation with Latin America. This fund would invest, in turn, in venture
capital funds to boost the region's technological and productive fabric,
and could be financed by the OECD and emerging countries, particularly the rest of the BRIC countries which, like China, are developing

international cooperation vehicles. Besides China, which we have already mentioned, India could also be involved given its growing interest in the region and its desire to position itself in the field of international cooperation. In this connection, in 2011, India announced the creation of the India Agency for Partnership in Development (IAPD), a cooperation agency similar to the agencies created by Spain and many other OECD countries in the DAC. This agency will have a budget of $11.3 billion to invest in the second half of the 2010s.

With an average annual international cooperation expenditure of $4 billion and a specialist agency, the Agência Brasileira de Cooperação (ABC), Brazil could also contribute to the promotion of this fund. Arab countries are becoming increasingly active and could also join the initiative. Saudi Arabia is currently, together with Kuwait and United Arab Emirates, the largest Arab player in international cooperation. In 2009, it provided $3.1 billion in aid (one of its main financial instruments is the Saudi Fund for Development).[18] Between 1973 and 2008, official assistance for development from Arab countries totalled an average of 1.5% of their GDPs, meaning it was above the famous United Nations target of 0.7% (which few OECD countries achieved).[19] Several of the region's international cooperation funds are worthy of note, including the Abu Dhabi Fund for Development, which operates in fifty-three countries throughout Africa and Asia,[20] and the Kuwait-based Arab Fund for Economic and Social Development.[21]

Ideas regarding the economics of development are currently undergoing a Copernican revolution with the spread of a more empirical approach led by economists such as Esther Duflo at MIT.[22] The growth of emerging economies and the conversion of many of them into providers of international aid is changing the traditional approaches. We are currently witnessing an unprecedented increase in the activity

---

[18] See www.sfd.gov.sa/.

[19] See ODI, 'Arab Donors: Implications for Future Development Cooperation', Policy Brief 13, March 2011. Available at www.edc2020.eu/fileadmin/publications/EDC_2020_-_Policy_Brief_No_13_-_Arab_Donors_Implications_for_Future_Development_Cooperation.pdf; see also the report by the LSE Kuwait Programme (London School of Economics): www2.lse.ac.uk/government/research/resgroups/kuwait/research/papers/donorship.aspx.

[20] See www.adfd.ae/pages/default.aspx.   [21] See www.sfd.gov.sa/.

[22] See the essay (and previous works) of Abhijit Banerjee and Esther Duflo, *Poor Economics: A Radical Rethinking of the Way to Fight Global Poverty*, New York, Perseus, Public Affairs, 2011.

of the BRICs and emerging countries in terms of international cooperation: they have gone from being mere recipients of aid to being providers. And this will continue in the near future – while the budgets of the OECD countries will suffer cuts as a result of the current debt crisis. China, India and Brazil, with more than $3,300, $350 and $300 billion in international reserves, respectively, have ample room to continue with their international cooperation and aid strategies.

It is highly likely that 2010–20 will see a radical shift in cooperation and changes in both hierarchy and approaches. While the USA remains the leader in international aid (providing $31 billion in 2010), the second in the ranking is no longer an OECD DAC country but China, which, according to data provided by the Wagner School at the University of New York, contributed $27 billion.[23] If India makes $2 billion available in aid via its newly created cooperation agency, it will then be on a par with Australia or Belgium in terms of international aid. According to other sources, BRIC and emerging countries together increased international aid by almost 145% between 2005 and 2008, to $11.2 billion a year before the crisis, i.e. more than 10% of the total provided by OECD countries.

Brazil, China, India, Saudi Arabia and Korea are some of the countries that have become important players in the field of international aid. There is scope for creating renewed cooperation networks, particularly with respect to Latin America – where Spain has a number of potential allies with which to promote triangular cooperation and further regional development.

Latin sovereign wealth funds

Particularly noteworthy among the possible instruments for boosting international cooperation are sovereign wealth funds. These public entities have both financial and economic development objectives. They could act as agents for international cooperation, something that

---

[23] See New York University Robert F. Wagner Graduate School of Public Service, *Understanding Chinese Foreign Aid: A Look at China's Development Assistance to Africa, Southeast Asia, and Latin America*, New York University, April 2008. See also the report by the US Congress on Chinese aid and cooperation for development at www.fas.org/sgp/crs/row/R40361.pdf. Regarding the institutional organisation of aid in China, see also www.oecd. org/dataoecd/27/7/40378067.pdf.

the World Bank's IFC already sought to promote with the creation of a fund for investments in Africa and Latin America (funded in part by contributions from sovereign wealth funds, including KIC from Korea). Many of these funds have also set up South–South cooperation arrangements and joint investments in Africa and Asia, resulting in the multiplication of initiatives in the 2000s.[24]

Sovereign wealth funds are more in vogue than ever in emerging countries and are acting as catalysts in the shift in world finances.[25] Almost 60% of the fifty or so sovereign wealth funds that exist today were created in just ten years between 2000 and 2010. A further fifteen countries are currently considering creating such funds: including Algeria, India, South Africa, Thailand, Indonesia, Japan and Israel. Following in the footsteps of veterans such as Singapore, other countries such as Malaysia, Russia, China and United Arab Emirates have already created several funds. Others such as Nigeria are redesigning their funds in view of previous failures. However, as various studies on the challenge of managing prosperity – particularly in terms of raw materials – show, there are a number of institutional challenges to overcome in the process.[26]

With the crisis affecting OECD countries and the loss by the USA of its AAA credit rating, many emerging countries are beginning to consider using their reserves more aggressively. This is the case of Thailand which, in the middle of 2011, decided that it was time to use part of its $180 billion in reserves more dynamically, opting for a sovereign wealth fund rather than investing solely in treasury bonds (particularly US bonds). Others such as Indonesia considered creating a stabilisation fund for fixed income (about $12 billion) in order to restrict international volatility in capital markets. The movements of

---

[24] See Javier Santiso, 'Sovereign Development Funds: Key Financial Actors of the Shifting Wealth of Nations', Paris, OECD Emerging Markets Network Working Paper, October 2008. Available at www.oecd.org/dataoecd/46/61/41944381.pdf.

[25] See Javier Capapé and Javier Santiso, 'Los fondos soberanos catalizan el re-equilibrio de la economía mundial', ESADEgeo Position Paper 18, July 2011. Available at www.esade.edu/research-webs/eng/esadegeo/publications/position. See also Javier Santiso (ed.), *Sovereign Wealth Funds Report 2012*. Madrid, ESADEgeo, KPMG and Invest in Spain, 2012.

[26] See Frederick van der Ploeg, 'Natural Resources: Curse or Blessing?', *Journal of Economic Literature*, 49(2), 2011, pp. 366–420; and Frederick van der Ploeg and Anthony Venables, 'Harnessing Windfall Revenues: Optimal Policies for Developing Economies', *Economic Journal*, 121, 2011, pp. 1–30.

these funds have been and continue to be essential for understanding the financial shift in the world; many have become global financial players and their influence will increase. The number of sovereign wealth funds and the size of their assets will continue to grow – the assets of the state oil fund of Azerbaijan should rise from $30 to $100 billion between 2010 and 2020.

Yet these funds are not specific to Asia or the Middle East. Such funds are already up and running in several African countries: Botswana was the first to create one and, more recently, Ghana and Angola have taken the plunge. Latin America has not been left behind; countries such as Chile, Trinidad and Tobago, and Venezuela have already created funds. Brazil joined them in 2010 with more than $250 billion in reserves, and, in 2011, Peru, Colombia, Panama and Bolivia began talks for the creation of similar funds. Panama and Colombia created their own sovereign wealth funds in 2011, Panama using income from the canal and Colombia using royalties from mining and oil. In both cases, the governance structures of the sovereign wealth funds of Norway and Chile were used as references for designing processes and decision making procedures. In 2012 Peru also started its own sovereign wealth fund.

In the midst of its crisis, during the years 2010–12, Spain has burst onto the scene with significant investments, particularly in Banco Santander and the Iberdrola electricity company, by Qatar Holdings, Qatar's sovereign wealth fund. In both cases, investment amounted to €2 billion, a sum unprecedented to date. Interest in Latin America was also behind these investments, and Arab funds in particular have sought to increase their commitment to this emerging region via companies that were previously quick to invest in a continent that is now being flirted with by all investors.[27] As a result of the 2008–12 crisis, sovereign wealth funds have generally sought to increase their exposure to emerging countries (even via OECD companies with significant investments in these markets, such as the Spanish companies mentioned above), investing more than 60% of their funds in these

---

[27] On the growing activity of sovereign wealth funds in emerging markets, and more recently their investments in Spain, see the Monitor report, *Braving the New World: Sovereign Wealth Fund Investment in the Uncertain Times of 2010*, Boston and London, Monitor Group, July 2011. Available at www.monitor.com/Portals/0/MonitorContent/imported/MonitorUnitedStates/Articles/PDFs/BTNW_Final.pdf; also the chapter on Spain in Santiso (ed.), *Sovereign Wealth Funds Report 2012*.

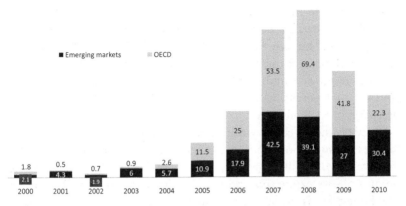

Figure 9.1 Sovereign wealth fund investment in emerging markets versus OECD markets, 2000–10.
Source: Monitor Group, 2011.

markets (an increase of almost 50% compared to 2008). Singapore's Temasek, which had $150 billion under management in 2011, has opened offices in Mexico and Brazil for the first time and, also in 2011, invested $300 million, with the South African Oppenheimer family, to create a $300 million fund for Africa. For its part, GIC, Singapore's other sovereign wealth fund, with almost $220 billion under management, did the same in Mumbai in 2011. Some 10% of this fund's total equity investment is already allocated to emerging markets and GIC intends to increase this amount in the future. For its part, United Arab Emirates' ADIA has set itself the target of allocating between 15% and 25% of its total portfolio to emerging markets[28] (Figure 9.1).

This interest in emerging markets has also been reflected in Latin America.[29] The huge investment in the region has been clearly demonstrated in a number of significant and recent investments. In October 2010, Singapore's sovereign wealth fund Temasek, with assets exceeding $150 billion, took a $400 million stake in Odebrecht, thereby positioning itself in a sector with great potential: that of (local) oil suppliers and Petrobras in particular. Sovereign wealth fund GIC has

[28] See Gawdat Bahgat, 'Sovereign Wealth Funds in the Gulf: An Assessment', LSE Kuwait Programme, July 2011. Available at www2.lse.ac.uk/government/research/resgroups/kuwait/home.aspx.

[29] See Javier Santiso, 'SWFs and Latin America in 2010 and 2011', in Monitor, *Braving the New World: Sovereign Wealth Fund Investment in the Uncertain Times of 2010*, Boston and London, Monitor Group, July 2011, pp. 50–3.

also invested in the region. In 2011, it took a stake of 5.3% in the capital of Aliansce, a Brazilian shopping centre manager. The fund is also participating, together with the Canadian Pension Plan fund, in a $650 million investment in six Cyrela Commercial Properties (CCP) real estate projects and, at the end of 2010, it formed part of a consortium that purchased 18% of the capital of BTG Pactual with an injection of $1.8 billion.

In 2011, the sovereign wealth fund Korea Investment Corp and one of the largest pension funds in Canada announced that they were each to invest $100 million in Brazil's Manabi Holding SA to participate in an iron-ore exploration project. For its part, China's CIC, one of the largest funds in the world, had 5.4% of its portfolio invested in Latin American listed companies at the end of 2010; this amount is still modest when compared to amounts invested by Asia, excluding China (almost 30%), or the United States (42%) but, according to its latest annual report, investments are increasing.[30] In 2010, its main transaction in Latin America was the investment of $300 million in the Brazilian bank BTG Pactual. In the middle of 2011, CIC reaffirmed its interest in the region by purchasing 30% of a subsidiary of the French multinational GDF Suez for €2.3 billion – of which €600 million was to be allocated for a 10% stake in the liquefied natural gas plant owned by the French multinational in Trinidad and Tobago.

In 2012, sovereign wealth funds from Arab countries increased even further their bet on Latin America. ADIA, one of the world's biggest sovereign wealth funds, based in Abu Dhabi, appointed Eduardo Favrin as head of Latin America in its internal equities department, in a clear move to muscle its Latin American teams. The move followed the decision of another Abu Dhabi fund, Mubadala Development Company, to invest $2 billion in Eike Batista's EBX Group Co. as the Brazilian billionaire was seeking cash to fund expansion. This transaction marked the first significant direct investment of Mubadala into one of the fastest-growing markets and is an important step in Mubadala's development of strategic opportunities in Brazil and Latin America. The deal also illustrated the international appetite of Brazilian multinationals and the diversification attempts away from commodities. As his commodity and logistics companies leave the pre-operational

---

[30] See the annual report, available on CIC's website: www.china-inv.cn/cicen/include/resources/CIC_2010_annualreport_en.pdf?ickey=1.

phase, Batista is diversifying into segments such as sports and technology. EBX has entered the catering-services market through NRX-Newrest, a joint venture with Newrest Group Holding, and also started IMX, a partnership with IMG Worldwide Inc. focused on sports and arena management in Brazil. Batista is investing $2.5 billion in a plant to make electronic screens in Brazil through a joint venture with Chinese Foxconn, a maker of metal casings for Apple. Last but not least, EBX also signed an agreement with Egypt's Orascom Construction Industries for a fertilisers venture that may require $3 billion of investment.

It is a paradox of abundance that many Latin American countries now have significant reserves and are facing the challenge – particularly in Andean countries – of managing a raw materials boom. Their investments and exports continue to be concentrated in areas with little value added or employment. For this reason they intend to take advantage of their abundance and diversify their economies – an issue which is still pending. Sovereign wealth funds could be used as strategic vehicles for achieving this aim, provided that care is taken to equip funds with first-rate professionals and processes.

This is something that Chile did brilliantly. In the middle of the 2000s, it created two sovereign wealth funds with stringent rules and first-rate staff and institutional capital. Its efforts have made it a worldwide reference for sovereign wealth funds, on a par with Norway. Chile's funds are governed by a strict tax responsibility law, which was adopted in 2006 and requires surpluses for the previous year in excess of 0.5% of the GDP to be added to the first fund (pensions reserve fund); with the next 0.5% of the surplus above GDP to be allocated to capitalising the central bank; and any surplus generated after that to be allocated to the second sovereign wealth fund (the economic and social stabilisation fund).

Several lessons can be learned from this successful Latin American experience. The first is that this kind of instrument cannot be used without a stringent fiscal policy. Chile implemented these funds within a corset-like structure that is now seen as exemplary not only in the region, but in the world (this is also the reason why Chile had no difficulty joining the select OECD club in 2010). The second lesson, a derivative of the first, is that rigorous rules and regulations are useless without an institutional framework. Chile created very clear institutional and regulatory frameworks, particularly with respect to emerging countries. Lastly, it is equally essential to equip such institutions with suitable staff. In Chile's case, both the previous and the current government have been formed by top-rate professionals and economists, starting with the past and present finance ministers, Andrés Velasco and Felipe Larraín, who have supervised the funds. They both have economics doctorates and prestigious academic careers, particularly in the USA.

However, the Chilean funds are not strategic funds designed to promote business development and diversification; they have remained funds of a relatively conservative nature, e.g. stabilisation funds and resource management funds. Perhaps because of the failures of the region's industrial policy in the past, they have not been made to follow the path of more strategic funds, despite the fact that – as the University of Chicago economist Adair Morse points out in a paper published in 2011 – many sovereign wealth funds have industrial objectives as well as financial ends.[31]

Chile's funds, like those of Norway and Australia, have purely financial objectives. Some of the emerging countries such as the United Arab Emirates, Singapore and Malaysia have created strategic funds with the clear objective of contributing to business development and diversification. Chile could create a (third) sovereign wealth fund with such an aim in mind. The beauty of the Chilean model is that it potentially has a suitable incentive structure to do so: it is possible to envisage adding a fourth layer for a strategic fund over the three layers that it currently has for tax surpluses. This would only come into play once the first three levels had been satisfied and would therefore only be activated once a significant tax surplus had been generated. The strategic fund could then operate as a fund of funds, accelerating the diversification of production towards technological sectors or industrial sectors related with the mining industry.

It is noteworthy that, despite its position as the world's leading copper producer and exporter, Chile does not have a single world-scale multinational supplier of vehicles, excavators or explosives. All the existing firms are foreign: Caterpillar and Joy Global are listed on the

---

[31] See Alexander Dyck and Adair Morse, 'Sovereign Wealth Funds Portfolio', The University of Chicago Booth School of Business, Working Paper 11–15, February 2011. Available at http://papers.ssrn.com/sol3/papers.cfm?abstract_id=1792850##.

New York stock exchange, Komatsu on the Tokyo stock exchange, and Atlas Copco and Sandvik in Stockholm; Boart Longyear, Leighton and Orica are Australian, Weir Group is Scottish, Hatch is Canadian and Orica is South African. All these firms generate large-scale employment and add significant value. The Chilean company Codelco, the world's leading copper producer, employs just under 20,000 staff, a great deal fewer than the Swedish multinationals Sandvik (44,000) and Atlas Copco (30,000). Its revenues are seven times less than those of Caterpillar, which also employs five times more people.

The strategic funds of the United Arab Emirates (e.g. Mubadala) have investment policies very different from those of Malaysia (Khazanah) and Singapore (Temasek): the first buys stakes in foreign multinationals in order subsequently to promote industrial plants within its national base; the two Asian funds have opted to support national champions directly (and they have achieved this aim). In any case, between them they offer a wide range of options that could serve as inspiration for various Latin American countries, particularly those – such as Colombia – with a greater institutional capacity.

These Arab and Asian examples demonstrate the extent to which sovereign wealth funds can be strategic players in economic diversification and development. In the case of Latin America, Brazil – via the Brazilian Development Bank (BNDES) – has operated as a de facto instrument of this type, producing giants of the calibre of Vale and Petrobras in the raw material sectors, but also others in leading sectors such as the aeronautical sector, e.g. Embraer. BNDES has not only generated global champions; it has also increased the value of their subsidiaries. A Harvard University study shows that in the middle of the 2000s the industrial holdings of BNDES (via its subsidiary BNDESPAR) amounted to some $13.5 billion, i.e. almost 4% of the Brazilian stock exchange. In 2009, these shares still represented 4% of Brazil's stock market capitalisation with a value of more than $53.4 billion.[32] Countries such as Peru and Colombia are heavily dependent on raw materials and are now debating whether or not to create sovereign wealth funds. They could look to Chile when designing their

---

[32] See Sergio Lazzarini and Aldo Musacchio, 'Leviathan as a Minority Shareholder: A Study of Equity Purchases by the Brazilian Development Bank (BNDES), 1995–2003', Harvard Business School, Working Paper 11–071, December 2010. Available at www.hbs.edu/research/pdf/11-073.pdf.

strategies, but they could also look beyond, to the United Arab Emirates, Singapore or Malaysia, and design a scheme that would also enable the creation of a strategic fund, something that Chile itself may well be advised to consider.

FONPRODE, which we mentioned above, and which ultimately acts as a sovereign wealth fund for international cooperation, could also be used as an instrument to lever the interest of sovereign wealth funds from other emerging regions in Latin America. It could also link Latin funds to sovereign wealth funds and promote triangular cooperation in certain sectors (water, infrastructure, technologies) in which Spain could act as a catalyst and connection. In any case, sovereign wealth funds, with their investment horizons and appetite for comparable risk, actively encourage cooperation amongst themselves, as shown by Korea's KIC.[33]

KIC participated in the creation of the World Bank's IFC Sovereign Fund, a venture capital fund for investment in Africa and Latin America. KIC invested a total of $100 million in the fund, which raised a total of $600 million, making it one of the largest in the emerging markets (the IFC Asset Management Company, the subsidiary that manages the fund, had established an initial target of a billion dollars). Another example is the biotechnology fund promoted by Mubadala and the French sovereign wealth fund FSI. KIC has also invested in the fund created by Mubadala and General Electric for Northern Africa and the Middle East. The IFC continues with its strategy to raise venture capital funds for developing countries: in 2011 it laid the foundations for another venture capital fund for emerging economies, the IFC Global Infrastructure Fund. This fund focuses on infrastructures and, with a target of a billion dollars, seeks the support of pension funds and sovereign wealth funds. The World Bank, via the IFC, is committing $200 million (20%) to help anchor the initiative.

(Re)thinking Latin America

In any case, relations with Latin America should be reconsidered in the light of another decade in which emerging economies promise to be the

---

[33] See Scott Kalb, *The Growing of Cooperation among Sovereign Wealth Funds*, Seoul, Korea Investment Corporation, June 2011. Available at www.kic.go.kr/en/pr/pr030000.jsp?mode=view&article_no=474&pager.offset=0&board_no=44.

main players. As regards international cooperation, the business and economic growth of countries like Brazil and Chile has brought new opportunities for modernisation and triangular cooperation between OECD donors and Spain, whose companies and economy are also committed to the region. Spain could become a central axis for international cooperation with the region, focusing efforts to reinvent development aid within a modern, public–private framework that promotes business and employment.

Above all, Spain could promote a renewed strategy with respect to the region, and establish itself as the gateway to Europe for the multilatinas – as well as a springboard in the other direction, from Europe to Latin America. Promoting Spain as a Latin hub is a pending task; although some multilatinas are already settled in the peninsula, many (particularly from Brazil) have preferred to establish their European bases further north. Moreover, Spain's potential as a European and Latin American hub could be promoted with respect to European multinationals that are seeking to expand into or consolidate their position in Latin America, and those from emerging countries such as China, who are seeking simultaneously to enter Latin America and Europe.

Multilatinas will continue to grow over the next ten years. Table 9.2 shows an extraordinary development between 1970 and 2010: in 1970, Latin America accounted for a total of 0.5% of the world's FDI outflows and developing countries for just 1.2% of the world total. Thirty years later, Latin America accounted for 3.7% and emerging countries for 13.8% of the world total. Latin America now accounts for one-third (of a total that is growing at an enormous nominal rate) of the FDI outflows from emerging markets. If we exclude tax havens, Asia as a whole accounts for 16% of the FDI issued at a global level and Latin America and the Caribbean account for 4.3%. Both regions have become important global investment players. As mentioned earlier, although most FDI originating in Latin America is intraregional, more recently the multilatinas have extended their investments beyond the region and have even ventured into Europe.

So we see that emerging markets, including those of Latin America, are now important players and investors on a global scale. International investment by emerging countries amounted to $922 billion in 2010, 20% of the world total, compared to $280 billion in 2000, just 6% of the world total. In 2010, more than half of IPOs took

Table 9.2 *Distribution of worldwide FDI outflows, 1970–2009 (as percentage of total FDI outflows).*

	1970–9		1980–9		1990–9		2000–9	
	% in the world total	% in the total of developing countries	% in the world total	% in the total of developing countries	% in the world total	% in the total of developing countries	% in the world total	% in the total of developing countries
Developing countries	1.2	100	6.3	100	10.7	100	13.8	100
South, East and South east Asia	0.2	18.9	3.9	62.2	7.9	73.2	8.3	60.1
LAC	0.5	41.2	1.2	18.8	2.4	22.1	3.7	27
Argentina	0	0	0	0	0.3	2.6	0.1	0.8
Brazil	0.3	23.1	0.4	6.7	0.2	1.7	0.4	3
Chile	0	0	0	0	0.2	1.7	0.3	2.3
Colombia	0	0	0.1	1.7	0.1	0.9	0.1	0.8
Costa Rica	0	0	0	0	0	0	0	0
Mexico	0	0	0.1	1.7	0.1	0.9	0.4	3
Peru	0	0	0	0	0	0	0	0
Uruguay	0	0	0	0	0	0	0	0
Venezuela	0	0	0.1	1.7	0.1	0.9	0.1	0.8

Source: ESADEgeo, 2012; based on UNCTAD data.

place in emerging markets, with Brazil's Petrobras holding the world record with a transaction for more than $70 billion.[34] The bulk of flows (61%) are still portfolio investments by the central banks of emerging countries, but investments by other kinds of players – private individuals, companies and sovereign wealth funds – are rising and helping to change the international shareholding and business map (Figure 9.2).

---

[34] See McKinsey, *Mapping Global Capital Markets 2011*, Boston and Washington, DC, McKinsey Global Institute, August 2011. Available at www.mckinsey.com/mgi/reports/freepass_pdfs/Mapping_global_capital_markets/Capital_markets_update_email.pdf.

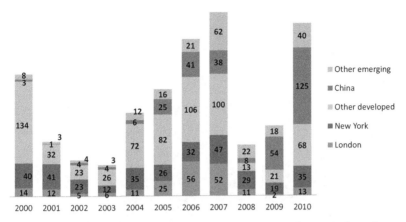

Figure 9.2 Volume of financial transactions (IPOs) in the capital markets, 2000–10.
Source: McKinsey Global Institute, 2011.

FDI from these markets amounted to almost $160 billion in 2010 and a large part was accounted for by multilatinas extending their horizons beyond the borders of the American continent. These multinationals now have access to capital at costs comparable to those of their OECD rivals: in 2010 alone, emerging multinationals issued corporate bonds for almost $280 billion for their national and international expansion. China and Latin America are leading the emerging market dynamic in foreign investment: in 2010 they accounted for $405 and $173 billion, respectively (Figure 9.3).

In the early 2000s the United States and Europe were still at the centre of the international capital flows network, but this is no longer the case. South–South relations have developed fast: in 2010, Latin America's cross-border transactions with Asia were on a par with its transactions with Europe. Multilatinas, like their counterparts in other emerging countries, have joined a race for internationalisation that is entering a new era: the rise of ever-more global multilatinas (or emerging multinationals). This will bring with it both challenges and opportunities for OECD countries. We must reprogramme our cognitive maps and say goodbye to Europe-centred visions.

With the rise of emerging multinationals, including multilatinas, business hierarchies are changing and they will continue to

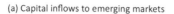

(a) Capital inflows to emerging markets

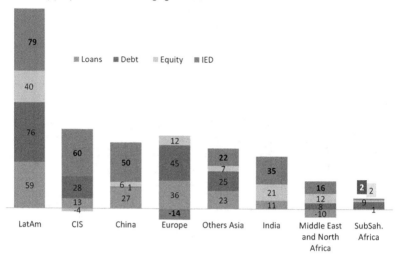

(b) Capital outflows from emerging markets

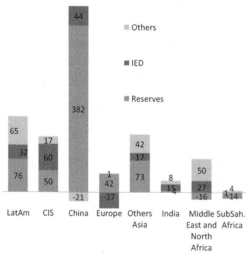

Figure 9.3 Emerging markets become international investors: capital flows in 2010 (in $ billion).
(a) Capital inflows to emerging markets.
(b) Capital outflows from emerging markets.
Source: McKinsey Global Institute, 2011.

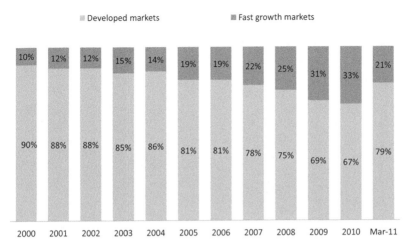

Figure 9.4 The thousand leading companies in the world, 2010 (market capitalisation value, as percentage of the total).
Source: Ernst & Young, 2011.

change, increasing the convergence between developed and developing economies.[35] In the early 2000s, only 10% of the top thousand multinationals came from emerging countries. In 2010, this figure was more than 31%, with BRIC countries accounting for 73% and Brazil and Mexico for 13% and 3% of the worldwide total, respectively. Brazil leads in terms of increase in sales, with an average annual growth of more than 22% since the middle of the 2000s[36] (Figures 9.4 and 9.5).

The current decade will require us to rethink relations between Spain and Latin America. These relationships are now more balanced than they were in the past and they will soon cease to be unilateral as the unstoppable rise of the multilatinas unfolds. These companies are the

[35] See the essay by the winner of the Nobel Prize for Economic Sciences Michael Spence, *The Next Convergence: The Future of Economic Growth in a Multispeed World*, New York, Farrar, Straus and Giroux, 2011.

[36] See Ernst & Young, *Globalization 3.0: Competing for Growth*, Ernst & Young, 2011. Available at www.ey.com/Publication/vwLUAssets/ Globalization-3.0-competing-for-growth/$FILE/Globalization-3.0-competing-for-growth.pdf.

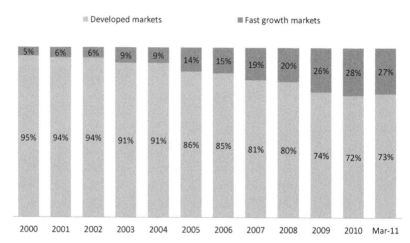

Figure 9.5 The thousand leading companies in the world in terms of market capitalisation, 2010 (number of companies, as percentage of total companies). *Source:* Ernst & Young, 2011.

new face of a continent that is no longer synonymous with dictatorships, crises and failure, and has become a land of democracy, growth and achievement, experiencing an impressive shift in terms of political economy.[37] This decade will see the reshaping of the developed world's relationship with a Latin American continent that has become a motor of change in the international business world.

---

[37] See for the nuances of this transformation the chapters published by Javier Santiso and Jeff Dayton-Johnson (eds.), *The Oxford Handbook of Latin American Political Economy*, Oxford University Press, 2012.

References

Abreu Campanario, Milton de, Eva Stal and Marcello Muniz da Silva, 2012, 'Outward FDI from Brazil and its Policy Context', Vale Columbia Center FDI Profiles, May. Available at www.vcc.columbia.edu/files/vale/documents/Profile-_Brazil_OFDI_10_May_2012_-_FINAL.pdf

Abu Dhabi Fund for Development. See www.adfd.ae/pages/default.aspx

Agtmael, Antoine van, 2007, *The Emerging Markets Century: How a New Breed of World-Class Companies Is Overtaking the World*, New York, Free Press

Alfaro, Laura, Sebnem Kalemli-Ozcan and Vadym Volosovch, 2007, 'Capital Flows in a Globalized World: The Role of Policies and Institutions', in Sebastian Edwards (ed.), *Capital Controls and Capital Flows in Emerging Economies: Policies, Practices and Consequences*, National Bureau of Economic Research, University of Chicago Press, May, pp. 19–72

América Economía, 2011, Ranking 500 Multilatinas. Available at http://rankings.americaeconomia.com/2011/500/

Arbatli, Elif, 2011, 'Economic Policies and FDI Inflows in Emerging Markets', IMF Working Paper, August. Available at www.imf.org/external/pubs/ft/wp/2011/wp11192.pdf

AT Kearney, 2010, Urban Elite Global Cities Index. Available at www.atkearney.at/content/misc/wrapper.php/id/50369/name/pdf_urban_elite-gci_2010_12894889240b41.pdf

AT Kearney, 2010, *Investing in a Rebound: The 2010 AT Kearney FDI Confidence Index*, Washington, DC, AT Kearney. Available at www.atkearney.com/images/global/pdf/Investing_in_a_Rebound-FDICI_2010.pdf

Avendaño, Rolando and Javier Santiso, 2011, 'Economic Fundamentals of the Relationship', in Adrian Hearn and José Luis León-Manriquez (eds.), *China Engages Latin America: Tracing the Trajectory*, London, Lynne Rienner Publishers, pp. 67–101

2012, 'Asian Opportunities and Diversification Strategies: An Outlook for Latin American Trade', in K. C. Fung and Alicia García Herrero (eds.), *Sino–Latin American Economic Relations*, London, Routledge, pp. 36–69

Bahgat, Gawdat, 2011, 'Sovereign Wealth Funds in the Gulf: An Assessment', LSE Kuwait Programme, 2011. Available at www2.lse.ac.uk/government/research/resgroups/kuwait/home.aspx

Banco de Bogotá, 2011, https://pbit.bancodebogota.com.co/Investigaciones/PresentacionPDF.aspx?PDF=42

Banerjee, Abhijit and Esther Duflo, 2011, *Poor Economics: A Radical Rethinking of the Way to Fight Global Poverty*, New York, Perseus, Public Affairs

Bareau, Pierre Yves, 2011, *Emerging Markets Debt Coming of Age*, London, JP Morgan Asset Management. Available at www.jpmorgan.com/pages/jpmorgan/investbk/solutions/research

de Barros, Octavio, 2011, www.fiesp.com.br/irs/cosec/pdf/transparencias_reuniao_cosec_13_06_11_-_octavio_de_barros_-_distribuicao_final.pdf

BBVA, Economic Watch Series, Peru, 2011, http://serviciodeestudios.bbva.com/KETD/fbin/mult/110726_EconomicWatch_Peru-Brazil_tcm348-264701.pdf?ts=882011

di Bella, Gabriel, 2011, 'The Impact of the Global Financial Crisis on Microfinance and Policy Implications', IMF Working Paper 11–175, July. Available at www.imf.org/external/pubs/ft/wp/2011/wp11175.pdf

BID, Inter-American Development Bank (IADB), 2010, *Ten Years after the Take-off: Taking Stock of China – Latin America and the Caribbean Economic Relations*, Washington, DC, IADB. Available at http://idbdocs.iadb.org/wsdocs/getdocument.aspx?docnum=35410652
2010, *From Multilatinas to Global Latinas, 2010: The New Latin American Multinationals (Compilation Case Studies)*, Washington, DC, IADB

Blackrock, 2011, *Introducing the Blackrock Sovereign Risk Index: A More Comprehensive View of Credit Quality*, New York and London, Blackrock. Available at www2.blackrock.com/webcore/litService/search/getDocument.seam?venue=PUB_IND&source=GLOBAL&contentId=1111142235

Blázquez, Jorge and Javier Santiso, 2006, '¿Ángel o demonio? Los efectos del comercio chino en los países de América Latina', *Revista de CEPAL*, 90, December, pp. 17–43

Booz & Company, 2011, *The Global Innovation 1000: How the Top Innovators Keep Winning*, London and New York, Booz & Company. Available at www.booz.com/media/file/sb61_10408-R.pdf

Boston Consulting Group (BCG), 2008, *The 2008 BCG 100: New Global Challengers. How Top Companies from Rapidly Developing Economies Are Changing the World*, Boston, BCG. Available

at www.bcg.com.cn/export/sites/default/en/files/publications/reports_
pdf/New_Global_Challengers_Feb_2008.pdf

2009, *The 2009 BCG Multilatinas*, Boston, BCG. Available at www.bcg.
com/documents/file27236.pdf

2010, *Innovation 2010. A Return to Prominence – and the Emergence of
a New World Order*, Boston, BCG, April. Available at www.bcg.com/
documents/file42620.pdf

2010, *Swimming against the Tide: How Technology, Media, and Telecommunications Companies Can Prosper in the New Economic Reality*,
Boston, BCG. Available at www.bcg.com/documents/file59590.pdf

2010, *The 2010 Value Creators Report. Threading the Needle: Value
Creation in a Low Growth Economy*, Boston, BCG. Available at www.
bcg.com/documents/file59590.pdf

2011, *BCG Global Challengers. Companies on the Move: Rising Stars
from Rapidly Developing Economies Are Reshaping Global Industries*,
Boston, BCG. Available at www.bcg.com/documents/file70055.pdf

Brautigam, Deborah, 2009, *The Dragon's Gift: The Real Story of China in
Africa*, Oxford University Press

Brown, Clair and Greg Linden, 2009, *Chips and Change: How Crisis
Reshapes the Semiconductor Industry*, Cambridge, Mass., MIT Press.
Available at http://mitpress.mit.edu/catalog/item/default.asp?ttype=
2&tid=12005&mode=toc and www.irle.berkeley.edu/worktech/
greglinden.html

Bustos, Paula, 2011, 'Trade Liberalization, Exports, and Technology
Upgrading: Evidence on the Impact of MERCOSUR on Argentinian
Firms', *American Economic Review*, 101(1), pp. 304–40. Available at
www.crei.cat/people/bustos/Trade_Skill_PBustos.pdf

Capapé, Javier and Javier Santiso, 2011, 'Los fondos soberanos catalizan
el re-equilibrio de la economía mundial', ESADEgeo Position Paper
18, July. Available at www.esade.edu/research-webs/eng/esadegeo/
publications/position

Cárdenas, Mauricio and Adriana Kluger, 2011, 'The Reversal of the
Structural Transformation in Latin America after China's Emergence', Washington, DC, Latin American Initiative, August. Available
at www.brookings.edu/~/media/Files/rc/papers/2011/0802_structural_
transformation_cardenas/0802_structural_transformation_cardenas.pdf

Cárdenas, Mauricio and Eduardo Levy-Yeyati (eds.), *Latin America
Economic Perspectives: Shifting Gears in an Age of Heightened
Expectations*, Washington, DC, Brookings Institution, 2011. Available at www.brookings.edu/~/media/Files/rc/reports/2011/0408_blep_
cardenas/04_blep_cardenas_yeyati.pdf

Cardoso, Eliana and Márcio Holland, 2010, 'South America for the Chinese? A Trade Based Analysis', OECD Development Centre, Working Paper 289, April. Available at www.oecd.org/dataoecd/41/39/45041460.pdf

Casanova, Lourdes, 2009, *Global Latinas: Emerging Multinationals from Latin America*, London, Palgrave Macmillan

2011, 'El ascenso de las multilatinas en la economía mundial', *Revista ICE*, 859, March–April, pp. 21–31. Available at www.revistasice.com/CachePDF/ICE_859_21-32__AB6E846F8E555C313551E3D3F54FCE 10.pdf

Casilda, Ramón, 2011, *Multinacionales españolas en un mundo global y multipolar*, Madrid, ESIC

Castilla, Emilio, 2003, 'Network of Venture Capital Firms in Silicon Valley', *International Journal of Technology Management*, 25(1/2), pp. 113–35. Available at www.talentfirstnetwork.org/wiki/images/1/1a/Networks_of_VC_Firms_in_Silicon_Valley.pdf

CEPAL, 2011, *La inversión extranjera directa en América Latina y el Caribe 2010*, Santiago de Chile, CEPAL, May. Report available at www.eclac.org/noticias/paginas/8/33638/2011-283-IED-Presentacion-es.pdf

2011, *La República Popular China y América Latina y el Caribe: hacia una nueva fase en el vínculo económico y comercial*, Santiago de Chile, CEPAL, June. Available at www.eclac.cl/publicaciones/xml/6/43666/La_Republica_Popular_China_y_America_Latina_y_el_Caribe_trade.pdf

Cesa-Bianchi, Ambrogio *et al.*, 2011, 'On the Transmission of Global Shocks to Latin America before and after China's Emergence in the World Economy', Inter-American Development Bank, Working Paper. Available at www.iadb.org/res/centralBanks/publications/cbm58_649.pdf

China Development Bank. See www.cdb.com.cn/english/

China Foreign Aid (White Paper), 2011. Available at www.eu-china.net/web/cms/upload/pdf/nachrichten/2011-04-21Chinas-ForeignAid-WhitePaper.pdf

China Investment Corporation, Annual Report, 2010. Available at www.china-inv.cn/cicen/include/resources/CIC_2010_annualreprot_en.pdf?ickey=1

Comin, Diego and Bart Hobijn, 2010, 'An Exploration of Technology Diffusion', *American Economic Review*, 100(5), pp. 2031–59

2010, 'Technology Diffusion and Postwar Growth', Federal Reserve Bank of San Francisco, Working Paper 16, June. Available at www.frbsf.org/publications/economics/papers/2010/wp10-16bk.pdf

Comin, Diego, Norman Loayza, Farooq Pasha and Luis Servén, 2010, 'Medium Term Business Cycles in Developing Countries', Harvard

Business School, Working Paper 10–029, September. Available at www.hbs.edu/research/pdf/10-029.pdf

Congressional Research Service, 2009. China's Foreign Aid Activities in Africa, Latin America and Southeast Asia. Available at www.fas.org/sgp/crs/row/R40361.pdf

Cooperación Sur–Sur. Programa Iberoamericano para el Fortalecimiento de la Cooperación Sur–Sur. See www.cooperacionsursur.org/

Coutinho, Luciano, Joao, Ferraz, André Nassif and Rafael Oliva, 2012, 'Industrial Policy and Economic Transformation', in Javier Santiso and Jeff Dayton-Johnson (eds.), *The Oxford Handbook of Latin American Political Economy*, Oxford University Press, pp. 100–33

Dabla-Norris, Era, Jiro Honda, Amina Lahreche and Geneviève Verdier, 2010, 'FDI Flows to Low-Income Countries: Global Drivers and Growth Implications', IMF Working Paper 10/132

Daude, Christian, 2010, 'Innovation, Productivity and Economic Development in Latin America and the Caribbean', OECD Development Centre, Working Paper 288, February. Available at www.oecd.org/dataoecd/4/36/44581147.pdf

Dedrick, Jason, Kenneth Kraemer and Greg Linden, 2010, 'Who Profits from Innovation in Global Value Chains? A Study of the iPod and Notebook PCs', University of California, Irvine, 2008, published in *Industrial and Corporate Change*, 19 (1), pp. 81–116. Available at http://web.mit.edu/is08/pdf/Dedrick_Kraemer_Linden.pdf

2011, 'Who Captures Value in the Apple iPad and iPhone?', University of California Irvine, July. Available at http://pcic.merage.uci.edu/papers/2011/Value_iPad_iPhone.pdf

Deloitte, Global Chinese Services. Available at www.deloitte.com/assets/Dcom-China/Local%20Assets/Documents/Services/Global%20Chinese%20Services%20Group/cn_CSG_MMChinaOutboundMA_301110.pdf

Devereux, M. P., B. Lockwood and M. Redoano, 2008, 'Do Countries Compete over Corporate Tax Rates?', *Journal of Public Economics*, 92, pp. 210–35

Douglass, John, Richard Edelstein and Cecile Hoareau, 2011, 'A Global Talent Magnet: How a San Francisco/Bay Area Global Higher Education Hub Could Advance California's Comparative Advantage in Attracting International Talent and Further Build US Economic Competitiveness', University of California, Berkeley, Center for Studies in Higher Education, Research and Occasional Paper Series, May. Available at http://cshe.berkeley.edu/publications/docs/ROPS.CalBayAreaHEHub.6.13.2011.pdf

Downs, Erica, 2011, 'Inside China, Inc: China Development Bank's Cross-Border Energy Deals', John L. Thornton China Center at Brookings Monograph Series 3, Beijing and Washington, DC, March. Available at www.brookings.edu/papers/2011/0321_china_energy_downs. aspx

Dyck, Alexander and Adair Morse, 2011, 'Sovereign Wealth Funds Portfolio', The University of Chicago Booth School of Business, Working Paper 11–15, February. Available at http://papers.ssrn.com/sol3/papers. cfm?abstract_id=1792850##

ECLAC, 2011, *La República Popular China y América Latina y el Caribe: hacia una nueva fase en el vínculo económico y comercial (The People's Republic of China and Latin America and the Caribbean: Ushering in a New Era in the Economic and Trade Relationship*, Santiago de Chile, ECLAC, June 2011. Available at www.eclac.org/comercio/ publicaciones/xml/4/43664/People_Republic_of_China_and_Latina_ America_and_the_Caribbean_trade.pdf

    2012, *Foreign Direct Investment in Latin America and the Caribbean 2011*, Santiago de Chile, ECLAC. Available at www.cepal.org/ publicaciones/xml/2/46572/2012-182-LIEI-WEB.pdf

Eichengreen, Barry and Hui Tong, 2011, 'The External Impact of China's Exchange Rate Policy: Evidence from Firm Level Data', IMF Working Paper 11–155, July. Available at www.imf.org/external/pubs/ft/wp/ 2011/wp11155.pdf

EMPEA and Coller Capital, 2011, *Emerging Markets Private Equity Survey 2011*, London, Coller Capital / EMPEA. Available at http://spanish. collercapital.com/uploaded/documents/News/2011/EMPEA_Coller_ 2011_Survey_-_final.pdf

Ernst & Young, 2011, *Globalization 3.0: Competing for Growth*, Ernst & Young. Available at www.ey.com/Publication/vwLUAssets/ Globalization-3.0-competing-for-growth/$FILE/Globalization-3. 0-competing-for-growth.pdf

    2011, *Restart: Ernst & Young's European Attractiveness Survey*, Ernst & Young, 2011. Available at www.ey.com/Publication/ vwLUAssets/Europe_attractiveness_2011_web_resolution/$FILE/ Europe_attractiveness_2011_web_resolution.pdf

    2012, *Globalizing Venture Capital*, Ernst & Young. Available at www.ey. com/FR/fr/Newsroom/News-releases/Communique-de-presse – Global -venture-capital-investment-trends-report-2012

ESADE, 2010, *La multinacional española ante un nuevo escenario internacional. Segundo informe anual del Observatorio de la Empresa Multinacional Española (OEME)*, Barcelona and Madrid, ESADE Business School and ICEX

Esteves, Rui Pedro, 2011, 'The Belle Epoque of International Finance. French Capital Exports, 1880–1914', University of Oxford, Department of Economics, Discussion Paper Series 534, February. Available at www.economics.ox.ac.uk/research/WP/pdf/paper534.pdf

Fairlie, Robert, 2008, *Race and Entrepreneurial Success: Black, Asian, and White-Owned Businesses in the United States*, Cambridge, Mass., MIT Press

Fairlie, Robert and Aaron Chatterji, 'High Technology Entrepreneurs in Silicon Valley: Opportunities and Opportunity Costs', University of California, Santa Clara, Department of Economics, October 2010. Available at http://people.ucsc.edu/~rfairlie/papers/

Ferchen, Matt, Alicia Garcia-Herrero and Mario Nigrinis, 2012, 'Evaluating Latin America's Commodity Dependence, on China', BBVA Research, Working Paper 12/08, May

Financial Times, 500 Global Companies Index, www.ft.com/intl/cms/95edc490-9d61-11e0-9a70-00144feabdc0.pdf

Flandreau, Marc, Juan Flores, Nicolas Gaillard and Sebastián Nieto-Parra, 2009, 'The End of Gatekeeping: Underwriters and the Quality of Sovereign Bond Markets, 1815–2007', NBER Working Paper 15128

Fleury, Alfonso and Maria Teresa Leme Fleury, 2011, *Brazilian Multinationals: Competences for Internationalization*, Cambridge University Press

FRIDE, 2010, *La tercera ola de actores del desarrollo*, Policy Brief, 60, www.fride.org/publicacion/818/la-tercera-ola-de-actores-del-desarrollo

Frot, Emmanuel and Javier Santiso, 2008, 'Development Aid and Portfolio Funds: Trends, Volatility and Fragmentation', OECD Development Centre, Working Paper 275

2009, 'Herding in Aid Allocation', OECD Development Centre, Working Paper 279

2010, 'Crushed Aid: Fragmentation in Sectoral Aid', OECD Development Centre, Working Paper 284. Available at www.oecd-ilibrary.org/development/crushed-aid_218465127786Furtado, Claudio. Published in 2011: www.anbima.com.br/eventos/arqs/eventos_anteriores/6-fundos-1/workshop2_cfurtado.pdf

Fundación Carolina, 2009, 'Cooperación Sur–Sur: innovación y transformación en la cooperación internacional'. Available at www.fundacioncarolina.es/es-ES/nombrespropios/Documents/NPBAyllón0912.pdf

Fundación MicroFinanzas BBVA. See www.mfbbva.org/castellano.html

Fung, K. C., Alicia García-Herrero and Mario Nigrinis Ospina, 2012, 'Latin American Commodity Export Concentration: Is There a China Effect?', BBVA Research Working Paper 12/07, May

Gallagher, Kevin, 2010, 'China and the Future of Latin American Industrialization', Boston University Issue Brief, 8. Available at www.bu.edu/pardee/publications/issues-in-brief-no-18/
  2012, 'A Catalyst for Hope: China's Opportunity for Latin America', in Javier Santiso and Jeff Dayton-Johnson (eds.), *The Oxford Handbook of Latin American Political Economy*, Oxford University Press, pp. 233–61

Gallagher, Kevin, Amos Irwin and Katherine Koleski, 2012, 'The New Banks in Town: Chinese Finance in Latin America', *Inter-American Dialogue Report*. Available at www.thedialogue.org/PublicationFiles/TheNewBanksinTown-FullTextnewversion.pdf

Gallagher, Kevin and Roberto Porcekanski, 2010, *The Dragon in the Room: China and the Future of Latin American Industrialization*, Stanford University Press

García, Jaime, 2011, Países Árabes, http://idei.pucp.edu.pe/docs/2011-paises-arabes-jaime-garcia.pdf

García Canal, Esteban and Mauro Guillén, 2008, 'The Expansion of Spanish Businesses into Latin America: An Analysis', *Journal of Globalization, Competitiveness, Governability, Georgetown University*, 2(2), pp. 18–45. Available at www.unioviedo.es/egarcia/GCG.articulo_91_1216827229514.pdf

García-Herrero, Alicia, 2010, 'China – Latam: Going beyond Conventional Wisdom', Hong Kong, BBVA Research, presentation made at the China–Iberoamerican Dialogue, Madrid, SEGIB, September. Available at www.bbvaresearch.com/KETD/fbin/mult/101007_AliciaChina-LATAM_tcm348-234062.pdf?ts=27122010
  2010, *China's outward FDI: What Explains Geographical Destination? Some Thoughts for Europe*, Madrid and Hong Kong, BBVA Research, December. Available at www.iberchina.org/frame.htm?images/archivos/ChinaoutwardFDI_agh_bbva.pdf
  2011, 'Who Are the Eagles? Driving Global Growth for the Next Ten Years', February, BBVA Research. Madrid and Hong Kong. Presentation available at: www.bbvaresearch.com/KETD/fbin/mult/110214_BBVA_EAGLES-ESADE_tcm346-246602.pdf

Garroway, Christopher, Burcu Hacibedel, Helmut Reisen and Edouard Turkisch, 2010, 'The Renminbi and Poor Country Growth', OECD Development Centre, Working Paper 292, September. Available at www.oecd.org/dataoecd/22/55/45950256.pdf

General Electric, Global Research. See http://ge.geglobalresearch.com/locations/bangalore-india/

Ghemawat, Pankaj, 2011, *World 3.0: Global Prosperity and How to Achieve It*, Boston, Harvard Business Review Press.

Glaeser, Edward, 2011, *Triumph of the City: How Our Greatest Invention Makes Us Richer, Smarter, Greener, Healthier, and Happier*, New York, Penguin Press

Goldman Sachs, 2009, *The Long Term Outlook for the BRIC and N-11 post Crisis*, London and New York, Goldman Sachs Global Economics Papers 192. Available at www2.goldmansachs.com/ideas/BRIC/long-term-outlook-doc.pdf

2010, *Emerging Markets Equity in Two Decades: A Changing Landscape*, New York and London, Goldman Sachs Global Economics Papers 24, September

2010, *Revisiting our BRIC Nifty 50 Baskets*, New York and London, Goldman Sachs

Goldstein, Andrea, 2007, *Multinational Companies from Emerging Economies: Composition, Conceptualization and Direction in the Global Economy*, London, Palgrave Macmillan

Goldstein, Andrea, 2010, 'The Emergence of Multilatinas: The Petrobras experience', *Universia Business Review*, pp. 98–111

González-Vicente, Ruben, 2012, 'Mapping Chinese Mining Investment in Latin America: Politics or Market?', *China Quarterly*, 209, March, pp. 35–58

Government of Colombia and OECD. Available at http://www.oecd.org/dataoecd/14/39/46080702.pdf

Grandes, Martín, Demian Panigo and Ricardo Pasquini, 2007, 'The Cost of Corporate Bond Financing in Latin America', Center for Financial Stability, Working Paper, 20 July. Available at www.cefargentina. org/files_publicaciones/16-36wp20-cob-grandes-panigo-pasquini-julio-2007.pdf

2007, 'The Cost of Equity beyond CAPM: Evidence from Latin American Stock Markets 1986–2004', Center for Financial Stability, Working Paper, 17 March 2007. Available at www.cefargentina.org/files_publicaciones/16-33wp17-coe2-jan-2007.pdf

Guillén, Mauro, 2005, *The Rise of Spanish Multinationals: European Business in the Global Economy*, Cambridge University Press

Guillén, Mauro and Esteban García Canal, 2010, *The New Multinationals: Spanish Firms in a Global Context*, Cambridge University Press

Guler, Isin and Mauro Guillén, 2010, 'Home Country Networks and Foreign Expansion: Evidence from the Venture Capital Industry', *Academy of Management Journal*, 53(2), pp. 390–410. Available at www.unc.edu/~guleri/Guler%20Guillen%20AMJ.pdf

'Knowledge, 2010, Institutions and Foreign Entry: The Internationalization of US Venture Firms', *Journal of International Business Studies*, 41, pp. 185–205

2010 'Institutions and the Internationalization of US Venture Capital Firms', *Academy of International Business*, 41, 2010, pp. 185–205

Hanson, Gordon, 2010, 'Why Isn't Mexico Rich?', *Journal of Economic Literature*, 48(4), pp. 987–1004

Hanson, Gordon and Raymond Robertson, 2010, 'China and the Manufacturing Exports of Other Developing Countries', in Robert Feenstra and Shang Jin Wei (eds.), *China's Growing Role in World Trade*, University of Chicago Press and NBER, pp. 137–59. Available at http://irps.ucsd.edu/assets/022/8776.pdf

Harvard Business School, 2009, *How GE Is Disrupting itself*, Boston, HBS Review, October. Available at http://hbr.org/2009/10/how-ge-is-disrupting-itself/ar/1. The case study of Harvard is available at www.gereports.com/reverse-innovation-how-ge-is-disrupting-itself/

Havro, Gøril and Javier Santiso, 2008, 'To Benefit from Plenty: Lessons from Chile and Norway', OECD Development Centre Policy Brief 37, OECD Development Centre, September. Available at www.oecd.org/dataoecd/23/12/41281577.pdf

2011, 'Benefiting the Resource Rich: Can International Development Policy Help Tame the Resource Crisis?', IDS Working Paper 35, February. Available at http://papers.ssrn.com/sol3/papers.cfm?abstract_id=1761007 and http://www.ids.ac.uk/go/bookshop

Hearn, Adrian and José Luis Márquez (eds.), 2011, *China Engages Latin America: Tracing the Trajectory*, Boulder, Colo., Lynne Rienner Publishers

HSBC, 2011, *The Southern Silk Road: Turbocharging South South Economic Growth*, London and New York, HSBC Global Research. Available at www.research.hsbc.com/midas/Res/RDV?p=pdf&key=WZnyWSIf38&n=299714.PDF

2011, *The World in 2050: Quantifying the Shift in the Global Economy*, London and New York, HSBC Global Research, 2011. Available at www.research.hsbc.com/midas/Res/RDV?p=pdf&key=ej73gSSJVj&n=282364.PDF

IESE, 2011, *The Global Venture Capital and Private Equity Country Attractiveness Index*. Available at http://blog.iese.edu/vcpeindex/

Izquierdo, Alejandro and Ernesto Talvi, 2011, *One Region, Two Speeds? Challenges of the New Global Economic Order for Latin America and the Caribbean*, Washington, DC, IADB. Report available at http://idbdocs.iadb.org/wsdocs/getdocument.aspx?docnum=35816781

Jenkins, Rhys and Alexandre de Freitas Barbosa, 2012, 'Fear for Manufacturing? China and the Future of Industry in Brazil and Latin America', *China Quarterly*, 209, March, pp. 59–81

JP Morgan, 2011, *The Domino Effect of a US Treasury Technical Default*, New York, JP Morgan Research. Available at www.jpmorgan.com/pages/jpmorgan/investbk/solutions/research

Kalb, Scott, 2011, *The Growing of Cooperation among Sovereign Wealth Funds*, Seoul, Korea Investment Corporation, June. Available at www.kic.go.kr/en/pr/pr030000.jsp?mode=view&article_no=474&pager.offset=0&board_no=44

Kauffman Foundation, 2011, *The Grass Is indeed Greener in India and China for Returnee Entrepreneurs*, Kansas City, Kauffman Foundation, April. Available at www.kauffman.org/uploadedfiles/grass-is-greener-for-returnee-entrepreneurs.pdf

Krauze, Enrique, 2011, *Redeemers: Ideas and Power in Latin America*, New York, Harper

Latin America Venture Capital Association. Available at www.lavca.org/

LAVCA Scorecard, 2011. Available at http://lavca.org/wp-content/uploads/2011/07/2011-LAVCA-Scorecard-update.pdf

Lazzarini, Sergio and Aldo Musacchio, 2010, 'Leviathan as a Minority Shareholder: A Study of Equity Purchases by the Brazilian Development Bank (BNDES), 1995–2003', Harvard Business School, Working Paper 11–071, December. Available at www.hbs.edu/research/pdf/11-073.pdf

Lerner, Josh, 2009, *Boulevard of Broken Dreams: Why Public Efforts to Boost Entrepreneurship and Venture Failed and What to Do about It*, Princeton University Press

Lerner, Josh *et al.*, 2009, *The Global Economic Impact of Private Equity Report 2010*, Geneva, World Economic Forum. Available at https://members.weforum.org/pdf/FinancialInstitutions/PrivateEquity_VolIII_WorkingPapers.pdf

Levy-Yeyati, Eduardo, 2010, 'Emerging Economies in the 2000s: Real Decoupling and Financial Decoupling', Universidad Torcuato di Tella, Work Document (not published), June. Available at www.bde.es/webbde/GAP/Secciones/SalaPrensa/Agenda/Eventos/10/Jul/04.Levy-Yeyati.pdf

Lin, Justin, 2011, 'From Flying Geese to Leading Dragons: New Opportunities and Strategies for Structural Transformation in Developing Countries', *World Bank Policy Research Working Paper 5702*, June. Presentation available at http://siteresources.worldbank.org/DEC/Resources/Uzbekistan-final.pdf

LSE Kuwait Programme (London School of Economics). Available at www2.lse.ac.uk/government/research/resgroups/kuwait/research/papers/donorship.aspx

McKinsey, 2010, *Lions on the Move: The Progress and Potential of African Economies*, Boston, McKinsey Global Institute, June. Available at www.mckinsey.com/mgi/publications/progress_and_potential_of_african_economies/index.asp

2011, *Building Globally Competitive Cities: The Key to Latin American Growth*, Boston and Washington, DC, McKinsey Global Institute, August. Available at www.mckinsey.com/mgi/publications/Building_globally_competitive_cities/PDFs/MGI_Latin_America.pdf

2011, *Mapping Global Capital Markets 2011*, Boston and Washington, DC, McKinsey Global Institute, August. Available at www.mckinsey.com/mgi/reports/freepass_pdfs/Mapping_global_capital_markets/Capital_markets_update_email.pdf

McMillan, Margaret and Dani Rodrik, 2011, 'Globalization, Structural Change and Productivity Growth', Harvard University, Kennedy School, Working Paper, February. Available at www.hks.harvard.edu/fs/drodrik/research.html

Mesquita, Mauricio (ed.), 2010, *India: Latin America's Next Big Thing?*, Washington, DC, Inter-American Development Bank (IADB). Available at http://idbdocs.iadb.org/wsdocs/getdocument.aspx?docnum=35239272

Ministerio de Relaciones Exteriores, 2011, *La inversión directa de capitales chilenos en el mundo, 1990–2010*, Santiago de Chile, Ministry of Foreign Affairs, Directorate General of International Economic Relations. Available at www.direcon.gob.cl/bibliotecas/scategorias/list/1937

Mlachila, Montfort and Misa Takebe, 2011, 'FDI from BRIC to LICs: Emerging Growth Driver?', IMF Working Paper 11–178, July. Available at www.imf.org/external/pubs/ft/wp/2011/wp11178.pdf

Mold, Andrew, Annalisa Prizzon, Emmanuel Frot and Javier Santiso, 2010, 'Flujos de ayuda en tiempos de crisis' ('Aid Flows in Times of Crisis'), presentation at the Conference on Development Cooperation in Times of Crisis and on Achieving MDGs, IFEMA Convention Centre, Madrid, 9–10 June. Available at www.eu2010.es/export/sites/presidencia/comun/descargas/agenda/agenda_junio/pdf_grupo/ES/Mold_xFlujos_de_ayudax.pdf

Monitor, 2011, *Braving the New World: Sovereign Wealth Fund Investment in the Uncertain Times of 2010*, Boston and London, Monitor Group. Available at www.monitor.com/Portals/0/MonitorContent/imported/MonitorUnitedStates/Articles/PDFs/BTNW_Final.pdf

Mori Foundation, 2009. Available at www.mori-m-foundation.or.jp/english/research/project/6/pdf/GPCI2009_English.pdf

Musalem, Alberto R. and Fernando Baer, 2010, 'Latin American Pension Funds Investing in Private Equity and Venture Capital', Centro para la Estabilidad Financiera, Working Paper 36. Available at www.cefargentina.org/files_publicaciones/12-00wp-n%BA36-abstract-espaxol.pdf

Nanda, Ramana and Tarun Khanna, 2008, 'Diasporas and Domestic Entrepreneurs: Evidence from the Indian Software Industry', Harvard Business School Working Paper 3. Available at www.hbs.edu/research/pdf/08–003.pdf

NAVCA, 2011, *American Made: The Impact of Immigrant Entrepreneurs and Professionals on U.S. Competitiveness*, Arlington, Virginia, NAVCA. Available at www.nvca.org/index.php?option=com_content&view=article&id=254&Itemid=103

New York University Robert F. Wagner Graduate School of Public Service, 2008, *Understanding Chinese Foreign Aid: A Look at China's Development Assistance to Africa, Southeast Asia, and Latin America*, New York University Press

Niembro, Andrés, Daniela Ramos and Cecilia Simkievich, 2009, 'El papel del Mercosur en la llegada de la IED a Brasil y la internacionalización de empresas brasileñas', Fundación CENIT, Working Paper, May. Available at www.fund-cenit.org.ar/investigaciones/dt33.pdf

Noya, Javier and Fernando Prado, 2010, *Estudio reputación de España en el Mundo*, Madrid, Instituto de Análisis de Intangibles. See www.institutointangibles.com/

Observatorio Casa Asia. Available at www.iberoasia.org/

ODI, 2011, 'Arab Donors: Implications for Future Development Cooperation', Policy Brief 13. Available at www.edc2020.eu/fileadmin/publications/EDC_2020_-_Policy_Brief_No_13_-_Arab_Donors_Implications_for_Future_Development_Cooperation.pdf

OECD, 2010, China's Foreign Aid and Aid to Africa: Overview. Available at www.oecd.org/dataoecd/27/7/40378067.pdf

2010, *Colombia Economic Assessment*, Paris, OECD. Available at www.oecd.org/dataoecd/38/14/46797800.pdf

2010, *OECD's FDI Restrictiveness Index. 2010 Update*, Paris, OECD. Available at www.oecd.org/dataoecd/32/19/45563285.pdf

2010, *Perspectives on Global Development: Shift in Wealth*, Paris, OECD Development Centre

OECD, INSEAD and Fundación Telefónica, 2011, *Innovalatino: Fostering Innovation in Latin America*, Ariel / Fundación Telefónica. Available at www.innovalatino.org/

Pereira, Carlos and Agusto de Castro Neves, 2011, 'Brazil and China: South South Cooperation or North South Competition', Brookings Foreign Policy Paper Series 26. Available at www.brookings.edu/papers/2011/03_brazil_china_pereira.aspx

Perry, William, 2011, 'Growing Business or Development Priority? Multilateral Development Banks' Direct Support to Private Firms', Center for Global Development, CGD Brief, April. Available at www.cgdev. org/content/publications/detail/1424992/

van der Ploeg, Frederick, 2011, 'Natural Resources: Curse or Blessing?', *Journal of Economic Literature* 49(2), pp. 366–420

van der Ploeg, Frederick and Anthony Venables, 2011, 'Harnessing Windfall Revenues: Optimal Policies for Developing Economies', *Economic Journal* 121, pp. 1–30

Pozsar, Zoltan, 2011, 'Institutional Cash Pools and the Triffin Dilemma of the U.S. Banking System', IMF Working Paper 190. Available at www.imf.org/external/pubs/ft/wp/2011/wp11190.pdf

Proexport Colombia, 2010, Investment Report. Available at www. inviertaencolombia.com.co/Adjuntos/246_Reporte%20de% 20Inversion.pdf

ProsperAr Invest in Argentina, 2009, *Primer ranking de las multinacionales argentinas*, Buenos Aires and New York, ProsperAr and Vale Centre, Columbia University. Available at www.prosperar.gov.ar/es/ descargas/Publicaciones/Primer-Ranking-de-empresas-multinacionales-argentinas/

Puga, Fernando and Marcelo Nascimento, 2010, 'O efeito China sobre as importações brasileiras', Rio de Janeiro, BNDES, Visao do Desenvolvimento 89, December. Available at www.bndes.gov.br/SiteBNDES/ export/sites/default/bndes_pt/Galerias/Arquivos/conhecimento/visao/ visao_89.pdf

Rivera-Camino, Jaime, Víctor Molero-Ayala and Julio Cerviño-Fernández, 2009, '¿Quién interesa que invierta en España? La inversión extranjera directa de Latinoamérica en España. Tendencias recientes y perspectivas, 2009', *Journal of Globalization, Competitiveness and Governability* 3(2). Available at http://gcg.universia.net/pdfs_revistas/ articulo_124_1248713270240.pdf

Rose, Andrew and Mark Spiegel, 2009, 'The Olympic Effect', National Bureau of Economic Research Working Paper, Boston

Santiso, Javier, 2007, *Latin America's Political Economy of the Possible*, Cambridge, Mass., MIT Press

    2008, 'La emergencia de las multilatinas', *Revista de CEPAL*, 95, August, pp. 7–30

    2008, 'Sovereign Development Funds: Key Financial Actors of the Shifting Wealth of Nations', Paris, OECD Emerging Markets Network Working Paper. Available at www.oecd.org/dataoecd/46/61/41944381.pdf

    2009, *The Shifting Wealth of Nations*, Paris, OECD Development Centre. Available at www.oecd.org/dataoecd/52/31/41373888.pdf; and another version of 2008 at www.oecd.org/dataoecd/22/8/41125576.pdf

2011, *Brazil and the Shifting Wealth of Nations: The Re-balancing of the World towards Emerging Markets*, Madrid, ESADE Business School, Conference held at the Fundación Juan March, 25 January 2011. Available at www.march.es/Recursos_Web/Culturales/Documentos/conferencias/PP2714.pdf

2011, 'SWFs and Latin America in 2010 and 2011', in Monitor, *Braving the New World: Sovereign Wealth Fund Investment in the Uncertain Times of 2010*, Boston and London, Monitor Group, pp. 50–3

Santiso, Javier and Jeff Dayton-Johnson (eds.), 2012, *The Oxford Handbook of Latin American Political Economy*, Oxford University Press

dos Santos, Enestor and Soledad Zignano, 2010, 'The Impact of the Emergence of China on Brazilian International Trade', Madrid, BBVA Research Working Paper 22, September. Available at www.bbvaresearch.com/KETD/fbin/mult/WP_1022_tcm348–231940.pdf?ts=1082011

2012, 'The Impact of the Emergence of China on Brazilian International Trade', in K. C. Fung and Alicia García Herrero (eds.), *Sino–Latin American Economic Relations*, London, Routledge, pp. 224–53

Saudi Fund for Development. Saudi Arabian Government. See www.sfd.gov.sa/

Saxenian, Anna Lee, 2006, *The New Argonauts: Regional Advantage in a Global Economy*, Cambridge, Mass.: Harvard University Press

Schroders, 2011, *Emerging Markets Investments: Exploding the Myths*, London, Schroders. Available at www.schroderstalkingpoint.com/?id=a0j50000000u972AAA

2011, *Fragmentation in the Global Village: The Paradoxes of Our Increasingly Connected World*, London, Schroders. Available at www.schroderstalkingpoint.com/files/VMaisonneuve%20Fragmentation%20in%20the%20Global%20Village.pdf

2011, *What Is The Best Method of Gaining Exposure to Emerging Markets? Exploding the Myths*, London, Schroders. Available at www.schroderstalkingpoint.com/files/Exploding%20the%20myths%20Jun%202011.pdf

SEGIB, 2010, *Informe de Cooperación Sur–Sur en Iberoamérica 2010*, Madrid, SEGIB. Available at http://segib.org/actividades/files/2010/12/inf-coop-sur-sur-2010.pdf

SELA, 2011, 'Relaciones de ALC con el Medio Oriente'. Available at www.sela.org/attach/258/EDOCS/SRed/2011/03/T023600004688-0-Relaciones_de_ALC_con_el_Medio_Oriente.pdf

Senor, Dan and Saul Singer, 2009, *Start-Up Nation: The Story of Israel's Economic Miracle*, New York, Twelve

Spence, Michael, 2011, *The Next Convergence: The Future of Economic Growth in a Multispeed World*, New York, Farrar, Straus and Giroux

Standard Bank, 2009, *BRIC and Africa: Tectonic Shifts Tie BRIC and Africa's Economic Destinies*, Standard Bank, October. Available at http://ws9.standardbank.co.za/sbrp/LatestResearch.do

    2010, *BRIC–Africa in 2015: Tectonic Shifts Continue Apace*, Standard Bank, November. Available at http://ws9.standardbank.co.za/sbrp/search.do

Standard Chartered, 2010, *The Super Cycle Report*, London, Standard Chartered Global Research. Available at www.standardchartered.com/media-centre/press-releases/2010/documents/20101115/The_Super-cycle_Report.pdf

Stanford Graduate School of Business, 2010, Case Study Arcor. Available at https://gsbapps.stanford.edu/cases/detail1.asp?Document_ID=2876

    2010, Case Study Tenaris. Available at https://gsbapps.stanford.edu/cases/detail1.asp?Document_ID=2603

    2010, Natura: Exporting Brazilian Beauty. Available at https://gsbapps.stanford.edu/cases/detail1.asp?Document_ID=3354

Stanford University and World Economic Forum, 2011, *Global Entrepreneurship and Successful Growth Strategies of Early Stage Companies*, Stanford and Geneva, World Economic Forum. Available at www3.weforum.org/docs/WEF_Entrepreneurship_Report_2011.pdf

Start Up Chile. See www.startupchile.org/

Sunesson, Daniel, 2009, 'Alma Mater Matters: The Value of School Ties in the Venture Capital Industry', April. Available at http://69.175.2.130/~finman/Turin/Papers/Alma_mater_matters.pdf

Toral, Pablo, 2011, *Multinational Enterprises in Latin America since the 1990s*, London and New York, Macmillan

Trun, Khanna, 2008, *Billions of Entrepreneurs: How China and India Are Reshaping their Futures and Yours*, Cambridge, Mass., Harvard Business School Press

UNCTAD, 2011, *World Investment Report 2011*, Geneva, UNCTAD. Available at www.unctad.org/Templates/webflyer.asp?docid=15189&intItemID=6018&lang=1&mode=downloads

UNESCO, 2010, *National Science, Technology and Innovation Systems in Latin America and the Caribbean*, Paris, UNESCO. Available at http://unesdoc.unesco.org/images/0018/001898/189823e.pdf

    2010, *Science Report 2010*, Paris, UNESCO. Available at www.unesco.org/new/en/natural-sciences/science-technology/prospective-studies/unesco-science-report/

Vale Columbia Center, 2010, EMPG Brazil Report. Available at www.vcc.columbia.edu/files/vale/documents/EMGP-Brazil-Report-2010-Final.pdf

Wayra. Available at www.wayra.org

World Bank, 2011, *Multipolarity: The New Global Economy*. *Global Development Horizons 2010*, Washington, DC, The World Bank

Yu, Yongzhen, 2011, 'Identifying the Linkages between Major Mining Commodity Prices and China's Economic Growth–implications for Latin America', IMF Working Paper 11–86. Available at www.imf.org/external/pubs/ft/wp/2011/wp1186.pdf

Index